the new
100 houses
x 100 architects

Dear Paul,
Thank you for the
opportunity to be involved.
Best in 2010,

Mark English

the new 100 houses

x 100 architects

images
Publishing

Published in Australia in 2007 by
The Images Publishing Group Pty Ltd
ABN 89 059 734 431
6 Bastow Place, Mulgrave, Victoria 3170, Australia
Tel: +61 3 9561 5544 Fax: +61 3 9561 4860
books@imagespublishing.com
www.imagespublishing.com

National Library of Australia Cataloguing-in-Publication entry:

The new 100 houses.

Includes index.
ISBN 9781864702668 (hbk.).

1. Architecture, Domestic - Pictorial works. 2. Interior decoration - Pictorial works.
I. Beaver, Robyn. II. Title : New one hundred houses.

728

Edited by Robyn Beaver

Designed by The Graphic Image Studio Pty Ltd, Mulgrave, Australia
www.tgis.com.au

Digital production by Splitting Image Colour Studio Pty Ltd, Australia
Printed by Everbest Printing Co. Ltd., in Hong Kong/China

CONTENTS

CONTENTS (continued)

1   Living and dining rooms
2   Kitchen with dining room beyond
3   View from dining room to foyer
4   Exterior from southwest
5   Third floor plan
6   Second floor plan
7   First floor plan
8   Lower level plan
Photography: Marty Peters

Studio Dwell Architects

915 NORTH WOLCOTT RESIDENCE
Chicago, Illinois, USA

This 4700-square-foot custom house is located on an unusually tight urban site, which was approximately 20 percent shorter than a typical Chicago lot. The site is bounded by a large multifamily building to the north, a garage tight to the site line on the east, and a noisy public alley to the south. || The goal was to create an urban retreat that provided privacy, yet was filled with natural light and had an open, spacious environment. || The solution called for breaking up a typical Chicago 'box,' with simple, yet aesthetically strong compositions—each volume defined by a different material. The massing of cubes creates **a modern composition of building materials** that flow from the exterior to the interior. || Rather than creating a blank wall to the alley, the architect used this façade to define the house's composition and to bring in natural light. The cubist volumes also helped deflect the noise (and headlights) from vehicles traveling in the alley. || The interior is designed with simple, layered volumes that create flowing spaces, both horizontally and vertically. An abundance of natural, yet indirect, light sources provide generous lighting. Of the approximately 48 windows in the house, only 11 offer views out for the inhabitants. The rest are frosted or are placed out of viewing height, either tight to the ceiling or at the floor line.

3

4

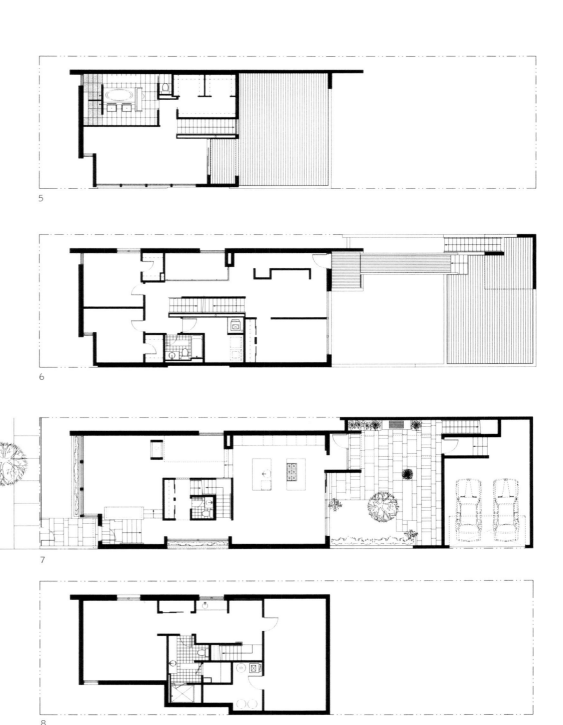

5

6

7

8

1

Hariri Pontarini Architects

ART COLLECTORS' RESIDENCE

Toronto, Ontario, Canada

Taking its inspiration from the owners' collection of glass art, this home explores qualities of **transparency, water, and light.** The interior is conceived to indulge the clients' passions, showcasing a vibrant collection of art and furniture, and establishing a private setting for health and wellness. In both massing and materiality, the exterior is designed to integrate with the natural landscape. || Lined with tall fir trees, the property is a 2-acre room enclosed by natural walls. Couched in the center of the site, the two-story, 12,700-square-foot house sits lightly in the landscape and takes advantage of views to large, existing trees. The house's L-form delineates an otherwise broad property into three exterior sectors, while preserving transparency from one sector to the other. || The living quarters are at the heart of the plan, relegating the non-domestic programs of art gallery and spa to each wing. The house's lower level is almost entirely transparent, holding the least private components of the house; the top layer is almost opaque, surrounding the most secluded rooms. || The external treatment of the house explores a finely honed language of natural materials: Algonquin limestone, copper detailing and awnings, rift-cut oak and teak windows, couched beside cascading fountains filled with

river rocks and plant life—evoking a sense of permanence, nature, and timelessness. || The interior is full of surprises. Essentially one room wide, it is almost void of doors and circulation spaces, enabling expansive views from one space to another, from the interior to the exterior, back in and out again. || The spa zone, which includes a fitness area, sauna, steam shower, swimming pool, and whirlpool is framed by limestone decking that forms a bridge between the interior and exterior water pools. On the interior, water cascades from the fitness mezzanine into the swimming pool, and on the exterior it falls from one level of fountain into another, bringing tranquility and sound into all areas of the house. The sense of water is carried further, with undulating ceilings over the art gallery and pool, suspending like heavy drops of liquid, and scooping light in waves overhead. || Throughout, clerestory windows, skylights, and floor-to-ceiling windows allow radiant, filtered light from multiple angles. Caught on a consistent backdrop of white plaster, French limestone, and walnut flooring, light ignites the house with a sense of flotation, movement, spirituality, and joy.

2

3

3   View in from the courtyard
4   Second-floor landing with undulating ceiling
5   Spa wing
6   Bath
7   Second floor plan
8   Ground floor plan

Photography: Steven Evans

4

5

6

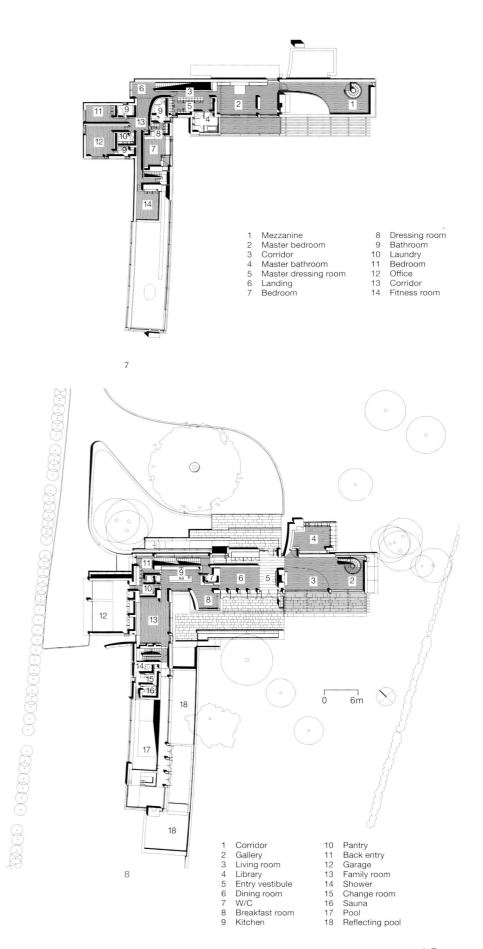

7

1	Mezzanine	8	Dressing room
2	Master bedroom	9	Bathroom
3	Corridor	10	Laundry
4	Master bathroom	11	Bedroom
5	Master dressing room	12	Office
6	Landing	13	Corridor
7	Bedroom	14	Fitness room

0   6m

8

1	Corridor	10	Pantry
2	Gallery	11	Back entry
3	Living room	12	Garage
4	Library	13	Family room
5	Entry vestibule	14	Shower
6	Dining room	15	Change room
7	W/C	16	Sauna
8	Breakfast room	17	Pool
9	Kitchen	18	Reflecting pool

1   Arthurs Point House as seen from the road below
2   North terrace framed by the louvered brise-soleil

1

Alexander Architecture

ARTHURS POINT HOUSE

Arthurs Point, Queenstown, New Zealand

The Arthurs Point House is a contemporary mountain dwelling situated between Queenstown and Arrowtown on New Zealand's South Island. It provides a 'platform for living on' with spectacular views into the Whakatipu Basin. It is both open to its environment and a very private home. Terraces to the north and east provide outdoor living and a horizon pool along the north edge of the house adds the sound of running water to the quiet mountain setting. || The concept for the house is **a simple composition of hillside forms**. The lower element is an Oamaru stone box, upon which a lighter form sits and cantilevers toward the valley beyond. The forms are simple and minimal, their lines generated by the site contours and a desire to 'turn toward the sun.' The upper element containing the main living area, dining area, kitchen, and master bedroom turns toward the view and is largely glazed. The ceiling plane flows out into a louvered brise-soleil, leading the eye to river and mountain views. || The interior is

conceived of as a subtle backdrop to river and mountain views. Materially the interior is rich, with heated concrete floors, travertine fireplace wall, marble bathrooms, American walnut wall panels, and original Art Deco light fittings set against modernist white walls. Automated curtains disappear into the walls when opened. The house is restrained but thoroughly detailed. A garage with a tussock roof garden is sited below the house. || The deceptively simple structural concept is an integral part of this contemporary composition. A deep head beam supported on two columns essentially frees the front façade of the upper level of the structure, enabling the roof to appear cantilevered in the master bedroom and dining area. The entire master bedroom floor cantilevers off the Oamaru stone form below. || Although overtly contemporary, this house sits comfortably in its mountain environment. It is a 'home with a view' and brings a sophisticated, contemporary, and slightly oblique house into the New Zealand landscape.

3

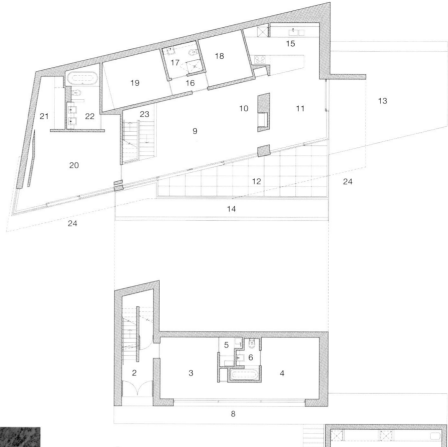

5

1	Double garage	13	North terrace
2	Entry lobby	14	Horizon pool
3	Studio lounge	15	Kitchen
4	Studio bedroom	16	Lobby
5	Kitchenette	17	Bathroom
6	Ensuite	18	Study
7	Access stair	19	Bedroom
8	Walkway	20	Master bedroom
9	Living area	21	Dressing room
10	Fireplace/travertine wall	22	Master ensuite
11	Dining area	23	Internal stair
12	East terrace	24	Line of brise-soleil above

4

6

3   Master ensuite features statuary vein marble and diffuse light from above
4   Dining area with view into Whakatipu Basin beyond
5   Floor plan
6   Self-contained studio with views to Coronet Peak

Photography: Jacqui Blanchard

1

2

0   10ft

Javier Artadi

BEACH HOUSE IN LAS ARENAS
Lima, Peru

Las Arenas is a gated community on the Peruvian coast, 100 kilometers to the south of Lima. This inhospitable desert landscape does not provide much in the way of context for new buildings and the uniform building regulations usually imposed by the governing bodies of such exclusive communities leave little room for individual expression. Fortunately, architect Javier Artadi was able to bend the rules to create a new typology for beach houses on this desert coast. || The 2300-square-foot house was designed as a holiday house for a couple with three children. Conceived as a series of box-like containers, the house is designed for flexible use and seamless integration of spaces, expanding the usual simple program of a beach house. Weightlessness and freedom were important characteristics that have been achieved by the use of **cantilevers, folded planes, framed views, suspension, and deep recesses**. Sunlight control has been achieved by strategic slicing of the building volume to produce shady outdoor rooms and indoor comfort. || The living–dining room is integrated with the terrace–swimming pool and the bedroom and services areas surround the main volume. The kitchen and the main bedroom are both connected visually with the terrace–swimming pool and, by extension, with the horizon.

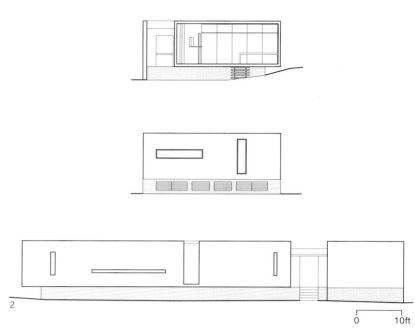

3

4

1   View on approach to entry
2   Top to bottom: west elevation, east elevation, south elevation
3   Main entrance
4   View from front terrace into house

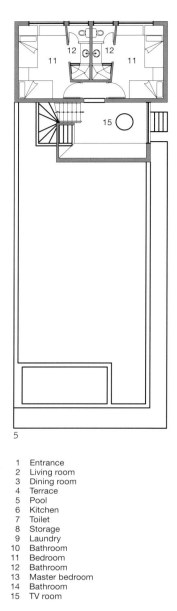

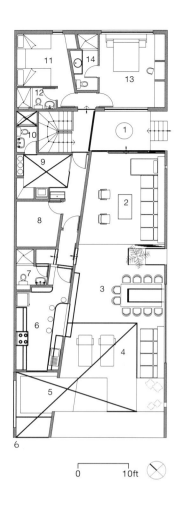

5

6

7

1 Entrance
2 Living room
3 Dining room
4 Terrace
5 Pool
6 Kitchen
7 Toilet
8 Storage
9 Laundry
10 Bathroom
11 Bedroom
12 Bathroom
13 Master bedroom
14 Bathroom
15 TV room

0   10ft

8

9

10

Photography: Alexander Kornhuber

1

2

Leuschke Kahn Architects Ltd

BEACHLANDS HOUSE

Auckland, New Zealand

A casual beachy look characterizes this two-level house designed as a first home for a young married couple. Located in Beachlands, in Auckland's eastern suburbs, it sits on a 1012-square-meter waterfront property that slopes down to a seawall with a public walkway and a small strip of beach. || The design is based on **simple symmetrical forms** with a double monopitch roof accenting the central volume. The exterior features two distinct cladding materials drawn from the traditional Kiwi bach vernacular. Stained timber weatherboards visually define the two-story central volume, while the elements on either side are finished in black-stained plywood and batten. Wrapped in black plywood, the south side of the house is closed off, while the north side is open to the sea, light, and views. || To accommodate the owners' love of entertaining, a covered loggia was created on the lower level of the house beneath the living room. It

incorporates an outdoor dining and barbecue area, a large exterior fireplace within a two-story bluestone chimney, and its own kitchenette. This frequently used space can be accessed directly from the front entrance and offers intimate views of the water through the trees. || The ground level also includes two bedrooms and a bathroom. Upstairs, an open-plan space contains the lounge, dining room, and kitchen, as well as the master bedroom and ensuite bathroom, and an office at the southern side of the house. || Extensive glazing and a high raking ceiling in the lounge offer views out to Waitemata Harbour and Rangitoto Island. The high stud creates an open, light feel and, although north-facing, trees on the site filter the sun and the space is sheltered by a large overhang. Pale Tasmanian oak floors with light walls and natural materials enhance the comfortable, relaxed atmosphere of this home.

1   Glazing, high ceilings, and balconies bring views and light into the living areas
2   Timber weatherboards define the raking roofline of the central volume
3   A sliding window beside the bath provides views through the bedroom to the water beyond
4   Ground floor plan
5   Upper floor plan
6   Tasmanian oak floors are complemented by relaxed neutral shades
7   The home features a relaxed open-plan living, dining, and kitchen area

Photography: Kallan MacLeod

3

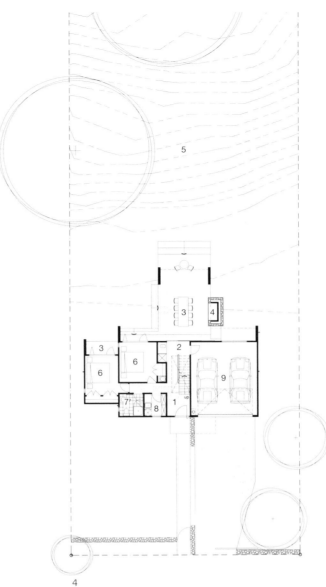

5

4

1 Entry
2 Kitchenette
3 Loggia
4 Outdoor fire
5 Bank
6 Bedroom
7 Bathroom
8 Laundry
9 Garage
10 Lounge
11 Indoor fire
12 Deck
13 Dining
14 Kitchen
15 Office
16 Ensuite

6

7

1

A-LDK: Anabela Leitão and Daiji Kondo

BELOURA HOUSE
Sintra, Portugal

This house is located on a new private allotment in the Quinta da Beloura complex near Sintra, Portugal. The clients' brief to the architects was for a light-filled house that takes advantage of its southwest orientation and incorporates a varied functional program and an indoor swimming pool. || The architects' response to the many varied program requirements was to distribute the interior organization of the 600-square-meter house among **seven half-floor uneven platforms**. Different functional areas and requirements for privacy are specifically allocated, and interconnect from the central core of the stairs, where all the routes around the house converge. || The space reserved for the swimming pool proved to be of the utmost importance for the functional and volumetric configuration of the house, because of its strategic positioning below the main volume. Wide sliding glass panels connect the pool directly with the adjacent lawn and contrast with the skyline, while sheltering the pool from the view of neighboring houses. || The openings located on the 'negative' spaces created on the stair volume allow views, from the interior, of different angles of the house and garden while shielding it from views from the outside of the property. Careful detailing of all interior spaces ensures an enhanced living experience. || The volumetric proposal took advantage of the characteristics of the aluminum panels used on the façades. The projection of light softens the impact of the substantial form of the house, and contrasts with the warmth of the wood panels in the entrance area. The north façade, directly facing the street, presents the image of an access portal to an exclusive enclave, which can only be enjoyed inside the perimeter of the garden. This front elevation gives only a hint of the multiple spatial relationships inside: spaces that exude comfort, privacy, and tranquility.

2

4

3

5

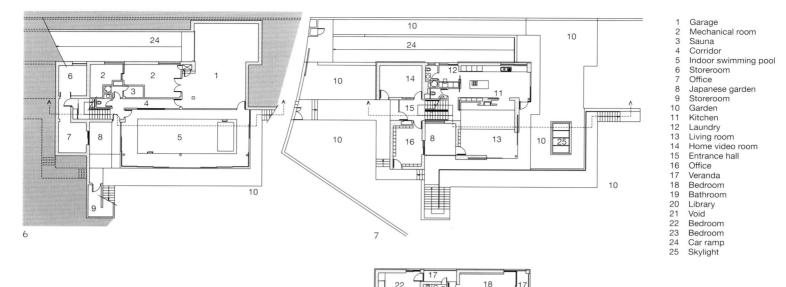

1	Garage
2	Mechanical room
3	Sauna
4	Corridor
5	Indoor swimming pool
6	Storeroom
7	Office
8	Japanese garden
9	Storeroom
10	Garden
11	Kitchen
12	Laundry
13	Living room
14	Home video room
15	Entrance hall
16	Office
17	Veranda
18	Bedroom
19	Bathroom
20	Library
21	Void
22	Bedroom
23	Bedroom
24	Car ramp
25	Skylight

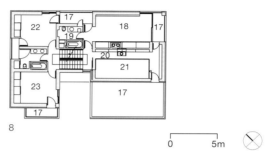

0   5m

6   Floor plan, levels –3 and –2
7   Floor plan, levels –1 and 0
8   Floor plan, levels 1 and 2
9   Kitchen
10   Living room
11   Library
12   Swimming pool interior with skylight above
13   Main bedroom ensuite

Photography: Rui Moraes de Sousa (1–5,9–11); Daiji Kondo (12,13)

10

11

12

13

1

2

Hudson Architects

BELPER HOUSE

Belper, Derbyshire, UK

Built into the hillside of the Derbyshire countryside, this house offers spectacular uninterrupted views of the Amber Valley. || The four-bedroom house was a study in material use and zoning. Local development restrictions meant that the house could not exceed 1 meter above the road level, necessitating a design that could slot into the hillside. With its north side built into the rock of the hill, the building's materiality becomes progressively light toward the south elevation, moving from solid red stone, to timber, and then glass. || A red stone boundary wall anchors the property into the landscape on the north side and runs into the interior, featuring extensively in polished form in the entrance hall. The 'cut from the rock' analogy continues in the master bathroom, where walls and floor are stone clad and the bath and utilities are embedded in a red stone plinth. || The roof is the primary elevation as viewed on arrival and its treatment was carefully considered. The heavy slate-tile roof wraps around and down the northwest wall; its tortoiseshell coloration is designed to pick up on the patchwork of roofs and fields in the valley below. It is **punctured with a 3.8-meter-diameter hole**, allowing light into the central sunken courtyard, creating shadows inside the house throughout the day. || Visitors arrive via a sunken forecourt through expansive woven stainless steel

automatic gates. Entry to the property is through an oak-paneled door into the hallway that leads through to the main reception spaces. All reception rooms are located on the ground-floor level, and the house is divided into three distinct zones that are characterized by their materiality. || Lighter aesthetics are apparent in the large open-plan space occupied by the kitchen, living, and dining areas. The kitchen features a custom-built double extractor, housed in a suspended stainless steel drum, the form of which complements the circular roof opening at the entrance. The living space is oriented toward a fireplace with brushed steel surround, drawing the eye to the southwest glazed elevation and the dramatic sun lounge and balconies. The lightness of the south-facing façade culminates in the spectacular two-story sun lounge, which protrudes from the house over the sloping grounds. Frameless fully glazed walls offer 180-degree views over the valley and town below, while the cantilever provides occupants with a sense of floating in space. || A small area in the attic of the sun lounge provides a quiet study space, separate to the rest of the house.

3

1 The roof is the primary elevation as viewed on arrival
and its treatment was carefully considered
2 The slate roof wraps down the northwest façade to
give protection and privacy from neighbors
3 View of the south corner of the property

4

5

6

7

8

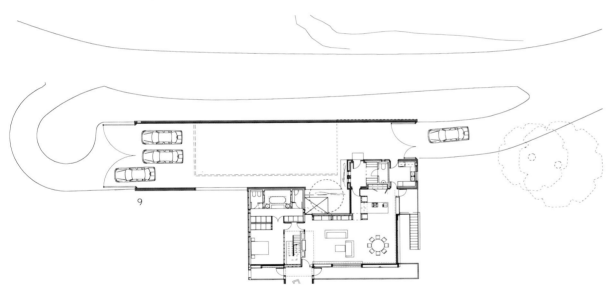

9

11

10

0   10m

1

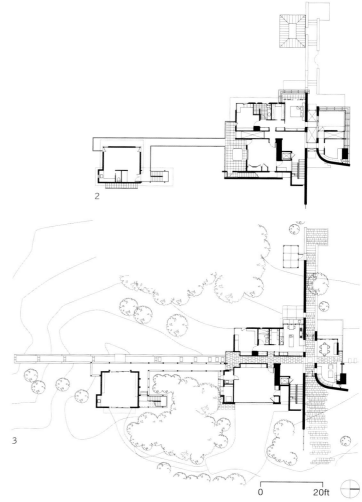

2

3

0   20ft

Olson Sundberg Kundig Allen Architects

BIRD WATCHERS' HOUSE

Puget Sound Region, Washington, USA

Creating a home **in tune to the rhythms of nature** was the primary design objective for this couple—avid bird watchers and lovers of nature. Site disruption was limited to the small area of the house, preserving as much of the 5-acre site's natural qualities as possible. Strategically sited on the forest edge, the house maximizes physical and visual connections with the adjacent meadow and forest. Axial in plan, the house stretches out into the site in the four cardinal directions. The cross axis forms the center of the house and is marked by a skylit 'cosmic' shaft connecting earth to sky. This central space, in addition to providing access to the other levels, also serves as a gallery for the couple's growing art collection. || The entry is formed from two large shot-crete walls (one of which is curved) that work their way into and through the interior of the house. The owners' casual lifestyle is picked up in the use of natural and understated interior finishes. Rooftop terraces provide space for gardening and for enjoying the outdoors. An elevated walkway connects the house to a small crafts studio and shop. Rainwater collected from the residence is incorporated into a 112-foot-long reflecting pool that is used to replenish newly established wetlands.

4

1   The house is designed to maximize connections to nature
2   Upper floor plan
3   Main floor plan
4   Daylight slipping into the stairwell is a reminder of the natural surroundings
5   The verticality of the house allows the owners to experience the rich variety of wildlife
    found in the surrounding forest and meadow
6   Soft, natural materials connect the house to its setting
7   Cozy alcoves provide protected spots from which to view nature

Photography: Paul Warchol, Tim Bies

Habif Mimarlik

BODRUM HOUSE

Bodrum, Turkey

This vacation house is in Bodrum, site of ancient Halicarnassus. With its beautiful harbor on the Aegean Sea and many traditional Turkish houses, Bodrum is one of southwest Turkey's most popular resort towns. ‖ The 1500-square-meter home is a contemporary interpretation of a traditional Bodrum house. The region's typically Mediterranean climate had a great influence on defining the physical environment and creating the major lines of the project. **Shadowed, open spaces and cool, spacious interiors** are the dominant features of the largely open-plan house, which can accommodate up to four families during the summer holiday period. ‖ Located on a sprawling 6500-square-meter site with stunning sea views, the house accommodates the various needs of its users while providing a comfortable and carefree holiday environment. The different effects of the sun are exploited to give spaces unique identities, depending on the time of day. The floors and walls are enlivened by bright sunlight and shadows that continually change as the sun interacts with shading devices. Deep recesses provide respite and shade. ‖ Simplicity is the dominant concept in the house and was the architects' starting point for creating a calm and quiet atmosphere. The use of different types and colors of wood was a deliberate choice, as was the simple geometry of the plan. ‖ Exposing the joins of the ceiling, walls, and the floor allows the elements to be seen individually. In this way, the importance of each element as an architectural object, not just as a construction tool, becomes evident.

3

4

3   Ground floor entrance
4   Living room
5   Basement home theater room
6   Exterior living room
7   Dining room
8   Bedroom
9   Bathroom

Photography: Gürkan Akay

5

6

7

8

9

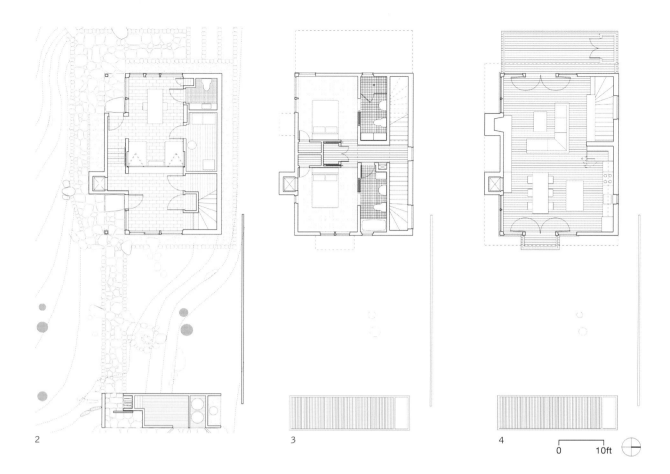

1

2

3

4

0   10ft

BOORA Architects

BOLES BEACH HOUSE
Neskowin, Oregon, USA

This house stands at a threshold between forest and ocean, shade and sun, intimate glade and distant vista. These defining dualities were observed at the beginning of the design process from a clearing at the western edge of the narrow sloping site. ‖ As a response to these conditions, the project strategically deploys service elements as opaque forms that direct diagonal views and define both communal and intimate spaces. Working with existing trees and topography, these forms **create areas of arrival, privacy, and shelter**. The occurrence of these consistently detailed forms on the interior and exterior of the house unites inside and outside through similar shapes, textures, and details. ‖ Primary spaces are arranged along the narrow bar to receive southern light filtered through spruce groves and to capture ocean breezes for maximum cross-ventilation. ‖ The first two levels of the house contain a studio and bedrooms. Concealed sliding wall panels and pocketed opaque glass doors contained within the opaque forms allow the spaces to offer maximum transparency or provide privacy when required. ‖ The highest level contains living, dining, and kitchen activities in a naturally lit space open to expansive views. Two decks extend this space further into the landscape—one toward the ocean, the other over the forest courtyard. ‖ Natural materials are used in the garden walls, site work, and architectural expression. A consistent and honest approach to detailing links inside and outside spaces while celebrating local skill and craft. All stone was found on site or obtained at a local quarry. Sensitive siting minimized soil disturbance; only two trees were removed.

5

6

7

8

1 The house takes in a panoramic view of the Pacific Ocean, while enjoying the shelter of a fir grove
2 First floor plan
3 Second floor plan
4 Third floor plan
5 The three-story beach house is located on a narrow infill site
6 Floor-to-ceiling windows in the main living space offer ample views of the ocean
7 Opaque service elements such as the fireplace wall direct diagonal views to the forest and ocean
8 A landscaped forecourt connects a covered car park with the entry

Photography: Laurie Black

1

2

1   Sweep of ceiling in living area conveys a sense of linearity
     and motion
2   Upper level with double curvature of glass/metal panel wall
Opposite:
     Night view from rear garden, showing sculptural massing of
     solid lower and light upper levels

Tony Owen NDM

BONDI WAVE HOUSE
Bondi, New South Wales, Australia

The brief for this house was simple: capture the spirit of Sydney's iconic Bondi beach in a home that is both a beach house and a stylish urban dwelling. The inspiration for this house comes as much from the culture of the surrounding streets as it does from the beach itself—the aim was to achieve **the ambience of a boutique or café** rather than a house. ‖ The swish of the roof echoes the soft lines of a surfboard and the curl of a wave. The line of the wave is the unifying element that runs all the way through the house. It forms an entry wing over the garage at the south and rises to give greater height to the living room at the north end. In between, the ceiling curves overhead at the main stair in the center where the lower and upper levels fold into one another. The wave re-emerges in the kitchen in the form of a single poured cantilevered concrete island bench. This bench, with its obtuse angle and curved geometry, forms the centerpiece of the living area. ‖ The lower level of rendered masonry is solid; the upper level, clad in translucent glass, reflects water. According to the architect, the house is all about the experience of space; the sensation of space should be tangible and should enhance the living experience—it should be felt and touched. In this house the experience of space involves slippage: one space slides into another space. This transition is enhanced by the use of different materials that signify different layers or

strata as in nature. This can be seen in the living area where layers of the curve slide over each other and blur the distinction between inside and outside. ‖ This idea is continued in the use of light. On the lower level highlight windows are used to bring in the sky. Upstairs the light is more diffuse; the translucent or metal walls act like a membrane, reflecting or distorting the light like the ocean. ‖ There is also a strong element of luxury in the house. The master bedroom has a wet bar and an open bathroom with a free-standing bath as the centerpiece; the shower and toilet are concealed behind a sliding translucent glass wall. Downstairs, the open timber decking and stone wall convey a sense of Bali. ‖ The form of the house, with its protruding carport and alignments, echoes those surrounding it. The form of the wing thrusts the main swish toward the street, exposing it to passersby, like an outdoor café. Yet the use of the translucent screen maintains a certain sense of privacy. ‖ The house was designed for a supplier of architectural glass who wanted show off his wares, hence the extensive use of glass on the interior. The walls of the main ensuite are either full-height mirror or color-backed glass. Timber veneer is used for the bench tops. The overall effect is a space that is ethereal, yet warm.

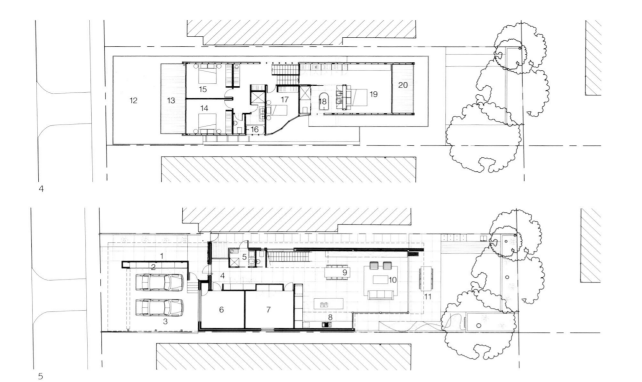

4   First floor plan
5   Ground floor plan
6   Living room with its sweep of wave ceiling relating to main
     stair and wall unit
7   Night view of the main living–dining area, showing the
     sweep of the ceiling and the sense of motion created by
     the geometry
8   Master ensuite with open layout to bedroom
9   Entry way to the house from the street at night
10   Kitchen with cast in-situ concrete cantilevered island bench

Photography: Brett Boardman

6

7

8

9

10

1

1   The house is wedged between a former church and a hall
2   Brookes Street house overlooking a public gathering space

James Russell Architect

BROOKES STREET HOUSE

Fortitude Valley, Queensland, Australia

Nestled between two 19th-century heritage-listed buildings, the Brookes Street house is a modern, raw, cubby-like home for a family of four. || A major challenge in constructing the project was to create a secure and green inner sanctum amid the chaos of two major arterial roads that link the city of Brisbane. The site was initially car parking space, wedged between the listed buildings. The site's total width is a mere 5.6 meters. || While high-density development was permitted under the planning scheme, it was decided that a small-scale proposal that enhanced the experience of the heritage-listed buildings was more appropriate. || The building is set back more than 16 meters from the street to create an entry across the forecourt. This unites the listed buildings, the office in front of the church, and the home. The new building is a tall, narrow structure grafted to the side of the church. With double-height glass facing the street, it recedes into the shadows of its neighbor. Tucked under the house is a small commercial space opening onto the landscaped forecourt. || Access to the house is via a staircase adjacent to the office. The entrance to the home is subtle: barely noticeable from the busy street. Once through the threshold, one enters a private and secure world. The stairs lead straight up into the heart of the home—a central, open courtyard of green grass bathed in sunlight. The house wraps around three sides of the grass, with the church wall and stained glass windows forming the fourth wall. Living spaces are on either side of the courtyard—one a less formal 'play room' and the other containing the kitchen and 'grown-up' lounge. || The sleeping areas are above the living areas—the children's bedroom is above the playroom, and the parents' room is suspended over the kitchen and lounge. A narrow bridge connects the two bedroom wings and overlooks the grass. Bathrooms and the laundry are concealed in cupboards running along the side of the bridge. || Walls of glass slide away completely at the edges of the living spaces, creating a fluid connection between the grassed and roofed areas. Upper-level windows are push-out timber flaps, which also act as eaves for sun and rain protection. Raw industrial materials of concrete and steel make up the shell of the building. These materials are enriched by the refined timber joinery of the interior. || The project reflects a **resourceful use of a limited space** to create a functional yet inspiring and sustainable space to live.

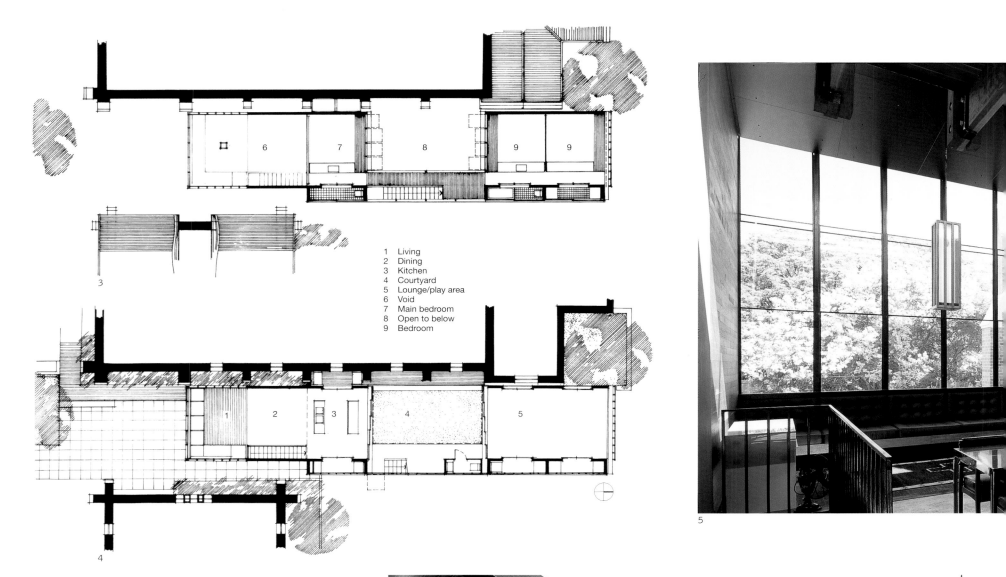

1 Living
2 Dining
3 Kitchen
4 Courtyard
5 Lounge/play area
6 Void
7 Main bedroom
8 Open to below
9 Bedroom

5

6

Photography: Jon Linkins

7

8

1

Iredale Pedersen Hook Architects

BROOME HOUSE

Broome, Western Australia, Australia

Broome, a town in northwest Australia, has a rich and fascinating history. Established as a pearling port in the 1880s, by the turn of the century it was the undisputed capital of the world's pearl shell industry, attracting workers from around the globe, and particularly from nearby Asian countries. Throughout Broome's colorful past, corrugated iron became the universal building material, especially in the district known today as Chinatown. The resulting structures added to a distinct and unique architectural heritage of which the town is justifiably proud. || The design of this house **responds to these early vernacular buildings of Broome**. Although the design does not follow the steeply pitched hip roof model of the pearlers' houses, it does pick up on the second-story gable roofs found on many of the old two-story buildings that were around Broome. Sadly, many of these buildings have been demolished and replaced with the newer style 'homestead' roofs (hipped with gable vents and lower pitched verandas) of Broome's modern subdivisions. || Broome's climate can include tropical, sub-tropical, Mediterranean, and desert conditions in any one year and thus requires a carefully considered design response. The two-pavilion plan form has been used to create outdoor courtyard spaces that have a strong relationship to the living spaces of the house. They form 'breezeway' spaces between the wings of the house, allowing the breezes to cross the site and to reduce the impact of the building on neighbors downwind from the cooling westerly breezes. All primary interior spaces are extended by a veranda area of a similar size, creating an 'outdoor house' wrapping around an 'inside house,' which can shut down when the weather conditions become too harsh. || The main living area has a hyperbolic paraboloid roof—the pitch varies across the roof, causing a curved plane effect. The roof reduces the height of the two-story section and provides low eaves to the northeast and northwest, reducing the heat gain of the house in the wet-season months. || The use of stumped floors, recycled jarrah, low-energy materials where possible, good breeze-catching features, and careful consideration make for an effective and unusual design that intelligently responds to Broome's climate and culture.

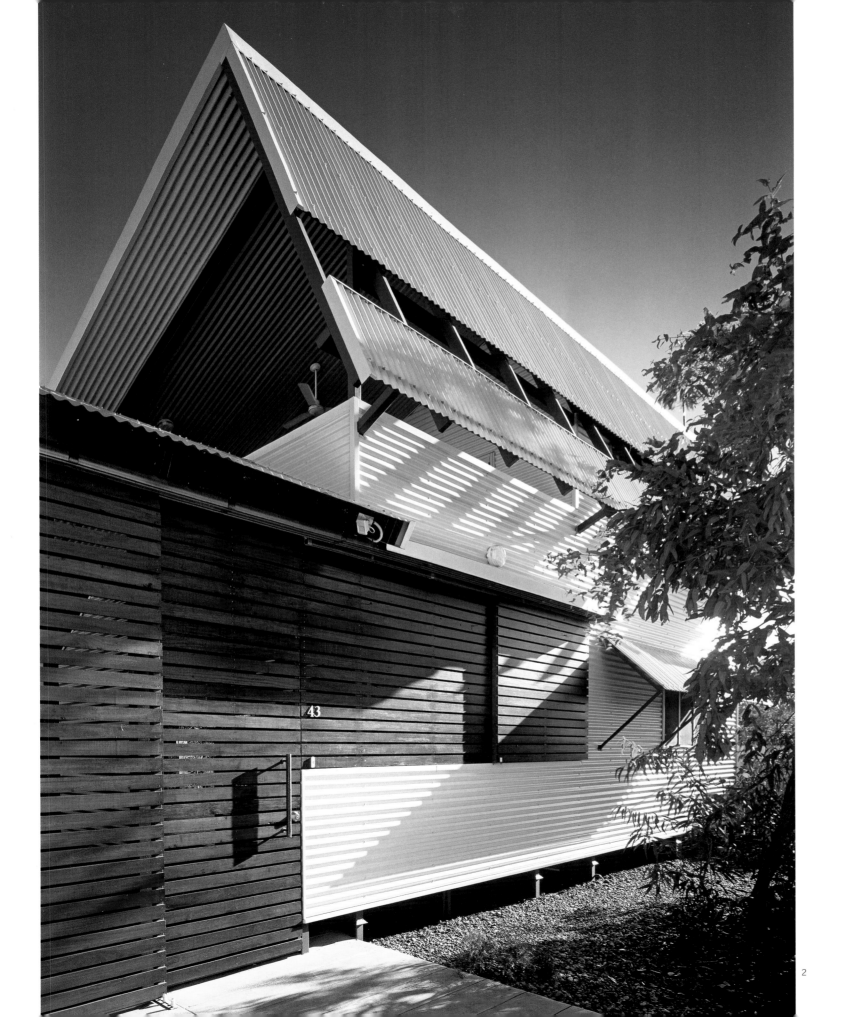

1 Entry
2 Carport
3 Outdoor shower
4 Veranda dining
5 Veranda lounge
6 Kitchen
7 Dining
8 Living
9 Toilet
10 Ground court dining
11 Laundry
12 Veranda
13 Bedroom
14 Bathroom
15 Workshop
16 Closet
17 Ensuite

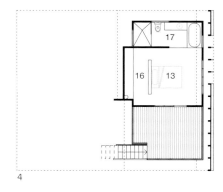

4

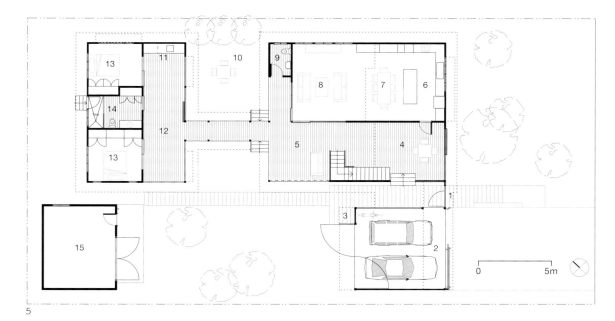

5

6

7

Opposite:
    Screened and light-filtered veranda space
4   Upper floor plan
5   Ground floor plan
6   Interior connection to veranda
7   Lounge veranda and outdoor shower

Photography: Shannon McGrath

Paul Cha Architect

C-I HOUSE

Germantown, New York, USA

Located in the historic Hudson Valley, the 4-acre site is situated two hours north of New York City. The picturesque countryside is highlighted by orchards, horse farms, and vineyards. The house is placed atop a gentle slope overlooking a pond and accessed by a private driveway, and is surrounded by dense vegetation to the south and north. Views include a vineyard to the east, and the distant Black Dome Mountain to the west. || The 2000-square-foot house is designed as a weekend retreat from hectic city life. After studying the programmatic, functional, and budgetary requirements, the proposal formed the plan for **a hybrid of the New England Salt Box typology**: a 50-foot-long x 20-foot-wide x 25-foot-high rectangular box with 11-foot-high public spaces on the first floor and 9-foot-high private rooms on the second floor. In accordance with the local ground conditions and building tradition, the construction consists of concrete foundation/footings, supporting a wood-framed enclosure with spatial layouts based upon standard modular construction dimensions. || On the approach to the house, an elevated ramp cuts through the manicured garden, leading up to the entrance through the first-floor concrete façade, which is formed by the foundation slab folding up vertically. This provides internal storage wall functions, and frames selected visual vistas through openings at different heights. The first floor's functional organization pivots around a square service core in the center of the rectangular box. Composed of a storage closet, a powder room, and the kitchen, the service core divides the first floor between the living room on one end and the dining room on the other. Beyond the concrete entry wall, the southwest façade dissolves into floor-to-ceiling metal-framed glass planes encasing the living room and dining room, providing a panoramic view of the scenery on all three sides. Opening the sliding glass doors allows access to the sun deck, which acts as an ethereal transition between the indoors and outdoors. || A two-story atrium with a staircase connects the first and second floors. Anchored to the staircase along the rear of the house, the bedroom hall provides circulation through the second floor. Light and sky filter into the hall through a continuous horizontal strip window along the upper third of the wall; the study and the bedrooms command specific views framed by larger square and rectangular windows. The combination of horizontal wood siding around the running strip windows and vertical wood siding surrounding the square and rectangular windows reinforces the expression of the different window types, and introduces different textures that disintegrate the Salt Box typology visually, even though its volumetric integrity is preserved. || Attention to human scale and material detailing is evident in the spatial proportions of public spaces and private rooms, along with detailing ranging from corner windows to concealed cabinetry. Similar in spirit to Shaker houses built in the Hudson Valley in years long past, the house's functional and contemplative character can be seen as a modern reinterpretation of the house on the prairie.

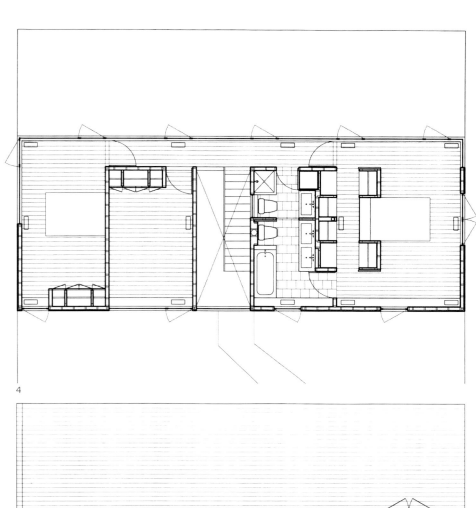

4

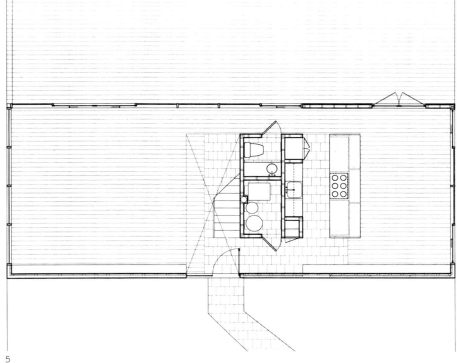

5

6

7

8

4 Second floor plan
5 First floor plan
6 Living room view of horizontal concrete wall/flooring with vertical entry/stair atrium
7 Open dining/kitchen with service core behind
8 Master bedroom with walk-in closet, master bathroom, and window opening to stair atrium

Photography: Dao Lou Zha

1

2

Line and Space, LLC

CAMPBELL CLIFFS

Tucson, Arizona, USA

Incised into solid bedrock below a sheer south face of the Santa Catalina Mountains in Tucson, Arizona, Campbell Cliffs is inspired by its surroundings. Details of this dwelling's sensitive integration with the desert and the mountains beyond are present at every scale of the project, allowing it to blend into the landscape. Despite the spacious interior volumes (more than 25,000 square feet), the home rises only 4 feet above the highest point on the property and is positioned to allow a sense of growth from its location within the 20-acre site and mitigate the influence on views from neighboring houses. ‖ Much care was taken during design and construction to minimize impact on the site, applying the philosophy that only the landscape within the building footprint should be traversed. This meant protecting natural areas, defining trails for people to walk, and storing on-site equipment only within driveway access paths. **Careful construction and a high level of craftsmanship** allowed for the conservation of both existing vegetation and rock outcroppings. ‖ The use of timeless and desert-appropriate materials unites the dwelling with its fragile site. When illuminated by natural light, these materials, including

stone, Douglas fir, glass, bead-blasted stainless steel, center score split face CMU, and exposed architectural concrete, foster a connection between inside and outside. The residence uses 14,000 square feet of Coconino sandstone from Ash Fork, Arizona for veneer on masonry wall planes and benches. These massive sandstone walls serve not only to block unfavorable views of surrounding neighborhood houses, but to create framed views of the desert and sky beyond, before they extend back into the interior space. Transitions within the house are seamless: the floor becomes a floating stone hearth or concrete bench. Glass walls up to 36 feet high provide incomparable views to the city and mountains while inviting the outside in. Windows are protected from the harsh summer sun by soaring cantilevered roof planes punctured to allow a gentle transition between the bright exterior and darker interior spaces. ‖ Extensive prototyping and detail development as well as a sensitive attitude toward the land ensured the highest levels of quality and resulted in interesting and unique relationships between materials and spaces that maintain harmony with the environment.

4

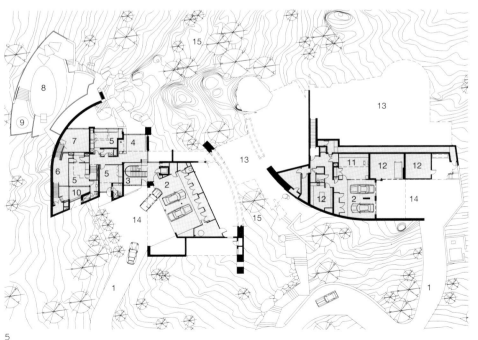

5

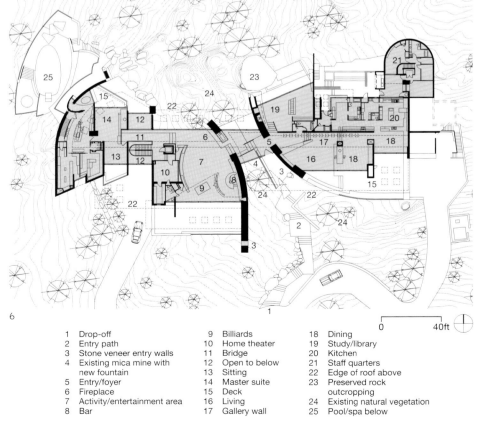

6

1	Driveway	9	Spa
2	Garage	10	Deck
3	Entry/garden	11	Workshop
4	Guest living	12	Storage/utility rooms
5	Guest bedroom	13	Footprint of main level above
6	Deck/gym terrace	14	Edge of roof above
7	Open to gym below	15	Existing vegetation
8	Pool		

1	Drop-off	9	Billiards	18	Dining
2	Entry path	10	Home theater	19	Study/library
3	Stone veneer entry walls	11	Bridge	20	Kitchen
4	Existing mica mine with new fountain	12	Open to below	21	Staff quarters
5	Entry/foyer	13	Sitting	22	Edge of roof above
6	Fireplace	14	Master suite	23	Preserved rock outcropping
7	Activity/entertainment area	15	Deck	24	Existing natural vegetation
8	Bar	16	Living	25	Pool/spa below
		17	Gallery wall		

0   40ft

1

2

John Lea Architect

CAPRI RESIDENCE

Gold Coast, Queensland, Australia

This 635-square-meter, three-level residence is located on a riverfront site in Surfers Paradise. || Entry to the house is via a 3-meter pivot door into a three-story-high lobby. A guest suite or home office is accessed directly from this lobby, which can also be entered independently from an external terrace. The lobby also provides direct access past a central courtyard into the principal living area of the house, overlooking the river. || The extensively glazed open-plan lounge, kitchen, and dining areas maximize exposure to internal and external views, natural light, and cross ventilation. Stacking bifold and cavity-recessed sliding doors allow the waterfront terrace, living, and courtyard areas to be linked as **one large, covered indoor/outdoor entertaining area**, or a combination of conjoined spaces. || The laundry, located adjacent to the kitchen, doubles as a secondary preparation kitchen and scullery with discreet direct access to the garage, the external herb garden, and the drying court. || The upper level comprises two distinct wings separated by the central courtyard, stair gallery, and a multipurpose gym/bedroom. High clerestory windows introduce natural light into the central zone of each wing and also contribute significantly to the efficiency of natural ventilation with all levels connected vertically through the central stair void. || The waterfront wing houses the master bedroom suite and is separated by the clerestory gallery from the home cinema/retreat. The master bedroom opens directly into a large ensuite bathroom that can be enclosed by concealed sliding walls that retract into pocket cavities. || The streetfront wing comprises the children's bedrooms and bathrooms, linked by a central activity space or media room. At river level, timber sundecks surround a horizon-edge swimming pool. A boat store extends across the full frontage of the residence and is also used for storage of pool and household equipment.

1   View from street
2   Entry lobby
3   Riverfront pool deck

3

4 Master ensuite opens onto main bedroom
5 First floor plan
6 Ground floor plan
7 Open-plan lounge, kitchen, and dining
8 Dining area overlooking river
9 Feature staircase
10 Riverfront terrace linking lounge to central courtyard

Photography: UBPhoto

4

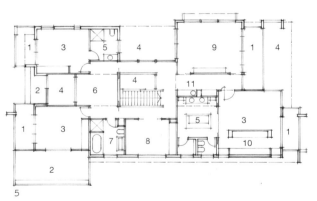

5

1 Balcony
2 Roof
3 Bedroom
4 Void
5 Ensuite
6 Media room
7 Bathroom
8 Gym/bedroom
9 Home cinema/retreat
10 Walk-in closet
11 Wet bar

7

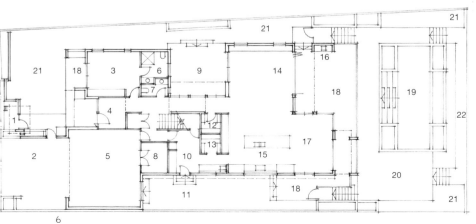

6

1	Entry gatehouse	12	Wine cellar
2	Driveway	13	Pantry
3	Bedroom	14	Living
4	Entry lobby	15	Kitchen
5	Garage	16	Wet bar
6	Ensuite	17	Dining
7	Powder room	18	Terrace
8	Workshop/store	19	Pool
9	Covered courtyard	20	Pool deck
10	Laundry	21	Garden
11	Drying court	22	River

8

9

10

1

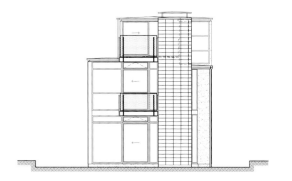

1   View of house from across the Avon River
2   Top to bottom: garage south elevation, house south elevation, garage north elevation, house north elevation
3   North elevation
4   View from landing to double-height sitting room

Wilson & Hill Architects Ltd

CARLTON MILL ROAD RESIDENCE

Christchurch, New Zealand

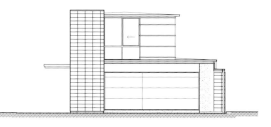

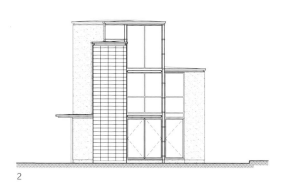

2

The brief for this project specified **a three-level house with an 'organic' feel**, to reflect its Avon River frontage with views over the river toward a nearby park. A separate garage building with a studio above, from which the client intended to run her business, was also required. Complying with town planning requirements was an important consideration in the design of the house. || The three levels of the house are divided into living areas on the ground floor, the master bedroom suite on the first floor, and guest bedrooms with a roof garden on the second floor. The ground-floor living and kitchen areas are in an open-plan arrangement; the sunny double-height sitting area flows into the dining/kitchen area, which opens onto an outdoor courtyard that in turn leads to the living area with views out to and up the river and park. Changes in floor level, ceiling heights, outlook, and flooring materials have been used to define each of these living spaces and to provide each with its own character. The double-height volume at the north end of the house ensures that sunlight penetrates deep into the plan, avoiding any shadow cast by the garage and studio in front. || Stacked, banded concrete block elements feature both internally and externally at each end of the house and studio. The blockwork element forms a spine through the house. The banding of the concrete blockwork, the use of timber as a trim material on the exterior, and the 'earthy' colors are further details that reflect the organic theme.

3

4

Photography: Stephen Goodenough

5

6

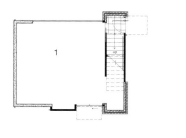

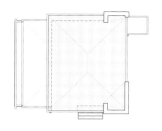

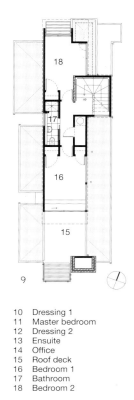

7

8

9

10

1	Garage	10	Dressing 1
2	Entry	11	Master bedroom
3	Sitting	12	Dressing 2
4	Dining	13	Ensuite
5	Living	14	Office
6	Kitchen	15	Roof deck
7	Laundry	16	Bedroom 1
8	Double-height void	17	Bathroom
9	Landing	18	Bedroom 2

11

12

1

2

House + House

CASA RENACIMIENTO
Atotonilco, Mexico

In the high desert landscape of Central Mexico two shells of an abandoned rattan factory sat decaying, surrounded by ancient mesquite trees and the soft sounds of a nearby river. What existed on the site was a 6000-square-foot warehouse, a 2000-square-foot shed, a well, remnants of walls, beautiful trees, and the dazzling clarity of the high plateau air. The client's program consisted of **a home with generous space for guests and a separate studio/gallery**. || The buildings themselves offered little inspiration. An alignment to the ancient World Heritage church of Atotonilco and a complex series of geometric moves led to the shapes of space and choreography of movement that formed this home. The driveway winds between mounds of earth that allow the approach to be a discovery. This circuitous journey continues along a sinuous path that penetrates to the center of the main building and the massive glass front door. Living, dining, kitchen, master suite, and writing studio occupy half of the main building, each spilling onto broad, curving terraces that step into the landscape. Each of the three guest suites is unique. A loft and roof-level mirador provide sweeping views to the mountains, the tropical thunderstorms, and glorious sunsets. || Terraces and gardens

weave together; a lap pool soars through the gnarled embrace of mesquite branches, its infinity edges drawing an invisible line between water and sky. Water trickles down a series of textured walls into the reflecting pool at the entry. A tiled vault sliced by a glass wall offers indoor or outdoor showers. An interior garden, accessible from the master dressing room, offers an alternative showering experience. || The owner's passion for ethnic folk art is evident everywhere. The studio/gallery serves as a workshop, a gathering space for events, and a place from which to discover the art of Mexico. || The flowing nature of the journey to and through this home is reflected in the forms of the windows, mantles, ceilings, terraces, and railings. Hand-made by a blacksmith, the doors and windows display skilled craftsmanship, as do the hand-made light fixtures, the bold tile murals, the railings, the cabinets, and the sculpted ochre, burgundy, and eggplant colored concrete sinks. Undulating mango-colored concrete roofs link the two structures and provide shade at the dining terrace. Cantera stone floors are locally quarried. The complex juxtaposition of colors draws the eye and guides the spirit as one moves through myriad shapes and experiences.

3

1   East façade from drive approach
2   Lap pool from upper terrace
3   Living terraces and lap pool

4

5

6

7

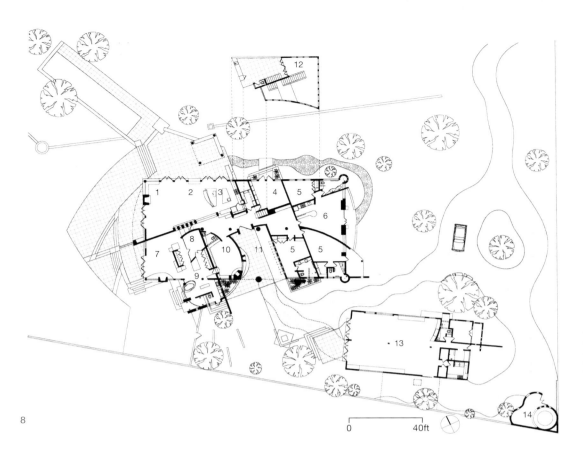

4 Steps from master bath to private garden
5 Gallery to guest suites
6 Entry with reflecting pond and fireplace
7 Custom-shaped concrete master tub
8 Site and floor plans
9 Master bedroom

Photography: Steven and Cathi House

1 Living
2 Dining
3 Kitchen
4 Study
5 Guest suite
6 Guest living
7 Master bedroom
8 Garden
9 Master bathroom
10 Library
11 Entry court
12 Mirador
13 Studio gallery
14 Mechanical

8

0   40ft

9

Peter Eising and Lucy Gauntlett

CRATER-LAKE HOUSE

Auckland, New Zealand

Perched on the rim of an inner-city crater lake, this house enjoys views through the trees out over the landscaped garden to the crater basin and harbor beyond. Over its 40-year history, the two-level family home had been subjected to several refurbishments, the previous one taking place in the early 1990s. || With this most recent upgrade, virtually the only elements that have been retained are the existing envelope of the house and the general layout. The living spaces are designed to create a lighter, more spacious feel and to improve the connection between the ground-floor living areas. The mezzanine on the upper level creates a double-height glazed gallery that runs adjacent to the pool area. || During the upgrade, all the interior finishes and fixtures, as well as the balustrades, doors, windows, and even the glazed façade facing the pool, were replaced. Soothing neutral shades and accents of **stainless steel, tensioned shipping rigging, and glass** feature throughout. The neutral decor provides an ideal backdrop for the owners' striking art collection, with the formal lounge incorporating custom-designed sculptural artwork screens. || The 4-meter-high brushed stainless steel front door with its diagonal motif introduces the theme of diagonal lines and metallic finishes that runs throughout the design. Inside the entrance, guests are greeted by a custom-designed water sculpture made of diagonal stainless steel tubes. The entrance is separated from the living areas by the sculptural wall. || This lower level of the house contains the open-plan living spaces, including the formal lounge, dining room, kitchen and laundry, family room, two offices, a guest bathroom, and a sunroom that completely opens out to the garden offering 180-degree sea and city views. || A focal point of the formal lounge is its 4-meter-long fireplace clad in dark-gray-and-gold-flecked metallic finished tiles, reminiscent of volcanic stone. The lounge opens out onto a gallery that takes visitors via the dining room through to the kitchen and family room. The gallery is punctuated by angled stainless steel columns that rise from the ground and pierce the mezzanine level as they extend to the ceiling, creating a dynamic sculptural form. || A sizeable underground wine cave, concealed behind a 'secret' wall, is located near the formal lounge. || The upper level contains the private areas of the home—the master bedroom with a deck and ensuite, two additional bedrooms, and a media room with a library. || The large outdoor entertainment areas look out onto the pool surrounded by palms and bromeliads, while terraced landscaping extends down the cliff with large vegetable gardens.

4

5

6

7

4 A 'secret' wall adjacent to the formal lounge conceals the wine cellar
5 The lounge features a fireplace and custom-designed artwork screens
6 A palette of black and metallic gray gives the kitchen a timeless appeal
7 An Italian crystal hand basin is a feature of the master bathroom
8 Ground floor plan
9 First floor plan

Photography: Lucy Gauntlett and Matt Stec

1 Sun room
2 Living room
3 Kitchen
4 Dining room
5 Storage
6 Lift
7 Laundry
8 Fireplace
9 Art screens
10 Lounge
11 Terrace
12 Study
13 Bathroom
14 Underground wine cave
15 Study
16 Water feature
17 Entry foyer
18 Pivot door
19 Entry
20 Garage
21 Cliff
22 Pool

8

9

1 Terrace
2 Master bedroom
3 Ensuite
4 Lift
5 Ironing/storage
6 Ensuite
7 Terrace
8 Bedroom 2
9 Void
10 Home theater
11 Library
12 Bedroom 3
13 Terrace
14 Ensuite
15 Closet
16 Void

0   10m

1 The exterior design references the protective armor of a beetle
2 Wide verandas surround the residence on three sides
Opposite:
   Rotation of the courtyard adds an enigmatic, erratic ridge edge to the house

HBO + EMTB

DE IULIIS HOUSE

Cessnock, New South Wales, Australia

The residence is located on a site that rises gradually from valley areas with generous woodland interspersed with open agricultural land planted with trellis grape vines. Spectacular distant mountain views, a foreground of vines, and dramatic weather changes from the northwest form the context of the site. || The design explores the **traditional rural veranda courtyard house**. Its nuclear plan of bedroom and living wings with wide verandas on three sides provides extensive views to the east and southeast over vineyards to distant mountains. This sheltered form is organized around a courtyard surmounted by a 'rain-operated' louver system, enabling the external courtyard to provide sun control and shelter from the rain. || To enhance this sense of protection, the house is arranged around three sides of the sheltered courtyard. The courtyard is slightly skewed to add an enigmatic, erratic ridge edge to the external form of the house and to bring the views more directly into the arc of the house. Main rooms respond to the various angles set up by the geometry of the courtyard; secondary rooms are orthogonal and protected from the harsh sun by the verandas. || The clients had specific requirements for the house, including weather-resistant materials and energy efficiency. The family also wanted a residence that was generous in size for entertaining, that would double as a gallery, and reflect their long appreciation and love of the surrounding landscape. || Responding to the client brief, the house is energy-efficient and automated, and can be operated remotely. Rainwater collected for household use is recycled as gray water for the garden; solar cells on the roof provide hot water; sewage is treated on site and recycled for agricultural use in the vineyard. || The metal plating on the exterior of the house references the protective armor of a beetle. The dense, shadowed exterior form contrasts with the light-filled, view-oriented interior and courtyard space. The veranda, cantilevered and strutted like an aircraft wing, features the adaptive reuse of sloping, tapered hardwood wharf posts to support the roof. || The client owns a regional steel fabrication plant and was responsible for all the steel elements in the house. A palette of robust materials including stone floors, white walls, expressed columns, a curved shelf providing indirect light, and extensive use of glass on the 'view' side of the site augment this elegant white steel frame. || Extreme weather conditions were considered when selecting external materials for the residence. The hardwood wharf posts, turned with stainless-steel yokes manufactured by the owners, give a calm yet robust external rural character using quite modern materials.

4

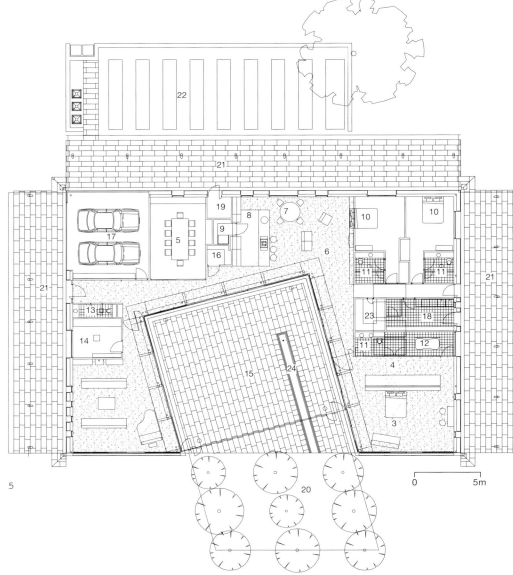

5

1	Entry	13	Wash room
2	Lounge	14	Study
3	Master bedroom	15	Courtyard
4	Dressing	16	Cellar
5	Dining	17	Garage
6	Family	18	Laundry
7	Breakfast	19	Plant
8	Kitchen	20	Orchard
9	Pantry	21	Veranda
10	Bedroom	22	Kitchen garden
11	Ensuite	23	Storeroom
12	Spa	24	Water feature

4   Accent lighting in corridor leading through to living area
5   Floor plan
Opposite:
    Sheltered courtyard surmounted by rain-operated louver system

Photography: Andrew Worssam

1

BBP Architects

DROMANA RESIDENCE

Dromana, Victoria, Australia

The brief for this new residence on Victoria's Mornington Peninsula was to design a medium-sized home that would ultimately become a permanent place of residence and accommodate visits from extended family and guests. || The result was a four-bedroom home with two living areas over two levels, a study room, and numerous bathrooms including a luxurious ensuite bathroom attached to a private master bedroom wing. || The house was in many ways informed by the **relationship to the views and the orientation of the site**. The main objective was to orient the residence to take full advantage of the panoramic views that exist from the site. || The house follows the fall of the land, with the lower level engaging with the site to create a base for the building. The main living area and master bedroom are on the upper level while the lower level, which contains additional bedrooms and living areas, is used only for children, grandchildren, and visitors. The house is entered from the upper (street) level and is accessed via a bridge overlooking a sheltered central courtyard. A two-level garage

accommodates five vehicles. || While the forms of this house are clearly modernist, the clean lines of the building are intentionally softened by the selection of materials, finishes, and colors. The house is primarily clad in timber and stone—these local materials were selected to engage with and reflect the context and colors of the natural coastal environment of the site. || Exterior spaces engage with the inside and can be used at various times depending on the weather. The front deck offers north sun and magnificent views while the courtyard offers a haven from the wind and days of extreme heat. All internal areas are organized so that views to the sea are optimized. || Solar orientation was carefully considered in the planning of the residence. Living areas are oriented to the north while considering the sun's patterns at various times throughout the day. Where required, eaves and overhangs complement the orientation; sun-control louvers and panels allow further solar control. Low-energy glass is used for energy efficiency and the house is insulated accordingly.

2

3

4

6

5

7

8

9

4   Bridge access to the front entry
5   The master bedroom window controls sun and
    views via an operable louver system
6   Main living space
7   Main living area includes an open-plan kitchen
    that captures the views
8   Horizontal forms are further expressed through
    the interior architecture
9   A stair void separates the two wings while
    addressing the view

Photography: Shania Shegedyn

1

2

1   The master bath is completely open to the view, yet privacy is protected by
    the natural rocks and topography
2   The living room expands toward the view
3   The roof opens up like an eagle's wings, with natural light penetrating the
    space through the clerestory windows
4   The play of light and texture throughout the house is inspired by the desert
    and its dynamic environment
5   Richly elegant, the Zen-type setting and accommodating guest suite also has
    direct access to the pool area

Photography: Arthur Coleman

Patel Architecture Inc.

EAGLE'S WINGS

Bighorn Mountain Estates, Palm Desert, California, USA

This house is on a hillside site at Bighorn-Premier Golf Community in Palm Desert California. The plan integrates the site and the program of the house; the 180-degree view over the valley provides the architectural inspiration. || The main roof is arched and is tilted down toward the valley to provide large overhangs to the outdoor living areas. The undulating and freely cut roof edge suits the dramatic setting of the rugged mountain surrounds and golf course with views down the valley. || The main great room, with a large clear-span roof, opens up like an eagle's wings, with natural light penetrating the space through the clerestory windows. The angled edges of the copper-clad roof accentuate the complex geometry. The rock outcropping is literally brought into the house as wall, screen, or furniture. The glass is inserted between the rock and the wood ceiling to create the envelope, undulating to animate the internal space and follow the shifting floor level. The existing rock outcropping at the entry courtyard was preserved; the guest house and the entry area were designed around it. || A welded, steel-plate trellis at the entry projects from the inside to the outside through glass to signify the entry door. The flagstone-paved entry courtyard is fragmented with water that defines

the arrival sequence. In contrast to the enigmatic arrival experience, the pool side of the house exposes internal spaces that spill out onto decks and terraces. || The master bedroom connects to two contrasting landscape experiences. On one side, the golf course is in the foreground, and there are distant views down the valley beyond. The other side is an up-close encounter with the rock outcropping penetrating through the glass and into the bedroom. The master bath is completely open to the view, yet privacy is provided by the natural rocks and topography. || The dramatic home theater is everyone's favorite room in the house. The fiber-optic studded ceiling, fully reclinable leather chairs, custom-designed wall lights, and state-of-the-art electronics make this an ultimate theater. || **Green design concepts are implemented to their full extent**. Solar orientation, a highly efficient mechanical system, water-conserving native landscaping, and a super-insulated building envelope are just some of the features. The natural air circulation system with motorized operable windows keeps the interior air quality at a healthy level and cuts the energy cost at the same time. The solar photovoltaic panels on the roof reduce the building's energy usage and carbon dioxide emissions.

3

4

5

Bates Masi Architects

ELIZABETH HOUSE

East Hampton, New York, USA

1   Southeast corner featuring cedar and concrete siding materials
2   South elevation featuring copper-clad fireplace and master bath deck above
3   Kitchen, dining, and living areas open directly onto the deck
4   The stair is made of the same mahogany decking used on the exterior
5   The dining area's window overlooks the north yard
6   Second floor plan
7   First floor plan

Photography: courtesy Bates Masi Architects

The change of seasons had a major impact on the designers of this house: the architect and his wife were particularly inspired by the seasonal experiences of the nearby lake. The same body of water they would kayak on in the summer is re-invigorated each year when it freezes over in the winter for ice-skating. They wanted their home to have the same flexibility and range, both in its use of space and in details that would interact with the environment and evolve over time. || This interaction began with a material palette that could be applied both indoors and out. Cedar, concrete, Santos mahogany decking, frosted glass, slate, aluminum, and copper slip easily from inside to out, blurring the line between the two. The front entry and interior stair are made from mahogany decking. Light seeps through the boards through two stories, giving a feel of openness. Mahogany decking from the private deck off the master bath becomes the shower floor and gives the already exposed space a more outdoor feel. The double-sided indoor/outdoor fireplace is faced with crimped copper that is already reaching a rich patina. A Spanish cedar entrance door is forever changing: it incorporates a window with a large air space into which small pieces of beach glass are deposited after daily walks on the beach, thus slowly changing the color and intensity of light as the collection increases. || As materials were selected to span between indoors and out, they were also adapted to perform in various applications. The jatoba floor in the kitchen wraps up the side of the island to double as a countertop. Its natural hardness and water-resistant OS Hardwax finish make it equally desirable for both applications. OS Hardwax is an environmentally friendly natural sealer that is water- and stain-resistant, safe for children, and produces no off-gassing. Accordingly, this oil was also appropriate for the mahogany veneer plywood lining of the MDF kitchen cabinets. || Over time, these oiled hardwood and veneered surfaces will slowly darken. Outside, rough sawn tongue and groove Western red cedar siding defines the spaces beneath the house's red-dyed concrete paneled shell. In contrast to the permanence and vibrancy of the panels, the boards will mature to a mellow, weathered, silvery gray conducting their own dialogue with the elements. **In and through time the house will mature and evolve.** It is designed to communicate with the environment and with its owners, changing in subtle ways only noticeable to those who really know it.

3

4

5

1 Writing
2 Rest
3 Rinse
4 Rinse balcony

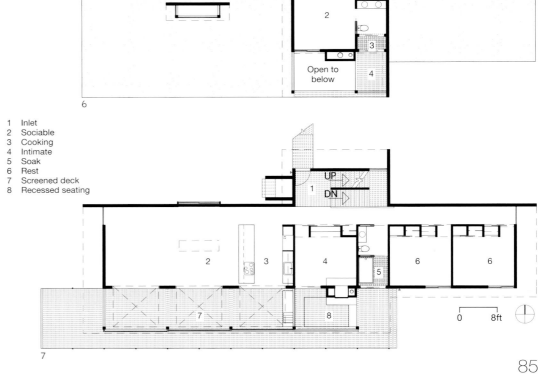

6

1 Inlet
2 Sociable
3 Cooking
4 Intimate
5 Soak
6 Rest
7 Screened deck
8 Recessed seating

DN

UP
DN

Open to
below

0   8ft

7

1

2

Utami Sugianto

EVERGREEN HOUSE
Singapore

This 560-square-meter house sits at the quiet end of a street facing a green school field. The site is a challenging narrow triangle made more complex by the presence of a dense residential area along one side and an electrical substation that partially blocks the site entrance. A further challenge is the site's steep slope, which results in the front being 5 meters lower than the back. The owners requested a home with a 'sense of space,' tranquility, and one that feels close to nature, yet functional and user-friendly. || To overcome the visual challenges, **spatial planning is driven by the views on offer**, with the daytime communal rooms facing the greenery and the sleeping quarters and bathrooms facing the less attractive views. To further guard privacy and block out direct tropical sun, mature foliage such as traveler's palm, bamboo, and flame trees have been planted to act as natural curtains. A split-level garden takes advantage of the sloping terrain and makes nature accessible from two floors. Vertical traffic is minimized though the upward layering of public to private spaces: first floor—dining, kitchen, and service; second floor—the living area; third floor—bedrooms and study. Formal dining or informal barbeque options are offered by the adjoining kitchen, dining room, and

terrace, separated by versatile sliding doors. || Spatial fluidity is exaggerated through visual and experiential manipulations. A significant portion of the house was designated as communal areas, resulting in a dining room of 100 square meters and a living area of 190 square meters. All unnecessary walls were torn down or replaced with full-length glass to allow natural light to enter. The minimalist interior contrasts starkly with the rich explosion of green shapes and shades of the various tropical flora bursting through the windows. An absence of visible furniture gives the spaces a uniform appearance, allowing personal objects to assume absolute visual eminence. Remote focal points constantly lure the eye to traverse the ends of each space: a smooth petrified wood from Kalimantan, a curved coffee table made of the outer trunk of a tree, and a massive stone Buddha head from Java. || The interplay of space and nature is balanced through the materials used: sand-colored tiles, and whitewashed plaster walls and ceilings that allow filtered sunlight to reflect softly and envelop the inhabitants in a peaceful ambience. Railway sleepers and bamboo branches are used both for their durability and raw beauty to bring nature inside the home.

3

1   Outdoor bath under a bamboo tree provides solace in nature
2   Dense foliage acts as a curtain to shield the harsh tropical sun
3   The light color scheme allows unique forms and textures to stand out

4 Borderless kitchen, dining area, and terrace allow for flexible entertainment
5 The study is dominated by Chinese marble and rosewood double-sided desk
6 The raw grain of the wood sleepers contrasts starkly with the smooth glass of the basin
7 Seamless indoor/outdoor living area amplifies the sense of space
Photography: Ying Yi

4

5

6

7

1

1 North elevation set against windbreak
2 Site plan
3 East elevation from field

2

0   200ft

Wendell Burnette Architects

FIELD HOUSE
Ellington, Wisconsin, USA

This house is located in an area of northeast Wisconsin dominated by crop fields and dairy farms, an 'altered landscape' that has been farmed for generations. Stoic utilitarian structures dot the predominantly agrarian scene, quarries harvest the whitest of limestone just below the ground, and native prairie grasses, wetlands, and forests compete for the remaining space. || The client, whose ancestors hail from Lithuania, has the changing seasons of the northern latitudes in his blood. His brief for the house was simply titled 'land, sky, and seasons' and demanded among other things, 'a sense … of space, of the farmland, of the prairie.' || The site is a 16-acre crop field; its context is understood as a garden with both natural and man-made field conditions. The rotation of crops, planted and fallow fields of corn, soybean, wheat, and oats, along with the apple orchards that hide the occasional pumpkin patch, heighten the sensation of seasonal change. || The field sits behind two existing houses. Turning off the county road, one first glimpses the field. Following the west tree line at the field edge for a

distance, a land bridge crosses the leading edge of a protected wetland, complete with flora and fauna indicative of Wisconsin. After this crossing, the gravel drive is focused between the tree line and the constructed apple orchard. The field is shielded for a time. In the distance, the house is a simple structure in the landscape, an object of utility that only reveals its purpose up close. || The haptic and other sensory qualities of time, memory, and space are subservient to architectural form. **The house is a simple 5000-square-foot box**, clad in a zinc-galvanized metal skin, akin to many constructed objects in the landscape, such as neighboring silos. Its apparent simplicity is articulated by specific moments of experience. These encompass notions of the house as a tunable instrument, to connect with and be responsible to the environment. Manifestations of these ideas include a gallery of 'the art and books of a lifetime,' and a silo ladder that ascends to a secret roof-top observatory whose geometry radiates to the heavens.

4

5

6

7

8

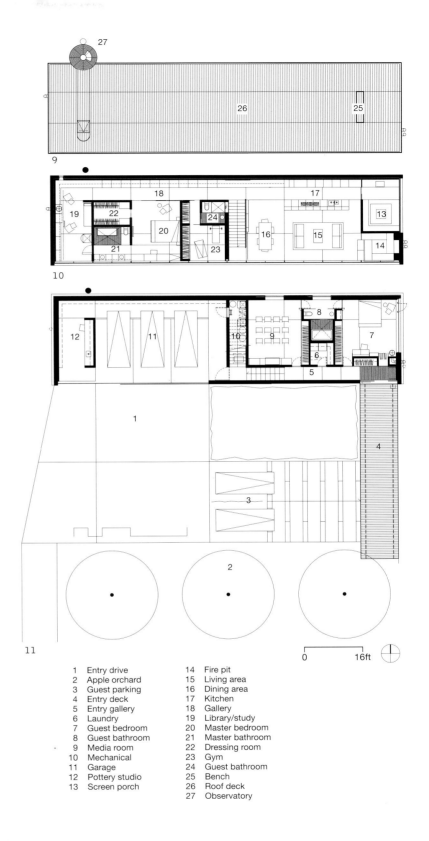

9

10

11

1	Entry drive	14	Fire pit
2	Apple orchard	15	Living area
3	Guest parking	16	Dining area
4	Entry deck	17	Kitchen
5	Entry gallery	18	Gallery
6	Laundry	19	Library/study
7	Guest bedroom	20	Master bedroom
8	Guest bathroom	21	Master bathroom
9	Media room	22	Dressing room
10	Mechanical	23	Gym
11	Garage	24	Guest bathroom
12	Pottery studio	25	Bench
13	Screen porch	26	Roof deck
		27	Observatory

4   South elevation with cedar 'barn door' entry
5   View from master bedroom to screen porch
6   Library at west end with silo ladder to rooftop observatory
7   Living space with kitchen of American black walnut
8   Upper loft from top of stair
9   Roof plan
10   Upper level floor plan
11   Lower level floor plan

Photography: Bill Timmerman

Peter L. Gluck & Partners, Architects

THE FLOATING BOX HOUSE

Austin, Texas, USA

This 14,000-square-foot house stands in a stunning native landscape of landmarked live oak trees and frames the modern urban skyline of Austin in the distance. ‖ The forms of the house consist of a floating box, the stainless steel structure on which it sits, and the partly buried base. The guest bedrooms, media room, and service areas are located in the buried section. An underground garage ensures that the landscape remains free of cars and driveways. The floating box, which is the top floor, contains the family bedrooms. ‖ Between the ground plane and the floating box, an entirely transparent glassed enclosure gives the living room, dining room, and kitchen unobstructed views of the natural surroundings on one side and the Austin skyline on the other. The stainless-steel structure holds the mechanicals for the house and produces the illusion of a wall-less space with a floating form above. ‖ An exterior rain screen protects the walls from extreme heat, UV light, and moisture. It is made up of resin-impregnated panels finished with mahogany veneer, which allow air to circulate and keep the walls cool and dry. Significant energy savings from the louvered upper box and buried spaces below more than offset any losses through the glass on the main level. ‖ An almost surgical excavation of 7000 yards of rock was necessary to protect the roots of the landmarked live oaks. The rock's stability permitted sharp vertical cuts so the house could be nestled close to the trees in a composition that **makes the building look as if it had always been there.** In an effort of reuse and cost reduction, the rock was sold for nearby highway construction. ‖ This is a very large house that appears small, with minimal impact on the site. 'Burying' the project works on multiple levels: it is energy efficient, it sits lightly on the landscape, and it creates an architectural tension between the clarity and purity of the exposed construction above the ground plan and the mystery and eccentricity of the spaces below.

4

5

6

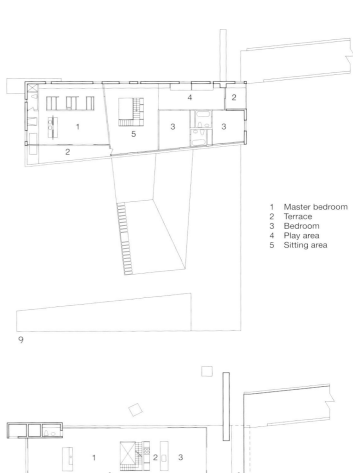

9

7

8

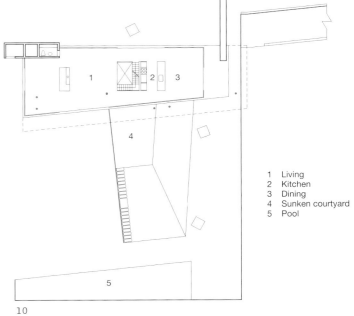

10

4   View of swimming pool through office
5   Living area
6   Dining room at night, with the lights of Austin beyond
7   Master bathroom
8   Interior stairway
9   Second floor plan
10 First floor plan

Photography: Paul Warchol

1

2

Jean Claude Maillard

THE FRENCH CASTLE
Marbella, Spain

Set in a 2.6-hectare plot, more than 300 meters up in the hills above Marbella, Spain, with views to the Mediterranean, the Sierra Nevada mountains and open countryside, this unique estate comprises two spectacular houses, two swimming pools, a garage complex, and paddle tennis court. The 950-square-meter, six-bedroom principal house is based in style on a classic Italian hunting lodge with two round turret rooms at each side, giving the feel of a castle. The structure incorporates **a stunning collaboration between the old and the new**. At its heart a monumental salon with one complete side in glass opens onto a 16-meter infinity swimming pool finished in slate. Most rooms, uniquely designed and decorated, connect from the main salon. Even the upper rooms are accessed from the main salon by a stunning cantilevered staircase. The whole structure was designed to create a synergy between modern contemporary materials such as glass and metal, melded with original historic and antique items built into the design, often built into the structure itself. These items include stone arches, ornate windows and inglenook fireplaces from a French chateau, magnificent iron gates,

imposing stone fireplaces, and rare and spectacular granite and marble floor coverings from Italy, Iran, and Greece. Every room offers something different and is a unique experience. Modern technology is not forgotten, with a high-tech stainless-steel kitchen, under-floor heating and cooling, plus a home cinema room. || The 450-square-meter guest house is just as spectacular, incorporating a large main salon with four pyramid-shaped glass encasements and large glass walls offering fantastic natural light into the room. The three bedrooms are all unique, again incorporating rare and unusual marbles, original cloisters, wooden doors, church spires, and a striking circular staircase to the upper-gallery bedroom. || The gardens contain formal areas, four antique fountains, an elevated knot garden on the garage roof, and a 100-meter drive lined with cypress trees. A lake serves as a self-sufficient source of water for the estate's plants and trees and is surrounded by an 'oasis' of 250 palm trees. Lemon, orange, walnut, wild olive, and cork trees also abound.

3

4

99

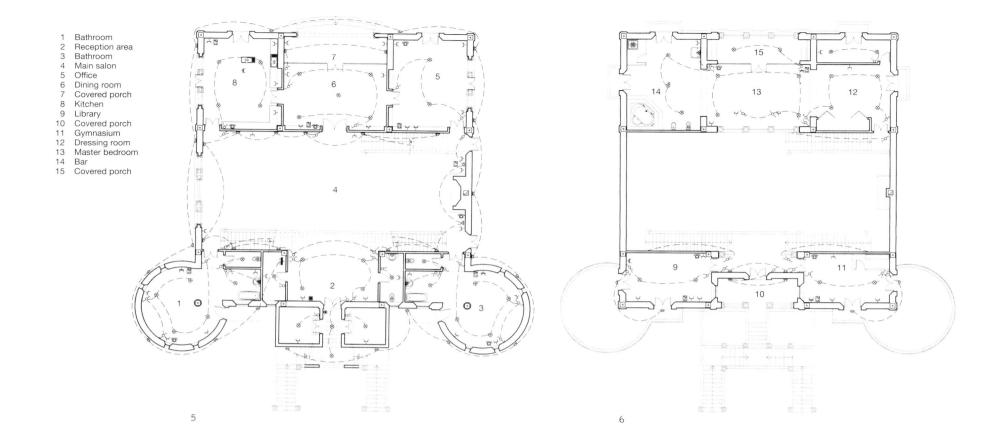

1 Bathroom
2 Reception area
3 Bathroom
4 Main salon
5 Office
6 Dining room
7 Covered porch
8 Kitchen
9 Library
10 Covered porch
11 Gymnasium
12 Dressing room
13 Master bedroom
14 Bar
15 Covered porch

5

6

7

8

9

10

11

12

5   Ground floor plan, main house
6   First floor plan, main house
7   Kitchen viewed from dining room
8   Main salon looking out
9   Master bedroom
10 Main salon
11 Guest house spiral staircase
12 Dining room looking into kitchen

Photography: Jean Claude Maillard; Mike Partridge

1

2

1   Wood-covered balcony features a polycarbonate element
2   The cladding of the different volumes is evident in this
      view from the patio
3   Wood accents enliven the polycarbonate volume

Graciastudio

GA HOUSE

Tijuana, Mexico

Tijuana is considered to be one of the world's most dynamic border areas, but quality architecture and urban design are still lacking. This house was designed by the architects as a vision of a 'new Tijuana,' and has had a significant impact. || The house is situated on a high, steeply sloping site, with extensive views. Geotechnical investigation found that it would be necessary to use a very expensive system of foundations with piles. This finding led the architect to consider the use of retaining walls for the same purpose; they have the added benefit of being an interesting design feature. || The architectonic program of the house was divided into two volumes connected by a third that acts as a link and as vertical circulation. Separating the volumes in this way generates substantial openings without sacrificing privacy and allows the maximum light and views to enter the house. || The volumes are further defined by the choice of materials. Low-maintenance white polycarbonate is used for

one major volume, which contrasts with the warm, dark wood used for the other. They are complemented by an industrial galvanized metal that covers the unifying volume. || The pure and clean design of the exterior is reflected in the interior spaces by materials that reflect those used on the outside. Careful location of openings results in an ever-changing effect of light and color and provides effective cross ventilation. The **integration of built-in furniture** was fundamental to the concept; all the joinery uses similar materials and its simple, functional, but aesthetically pleasing design complements the classic furniture chosen for the house. || The patio, generated from the 3-meter excavation necessary to access the street level, is one of the distinguishing aspects of the project's 'Zen garden.' This low-maintenance garden is accented by bamboo trees that frame the volumes, which in turn appear to 'float.'

5835

4   Second floor plan
5   First floor plan
6   Basement floor plan
7   Bamboo trees highlight the space below the access bridge
8   The office area in the polycarbonate-covered volume features the same
    material on the ceiling
9   Exterior materials are reflected indoors
10 Without walls and doors, the kitchen, dining and living rooms blend together

Photography: Eduardo de Regules (1,7–10); Pablo Mason (2,3)

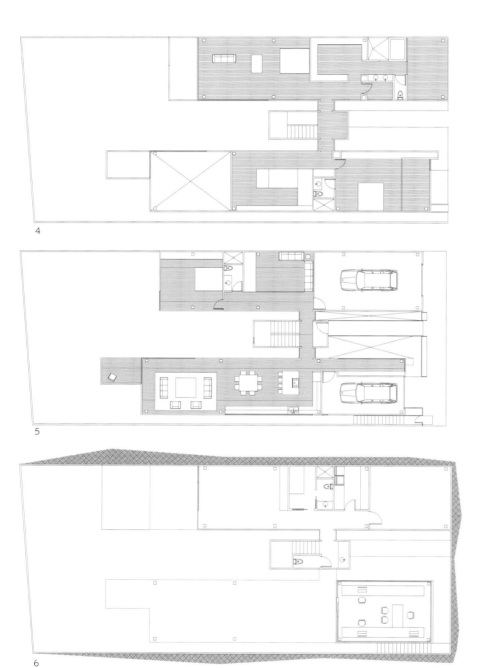

4

5

6

7

8

9

10

Ibarra Rosano Design Architects

GARCIA RESIDENCE

Tucson, Arizona, USA

This house is sited on a steep, north-facing slope in the foothills of the Tucson Mountains. The architects' first challenge was to design a structure that would appear to grow out of the desert hillside without dominating the landscape; not an easy task since the site is covered in low-lying vegetation and earth integration was out of the question. The second challenge was to create **an extraordinary space with ordinary materials**. || The axis of the 2150-square-foot house is set parallel with the site contours, creating three narrow bays that terrace up the hill, keeping the excavation and fill to a minimum. The terracing platforms contain the three zones of the house: living, circulating, and sleeping. The middle bay, the entry 'gallery,' was used for circulation and as an extension of the living spaces. The gallery is conceived as a tube-like space open at each end to frame the desert beyond, axially aligned with nearby mountain peaks to the west and saguaro views to the east. It invites the visitor down to the living, dining, and kitchen spaces on the lowest platform, while connecting the house to the bedrooms on the upper level. || The residence is intentionally loft-like. The house axis is intentionally broken and the main window rotated to frame fantastic views of the

Tucson city lights and the Catalina Mountains to the northeast. Here, the edge of the dwelling meets the desert floor, giving inhabitants a feeling of shelter and a connection to the land. || Sun from the south is introduced to the living spaces by splitting the bedrooms apart, creating a small, intimate courtyard. The courtyard serves as a sheltered, shaded exterior room with a view up the ridge and as a secret garden with brightly painted fuchsia walls and colorful bougainvillea. It invites warm solar rays in the winter, while in the summer it provides passive cooling for the house when the heavier cool air falls down the mountain through open windows in the courtyard into the house and out openings on the lowest level. || The material palette is simple, durable, and responsive to the desert climate, colors, and textures. The interior and exterior walls are sandblasted Integra® Block, an insulated concrete block system. The natural gray color complements the gray-green jojoba bush covering the hillside. Rusted steel echoes the iron oxide coloring found in the fieldstone while steel plate steps zigzag between the different dark gray concrete floor levels with birch plywood cabinets providing function and warmth.

5

6

7

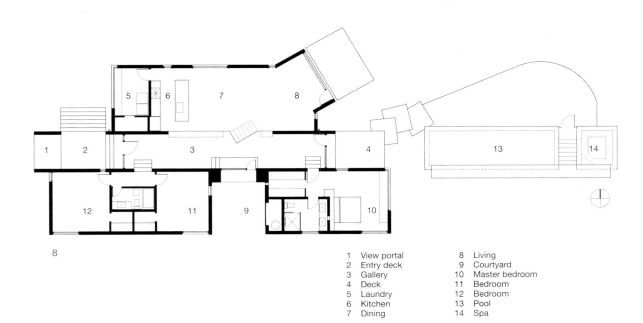

8

5   The living room was pivoted to capture city views and the Catalina Mountains
6   The courtyard celebrates the colors of desert flowers
7   The gallery separates the public and private areas
8   Floor plan
9   The narrow entry gallery spatially expands into the lower living area to the left and the uphill courtyard to the right
10   The lower level contains the living, dining, and kitchen areas

Photography: Bill Timmerman

1 View portal	8 Living
2 Entry deck	9 Courtyard
3 Gallery	10 Master bedroom
4 Deck	11 Bedroom
5 Laundry	12 Bedroom
6 Kitchen	13 Pool
7 Dining	14 Spa

9

10

1

Wadia Associates

A GEORGIAN COUNTRY ESTATE

Greenwich, Connecticut, USA

The scenic beauty of Greenwich's mid-country sets the stage for the formal grandeur of this magnificent country estate. The brick and limestone Georgian design was inspired by the owners' preference for something tasteful and conservative on the one hand, yet grand enough to readily accommodate the frequent large-scale entertaining required for the philanthropic and fund-raising work that the family is involved in. || In keeping with traditional Georgian style, the front façade of the house is elegant yet restrained, featuring relatively little ornamentation with the exception of limestone accents for the quoins, window surrounds, and entrance portico. **The rear of the house is undeniably grand**, with long sweeping views of the lawn and formal garden from the back terrace. Centered between bay windows topped with circular balustrades, the rear portico is proportioned exquisitely, and is given further emphasis by limestone pilasters and columns that continue up to the second floor. The prominence of the portico is enhanced by the entablature, which comprises a single slab of limestone that was so heavy it required special construction equipment to hoist into place. || The

interior of the house is equally as grand. The ample dimensions and luxurious details of the principal rooms bestow upon them an enviable elegance. A cupola above the central staircase leading off the entryway bathes the sweeping stair hall in sunlight. To give the space added distinction, the staircase was custom designed and the balusters were individually carved from mahogany. In keeping with the formal symmetry of Georgian architecture, the dining room and living room lead off either side of the stair hall. The dining room ceiling features delicate plasterwork in the Adam style. Its intricate ornamentation is painted in soft pastel shades, giving it a wonderful balance of formal grandeur and style. || Many of the rooms in the house were fitted with antique stone fireplaces procured from England; the library features custom-made burled oak paneling milled in England. The decorative motifs reflected in the paneling are recurring elements that can be found throughout the architectural design of the house. This continuity is essential to the symmetry of Georgian design, and provides the foundation for the refined elegance associated with this architectural style.

1 The front façade viewed from the motor court
2 Featuring the same materials and details, the pool house visually connects to the main house
3 The rear façade of the house overlooks the formal gardens and sweeping lawn

2

3

4

5

6

7

8

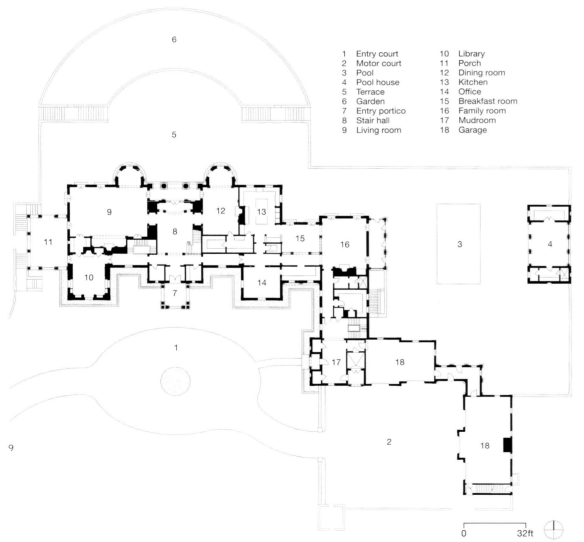

1	Entry court	10	Library
2	Motor court	11	Porch
3	Pool	12	Dining room
4	Pool house	13	Kitchen
5	Terrace	14	Office
6	Garden	15	Breakfast room
7	Entry portico	16	Family room
8	Stair hall	17	Mudroom
9	Living room	18	Garage

9

0   32ft

4   The private sitting room in the master suite
5   An axial view from the living room through to the dining room
6   The paneled entrance vestibule welcomes visitors
7   The family room includes built-in cabinets and bookcases
8   The library features an antique marble fireplace that was chosen to specifically fit with the architectural motifs that appear in the paneling
9   First floor plan

Photography: Jonathan Wallen

1

2

Bowen Architecture

GILBERT RESIDENCE
Telluride, Colorado, USA

This project is located in the Telluride ski area. Telluride, Colorado, is a Victorian-era mining town listed as a national historic district. Elements of this project recall the design vocabulary of mining structures prevalent in this region of Colorado. The project program explores the idea of merging vernacular architecture with the owner's strong preference for a modern space. An exposed steel structure contrasts with rigorously detailed ash wood paneling throughout the ceilings and walls, exemplifying this notion of **utility and precision modern detailing**. The site is situated along a ski run on a very steep aspen-wooded terrain with an attached narrow strip of property giving access to the nearby road. || The home is organized with separate living areas for adults and children. The lower floor has a media room and children's or guest bedrooms. The living area and master bedroom are elevated to enjoy mountain views. The master bedroom is arranged as a loft overlooking the living space. An entry and stairway is pulled away from the main part of the house and is connected by passages on lower floors and a bridge at the upper floor leading to the master bedroom.

3

4

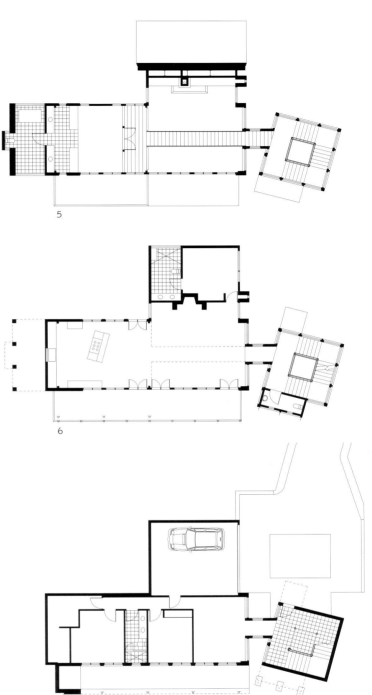

5

6

7

0   5ft

1   Entry
2   Rear façade
3   View toward stair from living area
4   View toward stair from master bedroom
5   Third floor plan
6   Second floor plan
7   First floor plan

Photography: Ron Semrod

1

David Jameson Architect

GLENBROOK RESIDENCE
Bethesda, Maryland, USA

Shaped largely by the site, the Glenbrook Residence is conceptually a courtyard inserted between two heavy walls. Threading the walls through the treescape to create distinct yet connected structures allows the house to be divided spatially into the most public, and most private spaces, and a living pavilion that can become either or both. The residual in-between spaces create outdoor rooms that engage the building. || The public and private wings of the 10,000-square-foot house make up the foundations of the design concept. They are thought of as being of the earth and are articulated through their materials and shape as heavy, static pieces. These wings define the bounds of the house and act as the backbone to support the various courtyards, upper roof canopies, and the dynamic living pavilion that sits between. || The living pavilion is the **centerpiece of the concept and glows like a crystal** between the heavy wall elements of the house and contains the cooking, eating, and living spaces. || Above each of the heavy wings floats a thin, folding roof canopy. More than a simple surface, this roof canopy is conceived as an entity where nothing is hidden and all six sides are exposed to view. The walls that contain the spaces beneath these canopies are made of glass to create the illusion of a floating roof and to blur the boundary between inside and outside. All of these elements adopt a language of angular, dynamic forms in order to be completely liberated from the solid elements of the house.

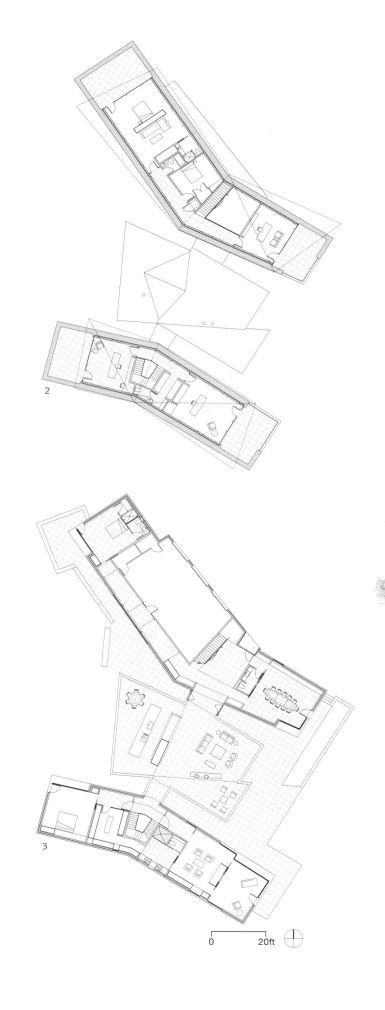

2

3

0   20ft

4

1   Front terrace
2   Level two floor plan
3   Level one floor plan
4   Central pavilion

5

6

5   Kitchen
6   Main entrance
7   Breakfast room
8   Front elevation
9   Entry hall
10 Central pavilion seating group
11 Central pavilion interior
Photography: Paul Warchol

7

8

9

10

11

1

Salmela Architect

GOLOB-FREEMAN RETREAT

Madeline Island, Wisconsin, USA

The Golob-Freeman Retreat was designed for a couple who live in the city of Minneapolis. Madeline Island, the largest of Lake Superior's Apostle Islands, is a four-hour trip from Minneapolis and is just off the north coast of Wisconsin. The island's built environment varies from trailer houses and self-built cabins to quaint bed and breakfast establishments. The architectural context can be described as 'diverse.' ‖ The clients wanted an economically straightforward modernist statement that would be easy to maintain, filled with light, and with transparent views. ‖ **The solution is two black-stained wood buildings:** a cabin and guest quarters. Various outdoor spaces are a step away, culminating with the abstract chimney fire wall. ‖ The black-stained wood recollects old practices of pine tar on seasonal wood structures. The painted wood interior also recalls post-immigrant times when it was fashionable to paint wood to make a more refined statement. ‖ The logic of this structure, the pure geometric planes and assembly of contemporary wood products, conveys a modernist vocabulary. The blending of this simple severity with the nostalgic wood finishes creates a quality of surprise and the warmth of the familiar.

2

3

4

5

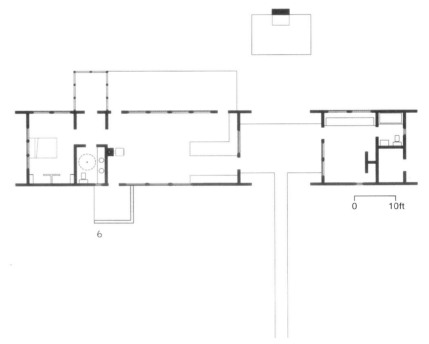

6

1   Exterior looking northeast
2   Northeast view from porch
3   Exterior looking northwest
4   Interior view to northeast
5   Southwest view of interior
6   Floor plan

Photography: Peter Bastianelli Kerze

1

1   A flat-roofed colonnaded portico connects the central two-story block to the front pavilions
2   The handmade stucco-over-brick Doric columns frame the Gulf views
3   From the water's edge, subtle geometries coalesce to endow this view with its magical countenance

Ken Tate Architect

GULFSIDE CLASSICAL

Gulfport, Mississippi, USA

Situated on a 1-acre site on the Gulf Coast, where the light is bright and clear, this house offers an etiolated study in classical motifs, here distilled to a purist palette and strong forms. Its front faces the expansive horizon of the water, viewed over a long, low wall that defines the motor court's perimeter. This wall hides the street behind, but underscores the continuity of the horizon, interrupted only at the entrance by the two flanking pylons. The house itself reflects this horizontality in the colonnade's forceful entablature, which stands in front of the central two-story block. Although such primary elements set the tone for the house, this is by no means a simple structure, but a complex compound. The main volume is flanked by hyphenated wings, further enhanced by an oceanfront pavilion as well as separate shelters for guests, automobiles, and poolside entertaining. While diverse in function, these outbuildings are **linked by a continuous architectural language** that includes Doric columns, segmental-arched openings, and a whitewashed, achromatic palette that allows the drama of the architecture and views to assume center stage. || The total building size (including front portico, front pavilion, rear lower loggia, rear upper porch, pool house loggia, golf cart building, and garage) is 11,478 square feet. The living area is approximately 8000 square feet.

2

3

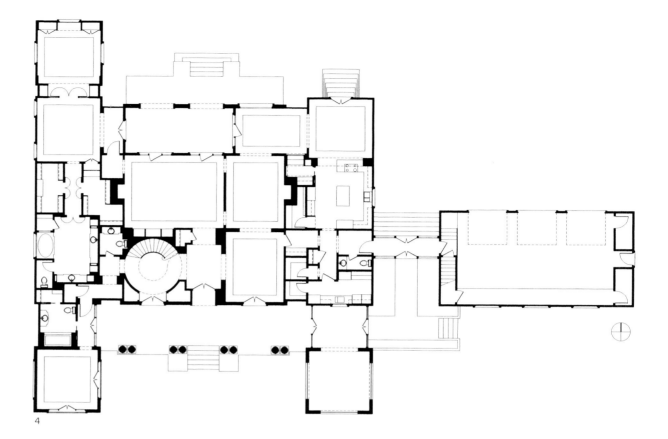

4   Floor plan

5   A sitting room off the breakfast room is an ideal spot from
      which to observe the rear courtyard and swimming pool

6   The curved stair, on axis with the foyer, receives light from
      the Gulf

7   The breakfast and sitting rooms are on axis with the loggia
      and the master bedroom beyond

8   Glass doors in the master bedroom open onto a private study

9   Loggia, sitting, and breakfast room axis has openings left and
      right to the pool, the living room, the parlor, poolhouse
      breezeway, and kitchen

Photography: Gordon Beall (1,2,5,7–9); Dan Bibb (3); Mick Hales (6)

4

5

6

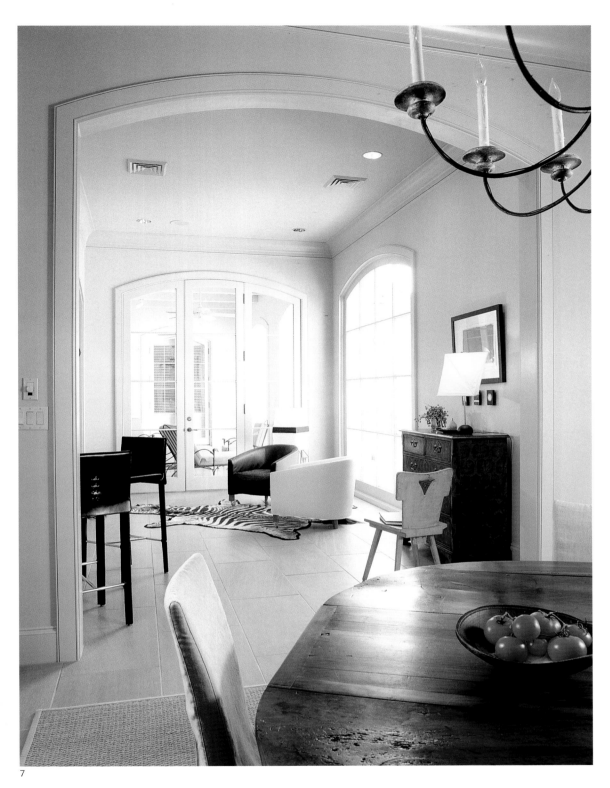

7

8

9

1

2

3

Bligh Voller Nield Pty Ltd

GULLY HOUSE
Yeronga, Queensland, Australia

Located in a gully near the river in Brisbane's inner southern suburbs, this small, 3200-square-foot house takes full advantage of its **secluded site and intimate views** over lush, sub-tropical vegetation. || The need to raise the living areas above ground-level overland flow paths, while retaining significant existing trees on the 7000-square-foot site, influenced the decision to arrange the house over three levels, maintaining a small footprint. The lower floor accommodates cars, storage, and rainwater tanks. The main floor, accessed by a long bridge across the gully, enjoys views to both the north and east over adjoining gardens. It accommodates large living areas, study, guest room, kitchen, laundry, and guest bathroom; the living areas open onto a large north-facing deck with stairs connected to the garden. The upper level, which overlooks the large, almost two-story-high living spaces, includes a generous master bedroom with bay window toward the river views and a mezzanine studio. || The character of the house and the method of construction respond to the particular physical characteristics of the site: the house straddles a stormwater and sewer line, neighbors to the west are in close proximity, the dense tree canopy casts high levels of shade over the site, and the soil conditions are fragile. The house employs a lightweight construction system supported on a grid of steel columns to the lower level with a hybrid timber and steel

frame to the upper levels. It is clad externally with black-stained plywood to diminish its apparent bulk; small aluminum cover strips at the plywood joints signify the constructed nature of the object. Other elements, including the fireplace, bay windows to the study and master bedroom, and an extension to the guest bedroom that protrudes from the main body of the house, are clad in zincalume sheet. Large expanses of glass allow maximum views over the surrounding gardens but are arranged to provide an appropriate level of privacy. || The interiors of the Gully House are deliberately simple and minimalist. This approach was influenced by the client's significant collection of contemporary art and an eclectic collection of contemporary and antique furniture. The interior spaces have been arranged for a high level of flexibility, allowing spaces to be joined together to afford larger views and better cross-ventilation. This is achieved by large sections of sliding walls, open balustrades, and louvers between rooms. Given that the house is only for two residents, the levels of privacy required within were relatively minimal. || Notwithstanding the restricted budget and the construction difficulties of the site, the house is remarkably private and enjoys a strong, but complementary, connection with the sub-tropical landscape.

1   North face of the house from adjoining garden
2   Western face of the house with entry bridge and front porch
3   Approach to the house from private laneway with pedestrian bridge to entry
4   View from southwest

4

5

5   Outdoor living room looking back to principal living/dining space
6   Principal living and dining space shows connection to outdoor living area
7   View from entry space through stair to principal living spaces
8   High volumes and permeable walls enhance natural ventilation
9   Upper floor plan
10 Mid floor plan
11 Lower floor plan

Photography: David Sandison

6

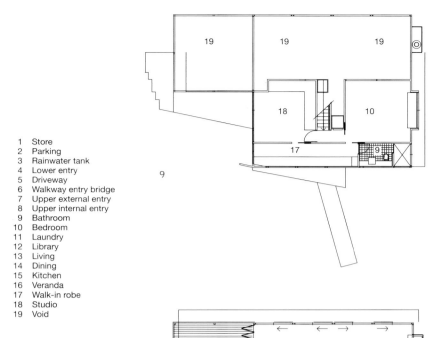

1 Store
2 Parking
3 Rainwater tank
4 Lower entry
5 Driveway
6 Walkway entry bridge
7 Upper external entry
8 Upper internal entry
9 Bathroom
10 Bedroom
11 Laundry
12 Library
13 Living
14 Dining
15 Kitchen
16 Veranda
17 Walk-in robe
18 Studio
19 Void

9

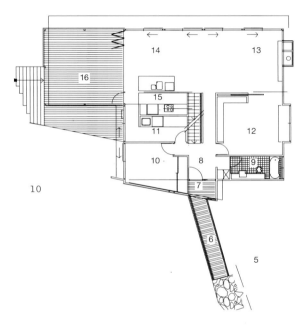

10

7

8

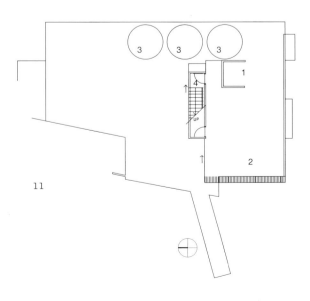

11

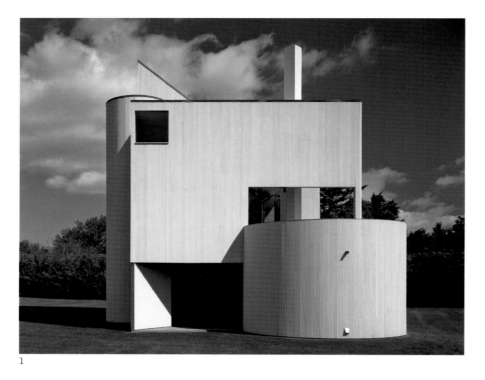

1

2

1   West façade
2   Living and dining rooms
3   Northwest corner
4   South façade at dusk
5   Master bedroom loft
6   Spiral stair

Photography: Scott Frances/Esto

Gwathmey Siegel & Associates Architects

GWATHMEY RESIDENCE AND STUDIO

Amagansett, New York, USA

At the time of design, this site was surrounded by undeveloped land. Future construction anticipated at the time has since occurred. Access to the property is from the south with views across the dunes to the ocean. The program of the original 1200-square-foot house included a living/dining space, kitchen, master bedroom/studio, two guest bedrooms, and a workroom. A year after completion, a second 480-square-foot structure was added, accommodating a guest room and full studio. || Within the limited budget, a design parti and vernacular were developed that set a precedent for later work. By organizing the house vertically, programmatic and site constraints were resolved through sectional as well as plan manipulations. The guest rooms, workroom, and covered terrace occupy the ground floor; the living/dining room and kitchen are on the second floor; the master bedroom/studio on the third floor balcony overlooks the double-height living space. Raising the 'public' spaces one level above grade capitalized on the extensive views and established a relationship between living areas and the ground plane that is unique to rural house architecture. By placing the continuously occupied portion of the habital house on a base of intermittent functions, the parlor floor was reinterpreted and a sense of privacy was established. || The addition of the studio extended and enriched the site/object relationship. The studio's section is derived from the house, but by siting it at a 45-degree angle to the original structure, a perceptual dynamic of corner versus façade was created. A second dynamic was established by the juxtaposition of structures and ground: whereas the house is clearly anchored, the studio is precarious and appears to be almost in motion. **The sense of duality, expectation, and change** adds a further dimension to the overall composition. || Both structures are composed of primary, minimal geometric forms that appear to be carved from a solid volume rather than constructed as an additive, planar assemblage. As they are manipulated in response to site, orientation, program, and structure, the intersections of these forms are defined by either erosion or natural light, or both. || The use of cedar siding on both the interior and exterior of the wood-frame buildings establishes a primary referential container from which secondary and tertiary elements are developed. Transparency, perceptual and literal extension, and volumetric interpenetration give this small building a unique sense of scale and presence.

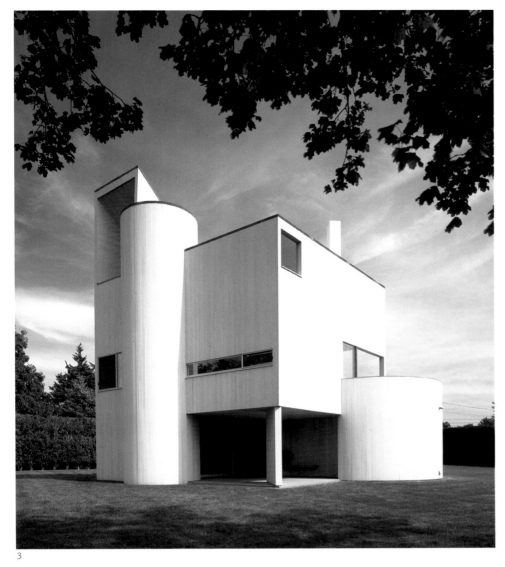

3

4

5

6

1

1   A rectangular pool is set on the side of the house,
    overlooking a small inlet
2   A long, open porch with views to the bay graces the
    back of the house
3   A series of gambrel-roofed volumes break up the scale
    of this L-shaped house

Austin Patterson Disston Architects

HAMPTONS HOUSE

Long Island, New York, USA

Set on a stunning waterfront site—a peninsula with 270-degree views—this Hamptons house is designed to take advantage of the views. The clients sought a house that could accommodate their family life and their entertaining needs. || The L-shaped rectangular house was designed with these requirements for views and entertaining in mind. The quieter section of the house is located to the east and includes the guest suite and octagonal library. The more formal public gathering spaces are set in the middle of the house: the entry foyer, living and dining rooms, and the more informal spaces—the kitchen, family room, screened porch, and exercise room—have access to the terrace and the pool to the west. || The 8600-square-foot, six-bedroom home is built in the **Shingle style, reflecting the Hamptons vernacular,** with a central double-gabled volume flanked by two pavilions on either side. A single-car garage is set within the main house, but the main garage and storage space are within the separate 2000-square-foot Shingle-style barn. This post and beam structure includes a wine vault, game room, and storage area, as well as garage space. || Materials used in the project include painted wood on the interior, stained red cedar shingles on the exterior siding and roof, white quarter-sawn oak flooring throughout, spruce paneling in the library, a walnut built-in bar, limestone fireplace surrounds, and an Esmeralda granite countertop in the kitchen.

2

3

4

4   A large island with a granite countertop is ideal for
    informal gatherings or a simple breakfast
5   Paneled screened porch
6   A painted floor complements the round dining table,
    creating a simple yet elegant dining room
7   The large master bath includes private shower and
    toilet and an ample soaking tub
8   Second floor plan
9   First floor plan

Photography: Tria Giovan

5

6

7

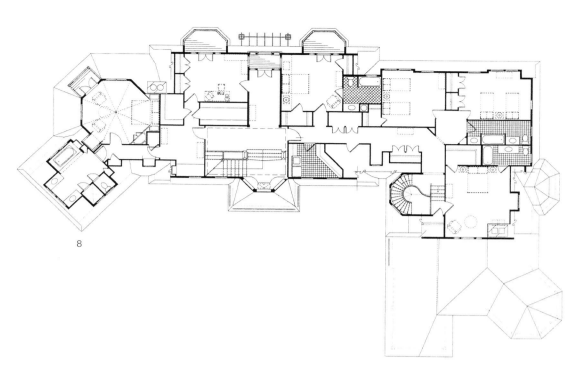

8

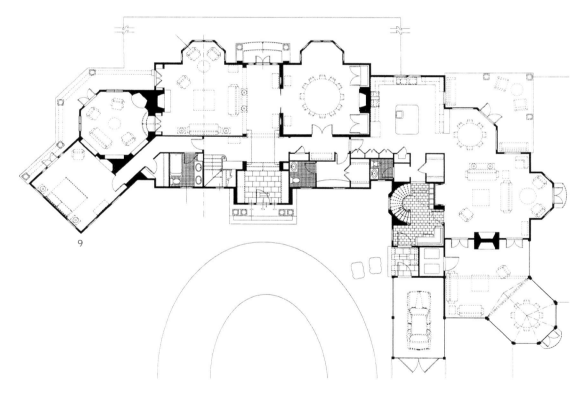

9

1   Front door and column detail
2   Front elevation

1

Harrison Design Associates

HAWN RESIDENCE
Atlanta, Georgia, USA

An estate home of formal grandeur, this residence recalls 1920's-era Atlanta, a period when the city's foremost families provided their homes with opulent public façades that could be enjoyed by all. Following Beaux-Arts design principles, the five-bay façade reaches a crescendo in the center with the giant order columned temple. The craftsmanship of sculpted limestone walls and trim is especially evident in the 27-foot Corinthian columns. Taking three years to quarry and sculpt in Indiana, they are the largest monolithic limestone columns in the city. The entry surround displays a composition of Italian Mannerist detailing with broken pediment, swags, cartouche, and strapwork over fluted Doric columns. The garden façade is inspired by 18th-century Neo-Palladian work in England. || The interior rooms are aligned in a formal layout with the entry axis terminating in the two-story salon. From the circular entry hall another cross axis connects the dining room with the library. The double cube height of the library with its walnut and iron circular stair is inspired by George Vanderbilt's Art Library in Biltmore House in Asheville, North Carolina. Jacques Brunet of Paris, former head of the French Iron Workers' Guild, designed the wrought iron and bronze openwork and handrails throughout the interior and exterior of the home. His most dramatic work occurs in the majestic stair balustrade composed of gilded birds, cherubs, and floral motifs. All entertainment spaces are accessed from the terrace level and include a billiard room and pub, wine cellar and tasting room, home theater, shooting gallery, and an outdoor swimming pool.

2

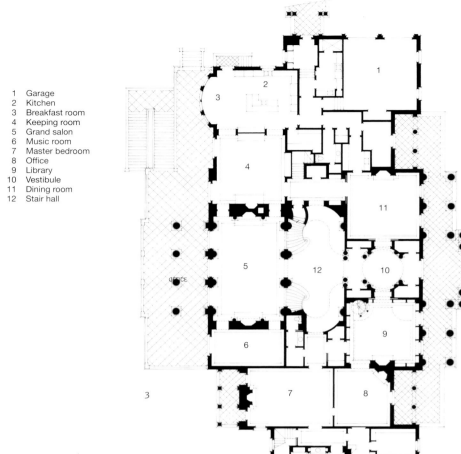

1   Garage
2   Kitchen
3   Breakfast room
4   Keeping room
5   Grand salon
6   Music room
7   Master bedroom
8   Office
9   Library
10 Vestibule
11 Dining room
12 Stair hall

Photography: John Umberger (1,2,7–9); Lynn McGill (4); Gil Stose (5,6)

8

7

9

Steve Domoney Architecture

HAWTHORN RESIDENCE

Hawthorn, Victoria, Australia

This new house is situated between two properties of historical significance within a heritage precinct. Defying pressure from the local council, the architects considered the best way to pay the required respect to the neighboring buildings was to avoid replication of their form or detail and instead establish a polite linking piece between. The building proudly celebrates its own place in history, is detailed and configured in a modernist manner, but is scaled and massed to maintain the integrity of the streetscape. || The new house recognizes the transition in height from the two-story Victorian house on its western flank to the single-story Federation home on its eastern side. Predominantly single-story, the house has a contained mezzanine component buried in the folds of the pitched roof. This hovers above a strong, horizontally arranged ground-level podium, setting its own agenda quite removed from that of its neighbors yet not competing with them. || The brief called for a family-friendly home with five bedrooms, an open feel to all living spaces, little formality, good natural light, and a strong connection to outdoor living spaces. The architectural response reflects the nature of the family—their open, friendly, and very Australian qualities. This honest and inviting air resonates throughout the home. || The living areas follow a meandering path, loosely connected to all internal spaces. Three defined private external spaces are generated by the plan. Bedrooms are aligned along the eastern boundary. They are more formally structured and are detached from the living areas to provide retreat and seclusion. || The hub of the house is the kitchen; its central position commands the best vantage point to survey all the living areas of the house as well as the external spaces. A playful inclusion was to elevate the level of the pool to beyond that of the adjoining living space. The glazed external wall of the building provides the support and separation to the pool. A mezzanine studio above the kitchen oversees the living areas. Its position allows the parents to engage in their work yet feel part of the social activities below. || Materials include timber flooring and external decking sourced from recycled stock. Maintenance of exterior finishes is minimized through the use of pressed metal fascias and soffit linings, Corten steel cladding to the walls, and colored cement renders. Most of the interior walls were plaster-glass finished and thus do not require painting. || This meandering geometric framework of internal volumes and embraced external space provides **a relaxed, yet dynamic and stimulating environment** for family living. It exemplifies how a contemporary building can integrate successfully within a heritage context.

3

1 Mezzanine studio
2 Guest bedroom
3 Bathroom

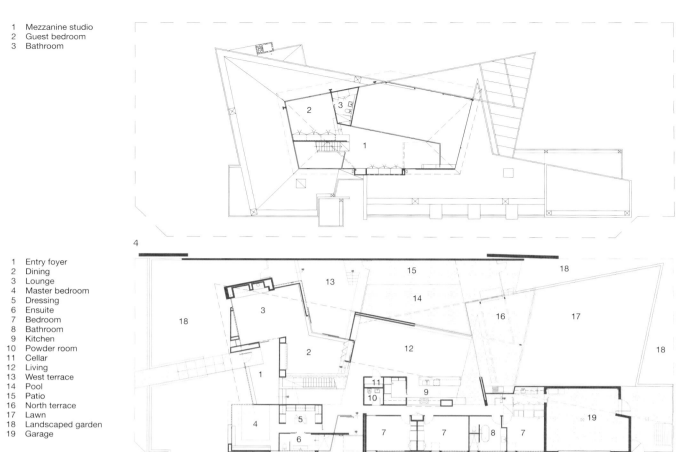

4

1 Entry foyer
2 Dining
3 Lounge
4 Master bedroom
5 Dressing
6 Ensuite
7 Bedroom
8 Bathroom
9 Kitchen
10 Powder room
11 Cellar
12 Living
13 West terrace
14 Pool
15 Patio
16 North terrace
17 Lawn
18 Landscaped garden
19 Garage

5

0   5m

6

7

8

Photography: Derek Swalwell

9

10

143

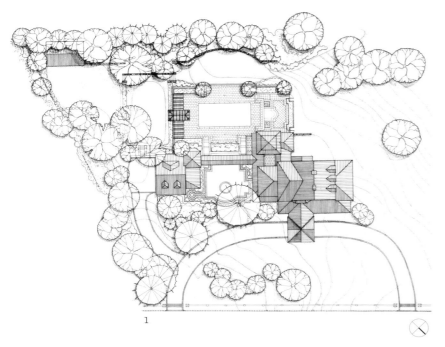

1

2

Peter Gisolfi Associates

HOROWITZ RESIDENCE
Englewood, New Jersey, USA

This house was a 14-room, 6200-square-foot relic of the 1890s, situated on a sloping, 2-acre site in suburban New Jersey. It was in a sad state of disrepair, covered in white asbestos shingles, with asphalt shingle roofs, and an interior plan that suffered from many unhappy alterations. The site was completely overgrown with little evidence of the original landscape remaining. || The interior was gutted and all the exterior building materials, except the frame, sheathing, and the original stonework, were stripped away. The interior plan now revolves around a new, three-story, open entry hall paneled with oiled mahogany surrounding a cascading staircase. The exterior is totally transformed. The asbestos shingles were replaced with cedar shingles and a porte-cochère, a surrounding veranda, and a major extension were added. A new guest house, potting shed, and garage were also added, and the second building was connected to the original house with a wooden arcade and lattice fence. The new buildings that now occupy the site have changed the former object in space into a group of buildings that engages a series of outdoor spaces. || The first major outdoor space is the front lawn, which is defined by a stone wall and fence along the street, a curving driveway, and the expanded edge of the house and guest house with the veranda and porte-cochère. The second major outdoor space is the sloping rear lawn, which connects seamlessly to the neighboring properties in the informal, Romantic landscape style. || The four smaller outdoor rooms are orthogonal in design. The most enclosed is the rose garden, which relates axially to the dining room and to the potting shed and is further defined by the lattice fence and the arcade. A fountain sits in the middle, on axis with the center of the dining room and the potting shed, and on the cross-axis with the swimming pool. || The second rectangular outdoor room contains elaborate planting beds and a swimming pool terrace. The long axis of the pool connects downhill to the third outdoor room—the outdoor spa. || The fourth outdoor room in this series is the croquet court, which is separated from the pool terrace on the uphill side by a wrought iron pergola. The orthogonal sequence—rose garden, pool terrace, croquet court, and spa terrace—is interconnected and separated from the informal landscape by a series of retaining walls. || **The house and garden form a uniquely American composition**—a remnant of the 1890s transformed 100 years later into a villa, surrounded by a Romantic landscape.

3

4

5

6

145

1

2

Polhemus Savery DaSilva Architects Builders

HOUSE AT POPPONESSET

Mashpee, Massachusetts, USA

The location of this striking house is highly sensitive, right on a Nantucket Sound beach. The lot is fairly narrow and restricted by conservation setbacks and coverage regulations. Fitting the house the clients desired, plus a garage, driveway, septic system and deck, within the coverage allowed by the regulations was a challenge for the architects. || The form of the house is volumetrically complex, particularly at the roof. The traditional architectural shapes that create the complexity primarily appear to be carved from a solid mass; more a reductive approach than an additive one. These characteristics make the house seem 'friendlier' than some of its boxy neighbors that may be smaller in size but have a bigger impact on the neighborhood. || Chunky, over-scaled details help make the overall seem smaller and help give an elemental sense of shelter, like something depicted in a child's drawing. The roof and its shapes are dominant, giving the house a 'top heavy' feeling like the great Queen Anne-style houses of the English countryside. This house is in the Shingle-style tradition, but it is **lighthearted and whimsical** as opposed to brooding and dark, or formal and serious. || First-floor rooms are set in an informal, irregular layout. The kitchen is at the center and the other public spaces revolve around it. All the major public rooms are open to one another to allow for casual flow, yet they are also defined by partial walls, ceiling shapes, built-ins, and color changes. The difference between the irregular plan shapes of the interior rooms and the regular perimeter of the house is taken up by a covered porch that faces the street and the ocean. || The complex plan and massing characteristics help create opportunities for the rooms to have multiple exposures. Natural light was very important in the design and all the major rooms have windows on at least two sides. This lengthens the amount of day in which sunlight penetrates, reduces the sense of glare that windows facing only one direction can create, and maximizes ocean views. A cupola and light shaft beneath it bring natural light from above through the center of the house all the way down into the kitchen. All major rooms have water views, even if they are through another space. || Materials include white cedar sidewall shingles; red cedar roof shingles and trim; Eagle aluminum-clad windows; white oak, bamboo, and tile floors; and painted wood cabinetry.

4

5

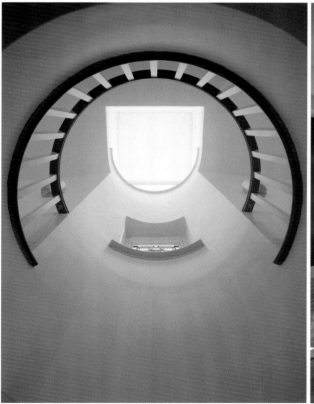

6

7

8

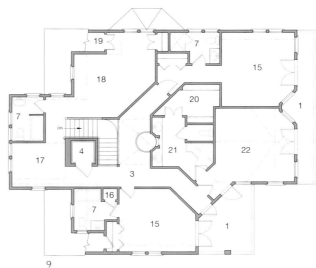

9

1	Porch	12	Dining
2	Entry	13	Kitchen
3	Hall	14	Deck
4	Elevator	15	Bedroom
5	Pantry	16	Linen
6	Laundry	17	Sitting area
7	Bathroom	18	Study
8	Shower	19	Attic
9	Home theater	20	Closet
10	Game room	21	Master bathroom
11	Living room	22	Master bedroom

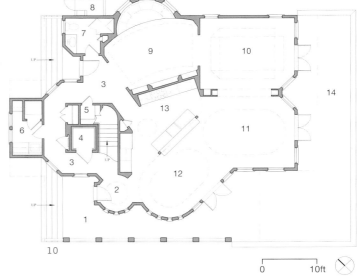

10

0   10ft

4   The view is enhanced when framed by playful architectural elements
5   The small entry hall provides a feeling of compression in contrast to the
     open spaces beyond
6   At the center of the kitchen one can look up through the house to where
     light floods in from the rooftop cupola
7   Curved lines in the ceiling and floor help organize the flowing spaces
8   The master bedroom and its balcony look out over the ocean
9   Second floor plan
10   First floor plan

Photography: Brian Vanden Brink

149

1   Kitchen with night view of downtown Naples
2   View of the living room toward the kitchen with sliding
    glass panel open

1

M Campi, L Giusti [GBC Architects]

HOUSE IN NAPLES

Naples, Campania, Italy

The clients' brief was for a house based on linear principles, simple geometries, minimum decoration, and muted colors. They wanted the wealth of light, noise, and color that characterize the city of Naples to provide the backdrop to the house. || The aim was to create a space where **rooms can flow without rigid definition** while maintaining clean lines and simple forms. This intention is evident right from the entrance hallway, where a large glazed aperture allows a flow of light that changes during the course of the day, and leads to a suite of rooms whose functions are not immediately obvious. || The large living area is the hub of the home. Here, a view of the city is framed by the windows surrounded by light wood paneling along the side walls. The living room supports several different functions: the lounge area with its comfortable L-shaped sofa, the dining area, and the kitchen. The kitchen features a peninsula work area with large glass and marble worktops. Large floor-to-ceiling sliding doors divide off the kitchen, or can be left open to see along the axis that leads from the dining room through to the studio. The study unit, sandwiched between the two bedrooms, can also be screened off in this way. || The outside edges of the functional rooms are 'traced' by large sliding walls, which make it possible to change and reinterpret the spaces, adapting them to different moments and moods of daily life. || Carefully modulated artificial light is also skilfully incorporated into the design: the light sources are hidden from view and become an integral part of the composition. Large, semi-transparent surfaces light up to provide a background to sculptures of ancient art; indirect ceiling lights illuminate edges before changing direction; little floor marker lights emphasize the main axes of the house. Small downlights illuminate the principal areas, imparting a soft glow through the apartment, while wayfinder spots set into the base of the walls indicate changes of direction. Various tones of white, transparent glass, and the natural textures of wood provide the muted, neutral backdrop. A French marble is used for the floors throughout.

150

2

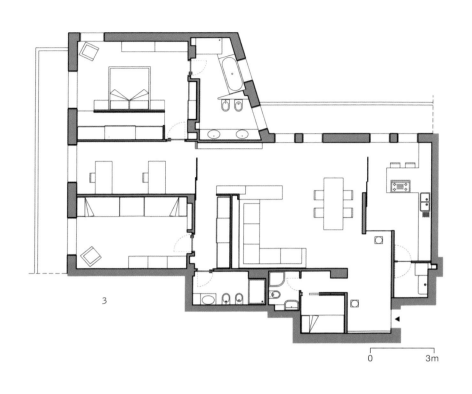

3

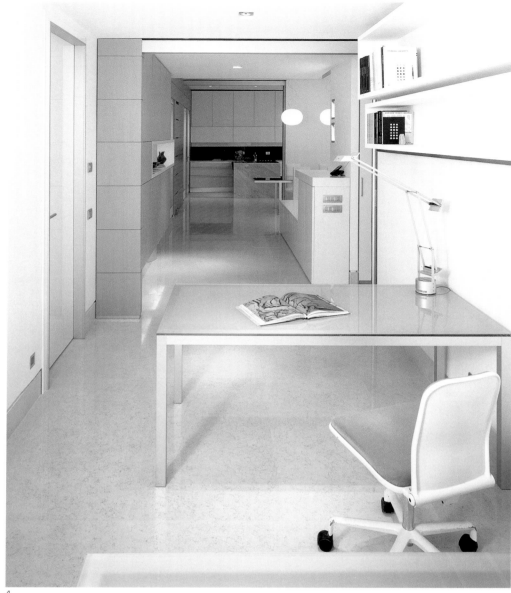

4

5

6

Photography: Luciano Pedicini

7

1   The three boxes are carefully placed upon the flat-roofed house
2   Axonometric
3   Evening view from the street

Daigo Ishii + Future-scape Architects

HOUSE IN NIGATA

Nigata, Japan

The extensive lush rice fields adjacent to this house were a major influence on its design, and are never far from view. || The transparent composition is a series of discrete 'huts' or boxes, with three small boxes sitting above the flat-roofed structure on the ground floor. The open ground-floor space is a 'public' area for entertaining friends. The rice fields provide the backdrop for all the activities in the ground-floor spaces. || The three boxes above are the 'private spaces', with bedrooms and utility areas. Each box has windows on all four sides, to provide maximum light and ventilation, and to allow a seamless connection to the outdoors. The placement of the boxes in relation to each other was carefully considered to allow each to receive the maximum light and breezes. || **Each box is distinguished by different materials** and the way the views are framed. The west box is finished in wood with a warm ambience. The central box has a metal interior and the scenery is framed by a large picture window. Mirrors and high-gloss paint characterize the interior of the east box; the scenery is reflected on the interior surfaces, further emphasizing the connection with the exterior. || The color and materials used on the exterior are typical of the area, and the volume of the architecture is similar to the surrounding houses, thus providing continuity with the townscape. The house's unique composition allows it to stand out in its own subtle way.

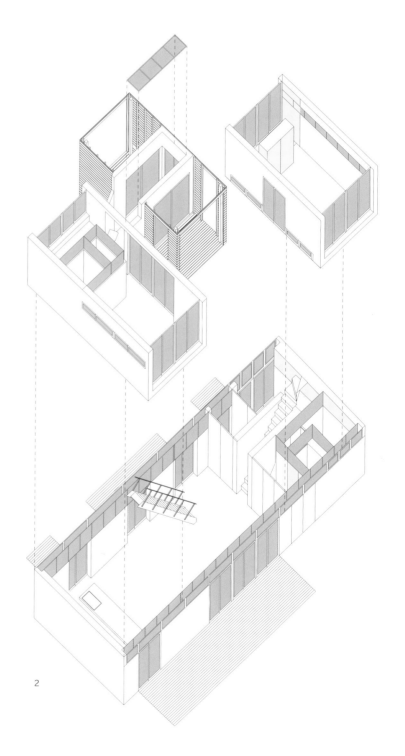

3

4   The central box is predominantly metal
5   Two staircases lead to the boxes on the upper floor
6   The central box has balconies on both sides
7   Scenery is reflected on the glossy surfaces and mirrors in the east box
8   Floor plan

Photography: K Torimura (1,3–5); Isamu Hirukawa (6,7)

4

5

6

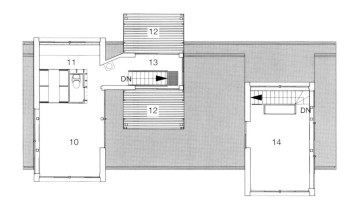

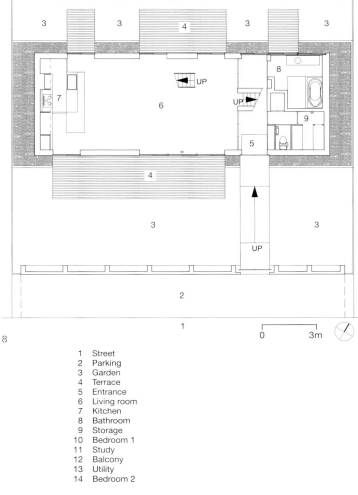

7

8

1 Street
2 Parking
3 Garden
4 Terrace
5 Entrance
6 Living room
7 Kitchen
8 Bathroom
9 Storage
10 Bedroom 1
11 Study
12 Balcony
13 Utility
14 Bedroom 2

0   3m

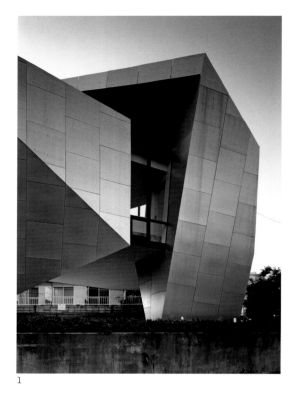

1

2

1   The house is raised on pilotis
2   Exterior at night
3   Southeast view of exterior

Satoshi Okada Architects

HOUSE IN WAKABADAI

Kanagawa Prefecture, Japan

Wakabadai is the last of the development areas in Tama New Town, the largest housing development in Japan, situated to the west of Tokyo. The site is at the end of a blind alley, a 4-meter-wide dogleg private road connected to the main street. It is bordered by a river on its south side, and has views over green hills on the other side. The site had been abandoned for some time because of its proximity to the river and its inconvenient location, set far back from the main street. || This small residence has a building area of less than 66 square meters. The clients, a couple in their mid-thirties, requested **'a house that is attractive and cool.'** They were happy to leave the details up to the architect, who believes that certain things are just so attractive that words cannot describe them; he calls this mysterious attraction the 'intensity of architecture,' and the house was an attempt to exemplify this notion. || The project began with considering the movement of cars within the site. The clients requested undercover parking for two cars, with space to manoeuver. Raising the house on pilotis allowed most of the site area of 116 square meters to be devoted to the cars. The small remaining area became the core, housing the entrance, staircase, and storage. || The scale of the outer shape of the building relates to its surroundings; the shape was defined by tilting and trimming volumes and surfaces. Special concern was given to the neighboring house to the west and the apartment building to the north. The living room window on the southeast corner of the house is open to a view over the hills on the opposite side of the river. Walls were tilted inward to allow unobstructed views. From the first floor and up, external walls were arranged so that the distance between the house and its neighbors gradually increases in an attempt to reduce the mass of the house. || The structure is a wooden construction, mostly comprising 2x4 members and laminated panels. Long piles were required because of the unstable ground. A patent-pending new wooden structural method developed by the architect, the Container Structure System, was used in this project. The house includes three structural elements that support the double-layered living section. The largest element in the Container Structure is the core accommodating the staircase, storage, and lavatory. The other two elements house utility pipes and wires. || The exterior walls were covered with 5-millimeter slit boards of rustproof, 1-millimeter steel sheet, placed 5 millimeters from the base steel plates to create heat-insulating air space in between, to keep the interior at a comfortable temperature during the summer.

3

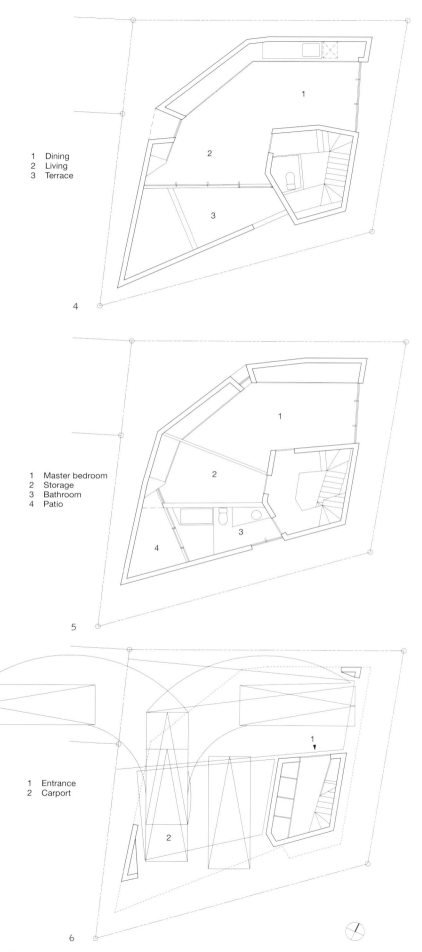

1 Dining
2 Living
3 Terrace

4

1 Master bedroom
2 Storage
3 Bathroom
4 Patio

5

1 Entrance
2 Carport

6

7

8

4 Second floor plan
5 First floor plan
6 Ground floor plan
7 Living area
8 The core accommodates the entrance to the house
9 View from living to dining area
10 Bathroom
11 Interior stair
12 Patio

Photography: courtesy Satoshi Okada architects; Nacasa & Partners

9

10

11

12

1

1   View from approach
2   Top floor plan
3   Main floor plan
4   Approach at night

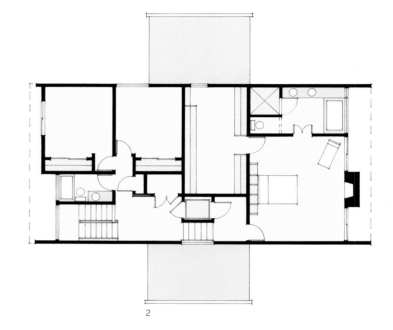

2

McInturff Architects

KALEIDOSCOPE HOUSE

Vienna, Virginia, USA

Built for a lively empty-nester couple who had always longed to build a house of their own, this project is like a kaleidoscope—a metal tube closed on its sides to very near neighbors and open on each end through colorful window walls to the tremendous length of its wooded site. Inside, **layers of colored walls** modulate the largely open interior, where, at the center, a wide-open kitchen acts as a sort of cockpit from which the owners can entertain in every direction. A tight budget dictated a simple form and straightforward material palette, but color is free, and the light and views of the woods are there for the taking.

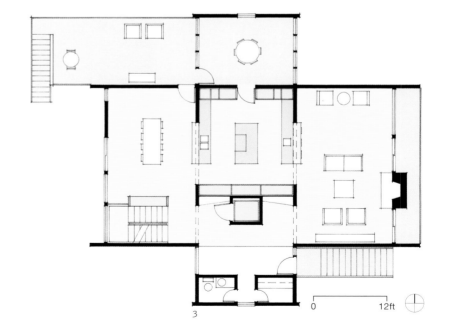

3   0   12ft

4

5

5   View of kitchen from living room
6   Dining room
7   Living room
8   Living room viewed from entry

Photography: Julia Heine

6

7

8

1

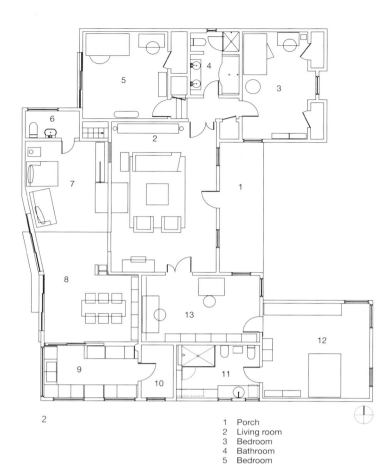

2

1   Porch
2   Living room
3   Bedroom
4   Bathroom
5   Bedroom
6   Powder room
7   Family room
8   Dining room
9   Kitchen
10 Laundry
11 Bathroom
12 Master bedroom
13 Office

Designed Real Estate

KAZOVSKY HOUSE

Los Angeles, California, USA

This property, bordering mountains in the Hollywood hills, is an urban retreat, visually and aurally isolated from the clamor and activity of nearby Hollywood. The house, the architect's own, is a design laboratory for prototyping, testing, and showcasing new ideas and products. || The 2400-square-foot home features a living room, family room, home office, kitchen, dining room, powder room, master bedroom with full master bathroom, and a children's wing with two bedrooms and a shared bathroom. Outdoor spaces include a dining area with kitchen, pool, spa, deck, fireplace, underground bathroom and laundry room, and patios. The home represents **a merging of old and new**—in building, design, and attitude. || The interiors were completely renovated, opening the kitchen, creating a dining room and powder room, and expanding the bathrooms. In the living room, the existing vaulted wood-beam ceiling and brick walls were retained, and new quartersawn white oak flooring was installed. A new glass-and-wood entry door ushers light liberally into the room. Brick wall openings into and out of the living room are outlined in steel. A new dining room was created by reducing the kitchen's original size and breaking down a wall to open the space. New stainless-steel appliances, granite countertops, limestone flooring, track lighting, and Italian black oak veneered cabinetry and panels give the kitchen a sophisticated look. || In the master bedroom, the charms of the existing house linger in the vaulted wood-beam ceiling. The existing master bathroom was nearly doubled in size, creating a charismatic, uneven ceiling line in the process. Applying her streamlined modern vision to the master bedroom, the architect carried through the white oak flooring and introduced clean-lined black oak wardrobes, drawer units, and storage units. || The north wing of the house comprises the children's wing—two bedrooms featuring beds, storage units, and accessories designed by the architect, and a full bathroom to which a shower, new bathtub, and two-basin counter were added. || In the front yard, the outdoor dining area looks onto a mosaic water feature that rests against the stark concrete wall of the above-ground pool. Terraced steps—illuminated at night by LED lights—lead up to the home's entrance and new heated lap pool with deck. Solar panels located on the roof above the master bedroom heat the pool for use during cooler weather. At night, fiber optic lights in the pool and spa illuminate the water in varying hues.

3

1   New lap pool features built-in benches
2   Floor plan of renovated house
3   The house is an urban retreat nestled in the hills

4

5

6

4 Brick wall openings are outlined in steel
5 Long windows—instead of backsplash—frame kitchen views
6 Dining and family rooms open onto back patio
7 Architect-designed headboard and suspended side tables
8 Surprise spaces display collections
9 Pocket door can separate kitchen from dining room
10 Children's bathroom features separate basins

Photography: Josh Perrin

7

8

9

10

1 Street elevation toward market
2 Section
3 Front elevation

1

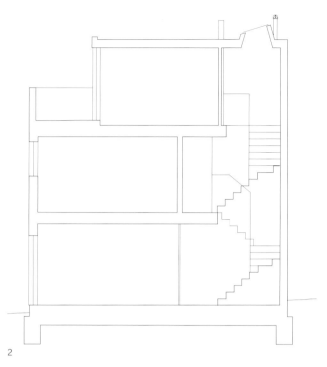

2

Richard Dudzicki Associates

LACON ROAD RESIDENCE
Dulwich, London, UK

The brief from the client for this project was a contemporary family house with a garden space. The house was to be **flexible and sustainable**, was to cost no more than £150,000 to build, and was to be built as quickly as possible. The site, measuring 45.5 square meters, is at the beginning of a Victorian residential street in inner London. It incorporated a derelict garage and adjoining single parking space. ‖ Planning was eventually granted following a committee hearing. Planning constraints did not allow any clear windows in the east, south, and north elevation due to amenity concerns; additionally, the architects did not want to embrace a view of a nearby substation. To resolve this, a large roof light was installed above the staircase to allow light into the depth of the building. The result is that the majority of the glazing is on the west elevation with a tiny amount that wraps around to allow views of the market street. ‖ The open-plan ground floor consists of a kitchen, lounge, and dining area overlooking an evening garden with an olive tree. A Pyroglass protected lobby leads to a well-lit staircase to the first floor. Two double bedrooms, each with storage walls and one with an ensuite bathroom, are on the mid-floor. The main bathroom is surprisingly large with a bath and walk-in shower fitting neatly under the stairs, utilizing all the available space. ‖ The top floor is light and airy, with large windows and patio doors leading onto a roof terrace. The floor is one large room, used as a study/lounge, although it could be turned easily into another bedroom. This looks out onto the Victorian 'bedknobs and broomsticks' roofscape of inner London while allowing views of the setting sun. Out on the terrace a bamboo screen is employed as a planning condition to prevent overlooking while provision has been made for a wind generator or solar panels. ‖ The soil conditions and type of building required a raft-type foundation; this thermal mass is used to help heat or cool the building by the use of under-floor wet heating, with the large overhead skylight allowing cooling by opening in the summer. The SIP panels are clad with a recycled glass Varotec board followed by a Sto render. No steel beams are used and the house is a 100 percent timber construction, the majority of which has been recycled. The roof and guttering are zinc.

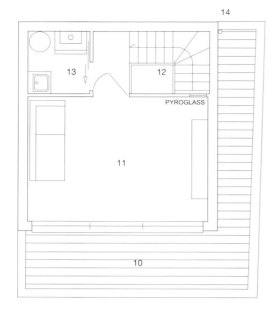

PYROGLASS

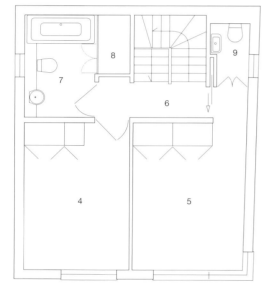

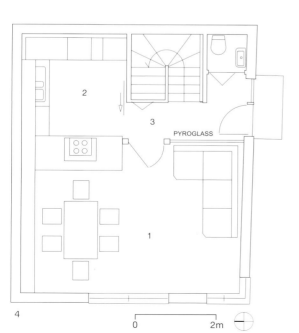

PYROGLASS

1 Living room
2 Kitchen
3 Hallway stairs
4 Bedroom 1
5 Bedroom 2
6 Hallway stairs
7 Bathroom
8 Shower
9 Ensuite
10 Terrace
11 Living room
12 Skylight
13 Utility room
14 Wind generator

0   2m

4

5

6

7

8

9

4 Floor plans, from bottom: ground floor, mid floor, top floor
5 Kitchen/dining area
6 Top-floor living room
7 Front garden
8 Glass to glass detail
9 Panoramic view from the top-floor living space

Photography: Timothy Soar; www.soargallery.co.uk

1

2

Lake|Flato Architects

LAKE AUSTIN RESIDENCE

Austin, Texas, USA

This 6000-square-foot modern 'village' is on a narrow, 1.7-acre site on Lake Austin. The site was made even tighter by an existing 30-foot-wide canal running along one edge of the property from the lake to the access road. The canal became the organizing element for the design of a 'fishing camp'—**a series of small pavilions clustered along a wooden boardwalk** that cantilevers out over the canal. || To reach the main house, the property is first entered through a long stone wall that connects two of the three guesthouses. The boardwalk is like an entrance hall, leading to the large screened boathouse, which is also the major gathering space. Water courts were created along the canal with excavated fill, creating a peninsula extending from the dining room and the impression of a building afloat. || The main house sits at the end of a long pier, lined

with three small guesthouses. It contains the communal spaces and three bedrooms and was designed to take advantage of the canal and water courts. Passage through the house provides glimpses and reflections of the outside at every opportunity. || Separate buildings for guests and office define the street entry sequence and front the canal. Stone garden walls face the street and adjacent property, creating courts at the master suite and along the pool, which extends from the master suite to the lakeside cabana. Beyond the glass wall of the master bath is a private Japanese garden courtyard. || Materials—limestone, cypress, and copper sheeting—unify the components, but their relationship to the surrounding water is what ties them together.

3

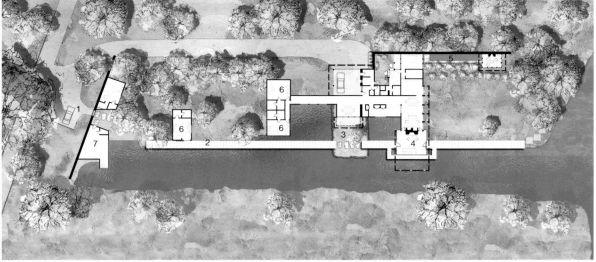

4

1 Entry gate
2 Boardwalk
3 Island
4 Screened boathouse
5 Pool
6 Guest
7 Studio

5

6

1 Boathouse interior
2 Screened boathouse
3 Boardwalk connects a guesthouse, bedrooms, and boathouse along the canal
4 Site plan
5 Copper fireplace in living room
6 Dining room

Photography: Hester + Hardaway (1–3); Atelier Wong Photography (5,6)

1
2

LAKE STREET RESIDENCE

San Francisco, California, USA

The challenge in remodeling a poorly planned, five-bedroom Victorian home in the Richmond district of San Francisco was to create a cohesive, well-lit, modern home for two. The solution lay in opening the interior to make new spatial connections while bringing in light and views. The wide, shallow, two-level residence had two sets of rooms—one facing the street and receiving southern light, the other with views of the wooded Presidio to the north but receiving less light. The rooms were closed off to one another, resulting in underutilized spaces with imbalanced light. ‖ With the help of skylights, windows, wall openings, and an open outlook between rooms, the new interior flows from front to back, as well as from left to right. The central staircase, which previously divided the house, was opened on both ends; formerly a dark object, it has become a dramatic, light-filled, two-story focal point. New rooms with new uses orient around the openings, creating clarity and flow. Art, sculpture, and light liberate the space. ‖ On the first level, a large, well-appointed kitchen flows into the dining and living areas—essentially one 50-foot-long space that looks out to the Presidio. Panels of mirror with wood verticals line the west wall, **bouncing light and views**. Along the street, a new media room and a piano room/library have replaced two of the previous bedrooms. Both new rooms have few walls and are open to the other spaces. Upstairs, skylights and large windows illuminate the new master suite and home office. The serene and luxurious master bath has a large, walk-in shower with walls of limestone and glass. Operable windows with high sills allow great views but no sight lines are allowed in.

1   Street frontage
2   Dining and living space
3   Living space with mirror panels on west wall

3

4

1 Master bedroom
2 Master bathroom
3 Closet
4 Study/home office
5 Office bathroom
6 Walk-in shower

5

1 Deck
2 Breakfast room
3 Kitchen
4 Dining
5 Living
6 Powder room
7 Stair and central hall
8 Guest bathroom
9 Guest bedroom
10 Piano room
11 Media room
12 Rear yard

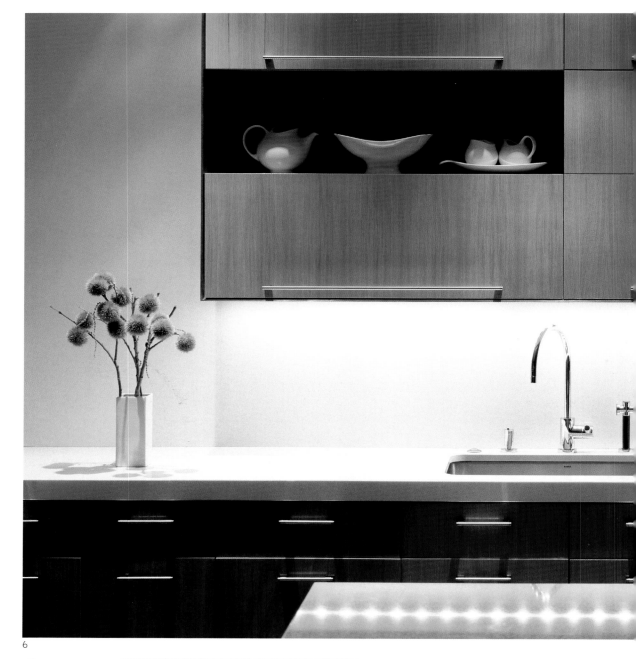

6

7

Photography: Joe Fletcher

8

Mark Dziewulski Architect

1   The form cantilevers over the man-made lake
2   The sculptural roof appears to float over the space
3   Mirror-like reflections appear in the still water at night

LAKESIDE STUDIO
California, USA

The owner of this property wished to create a tranquil and sheltered environment from which to enjoy a rich natural landscape and spectacular river views. The single interior space has a complex program: a combination of office, art studio, flexible living space, and gallery in which to show a rotating display of pieces from the owner's extensive sculpture and painting collection. || The relationship between the natural environment and the building is central to the design. **The sculptural form of the structure curves and twists** to take advantage of the river views. The stretching cantilevered floor carries the observer well over the lake, an experience that is reinforced by views down to the water through areas of transparent glass floor. Projecting over the water, the skeletal metal stair comes to land at a massive stone plinth set into the bank. || Uninterrupted glass walls open the room up to the landscape and the boundaries between exterior and interior are blurred. The space is shaded by the dramatically extended roof overhang. The sense of openness pushes the interior into the realm of the lush foliage of the exterior and the occupant feels fully immersed in a benign landscape. The effect is contemplative and peaceful. || The play of natural light is used in several ways.

Sunlight reflecting off the water dapples the ceiling with constantly changing patterns; skylights bring light deep within the interior and articulate the roof form. Continuing the sequence of roof penetrations, an oculus in the exterior roof allows a slowly moving circle of sunlight to animate the floor. A curved wall of angled translucent and transparent glass panels creates an optical louver that directs views toward the river and provides an illuminated backdrop for sculpture. || In effect the composition becomes a built object responding to the dynamics of a natural context. The form is integrated with this context and yet at the same time makes use of the contrast between the man-made and the natural. Building elements—the floor, roof, solid walls, glass, and piers—are expressed as independent planes, interwoven yet individual. The curved planes are distinctly architectonic yet they share their organic form with the natural world. The openness and apparent agility of the floating structure also alludes to the lightness and elegance of forms found in nature. || Although the final effect appears effortless and clean, it belies the substantial technical, structural, and detailing challenges required from each of the many participants.

4

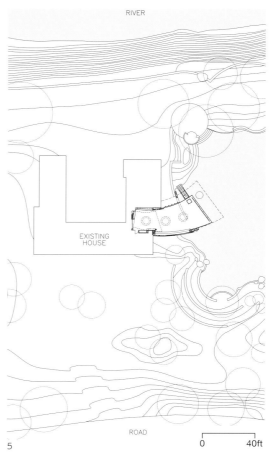

RIVER

EXISTING
HOUSE

ROAD

0   40ft

5

6

4   The space provides a tranquil setting for work
5   Site plan
6   The play of light animates the interiors
7   Clear and translucent glass panels create a louvered
      window wall
8   The translucent glass panels focus views toward the river

Photography: Keith Cronin

7

8

Arkhefield Architects

LANTERN HOUSE
Bardon, Queensland, Australia

Engaging with the bush views to the south while enjoying the northern aspect was the challenge in this design for a new house about 5 kilometers from the center of Brisbane. The architectural concept was a 'perched pavilion' that cantilevers over a heavy masonry base anchored into the site. The primary arrangement of space is vertical and linear, and is articulated by an east–west, metal sheet-clad service spine. ‖ This house hugs the site in a deliberate strategy to maximize the south yard and aspect to the bush. To the rear, the house cuts into the site, creating an 'introverted' space while the street façade presents as an 'extroverted' space. **The architecture is deliberately non-domestic** to challenge the postwar brick veneer vernacular of its neighborhood. ‖ The architects' belief that a house can contribute to its surroundings was a strong influence on the design of the house. The introduction of light, color, and transparency allows the house and occupants to engage with the street, and vice versa. The primary source of the color and transparency, and the most monumental element of the building, is the stunning glazed stairwell. Characterized by horizontal strips of jade and amber-tinted glass, the stairwell glows like a lantern at night, and animates the stairwell with brilliant color during the day. ‖ Bedrooms, bathrooms, and living spaces are all positioned on the south elevation. Generous glazing, which includes floor-to-ceiling double-hung windows, directs activity and outlook toward the street and bush views and allows all rooms to take advantage of solar orientation and the balmy climate. The main bedroom occupies the 'loft' space and also enjoys the north–south relationship. The double-height living room opens up from the adjacent dining area and kitchen. This room looks over the pool, to claim the view of gum trees beyond. A sheltered courtyard at the rear is at the center of a U-shaped plan formed by the kitchen, dining room, and study. Clad in honey-stained plywood, this space is the furthest away from the street, and is the most protected space in the house. ‖ The house has been designed around sound solar, illumination, and ventilation principles. A drought-tolerant and sustainable garden allows the house to blend into an area where native trees and scrub still flourish.

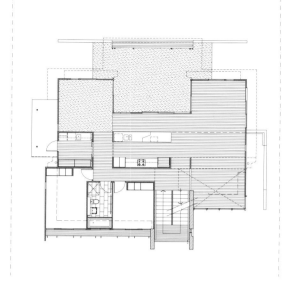

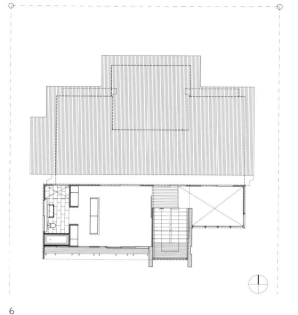

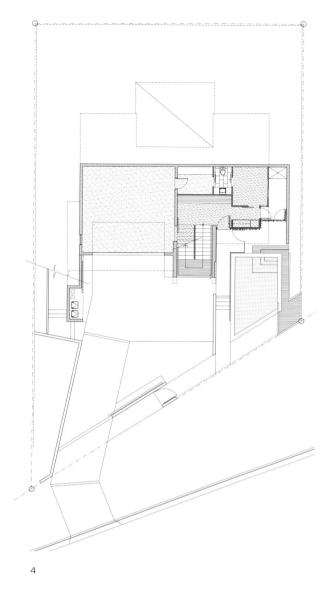

4

5

6

4 Ground floor plan
5 First floor plan
6 Second floor plan
7 View of bedroom bridge
8 Kitchen and dining area
9 Living area
10 Bedroom bridge and entry

Photography: Scott Burrows, Aperture Photography

7

8

9

10

1   Aerial context view
2   View of roof from neighboring property; glass panels with varying density
    are positioned according to daylight requirements in rooms below
Opposite:
    View from ground floor to first floor up main staircase

Gianni Botsford Architects

LIGHT HOUSE
Notting Hill, London, UK

This new 800-square-meter house, on an enclosed back-land site in Notting Hill, was designed for a family of two academics and their two children. The brief required a very private house for the family to live and work in, a suite of living rooms, a kitchen, two studies, a library, dining room, chapel, five bedrooms and bathrooms, a swimming pool, courtyard gardens, garage, wine cellar, laundry rooms, and plant rooms. || The orientation of the site runs almost east–west and is heavily overlooked and overshadowed on the south and west elevations. The key challenge of the project was to maintain privacy while optimizing daylight and sunlight penetration into the house. || The architects' starting point was to represent the site as a 3D grid of individual data points. Working with structural engineers Arup, a detailed environmental analysis for each point produced a database of solar and daylight conditions throughout the year. Specific weather patterns were also incorporated and the resulting data were analyzed using special database mining software. Alongside the client's preferences and lifestyle, this analysis formed the basis of the design process. || As a result, the section was inverted, with the bedrooms on the ground floor and the living spaces on the first floor. **Terraces and gardens create internal courtyard volumes** into which the surrounding spaces face. A completely glazed roof functions as an environmental moderator, filtering sunlight and daylight through layers of transparency and opacity. The roof has a highly effective solar coating, three different frit densities to the glass, electrically operated blinds, and opening vents, all of which contribute to a high level of control of the internal environment by the occupants. || The empty site was essentially a box: 40 meters deep and 15 meters wide, with brick party walls 8–10 meters high. No loading on the party walls was allowed, hence a requirement for very large planes of walls extending up to the top of the highest wall. In situ exposed concrete was a natural choice for the project—it acts as an environmental moderator (the house is naturally ventilated), the exposed finishes put workmanship on display, and structurally there was a requirement for large vertical cantilevers and beams. || A very restricted pallette of materials, consisting of stainless steel, concrete, glass, and aluminum was used throughout the house and includes polished concrete screed floors, stainless steel-lined swimming pool and bathrooms, exposed concrete structure to the walls and beams, stainless steel kitchen, aluminum-framed sliding doors and windows, and perforated corrugated stainless steel used as cladding, external screens, and doors.

4   First floor plan
5   Ground floor plan
6   View from study toward living room with dappled light from glass roof
7   View from kitchen to main first-floor terrace
8   View of stainless steel swimming pool; master bathroom at far end of pool
9   View of living room; sunlight is controlled from glass roof with retracting blinds and variable fritting to glass panels
10 Dressing room
11 View from master bedroom through dressing room to master bathroom formed from stainless steel and exposed concrete

Photography: Aeolens (1); Hélène Binet (2,p189,6–11)

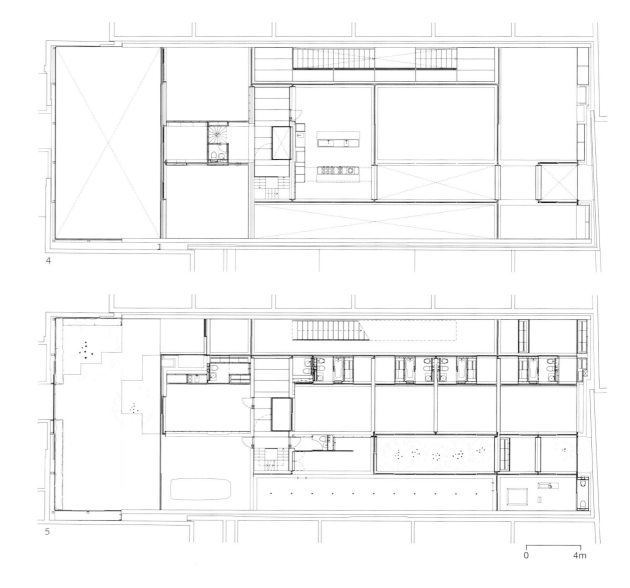

4

5

0   4m

6

7

8

9

10

11

1

Studio B Architects

LORD RESIDENCE

Aspen, Colorado, USA

This flat, 1-acre site lies at the entry to Aspen and enjoys panoramic views to Pyramid Peak and the striking Maroon Bells, one of the most famous sights in Colorado. Because of the site's proximity to the highway, and any building's likely impact on the area's views, the zoning authority required that the house be 'low in posture.' ‖ The result is a single-story, 9000-square-foot residence that **employs materials, textures, and hues** to minimize any impact it may have from the observer's perspective. The exterior material palette includes rammed earth, vertical rusted steel panels, sandblasted masonry block, and zinc roofing. ‖ The program is divided between a public zone, private wing, and a guest/children's area, with all spaces not only focused on the views, but the large outdoor gardens and terraces.

2

Photography: Paul Warchol (1,6,8); Aspen Architectural Photography (2,3,7,9,10)

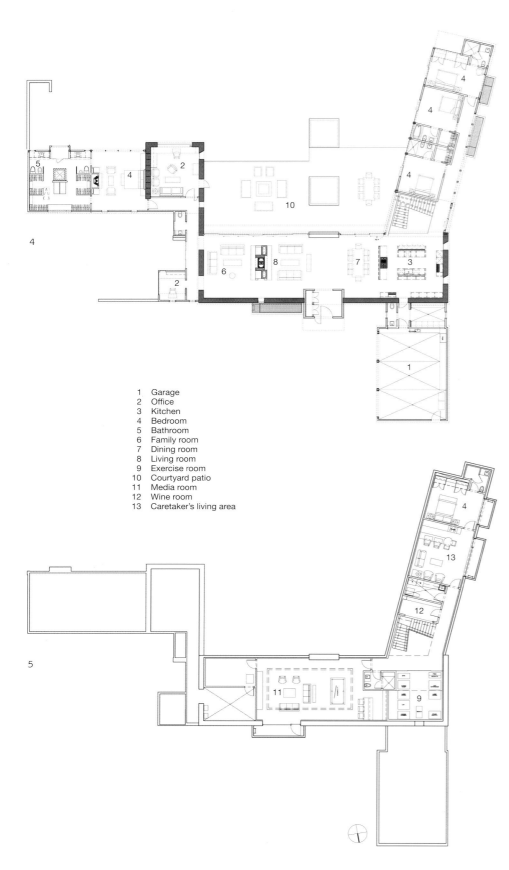

4

1   Garage
2   Office
3   Kitchen
4   Bedroom
5   Bathroom
6   Family room
7   Dining room
8   Living room
9   Exercise room
10   Courtyard patio
11   Media room
12   Wine room
13   Caretaker's living area

5

6

7

8

9

10

1

2

Higham Architecture

MACDONALD HOUSE

Christchurch, New Zealand

Located on a small, unusually shaped site in northeast Christchurch, this contemporary home presents a true reflection of client needs versus site constraints. ‖ The clients were moving from their large residence in Auckland, so the **challenge included creating a real sense of space** within the limited building footprint permissible on their new 522-square-meter site. Plenty of natural light, high ceilings (in selected areas) and light colors throughout helped achieve this. ‖ Spatial requirements from the clients, coupled with the site geometry, led to the design of two wings. The skewed 'service' wing is clad in dark-stained cedar weatherboards and is generally flat-roofed, contrasting with the pitched roof and white plaster finish of the 'living' wing. The entry is central, balancing the forms on either side. ‖ Both wings retreat from the north sun via deep recesses, giving visual depth and shading. The living wing features higher ceilings and large expanses of glass to capture natural light, warmth, and outlook. ‖ Hinuera stone features on the wall upon entry and also on the hearth of the open gas fireplace, giving a natural, solid appearance. The horizontal lines of the stonework are then subtly echoed

in the white-lacquered grooved kitchen joinery, while glass catches the light on selected panels, including the large splashback on the rear wall. A stunning wenge-wrapped central island unit adds a touch of luxury to the kitchen and provides a communal area for visiting family and friends. A lowered ceiling above helps define the kitchen space and a deep external window shroud shades the west-facing servery area. The clean, simple lines are continued in the open-plan living area, with recessed shelving and hi-fi components hidden in discreet cabinetry. ‖ The usually banal domestic hallway became a light-filled, wedge-shaped gallery space for the clients' extensive artwork collection, while a timber door with double-glazed panels gives views into the much-desired, super-insulated and climate-controlled wine cellar. ‖ The clients requested no carpet, so polished concrete flooring is warmed underfoot throughout, except in the master bedroom and ensuite where oak and tiles feature. A sloped ceiling over the spa bath follows the roofline and provides a sense of intimacy.

3

4

1   Driveway
2   Garage
3   Entry
4   Living
5   Dining
6   Kitchen
7   Ensuite
8   Dressing
9   Bedroom 1
10 Bedroom 3
11 Bedroom 2
12 Bathroom
13 Gallery
14 Wine cellar
15 Laundry

1   The well-stocked and climate-controlled wine cellar
2   Light-filled wedge-shaped hallway acts as gallery space
3   Glazed entry doors offer views to the gallery space beyond
4   Floor plan
5   A striking composition of forms at the roadfront
6   Oak flooring complements furniture in the master bedroom

Photography: Stephen Goodenough

5

6

1

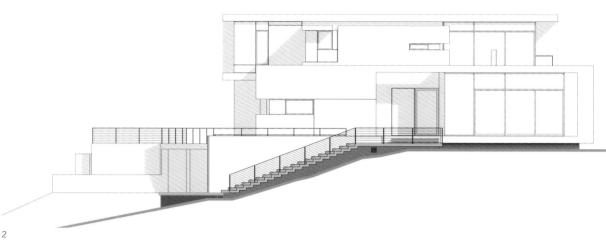

2

Kanner Architects

MALIBU 5
Malibu, California, USA

Vertically stacked and set into a hillside, Malibu 5 is a sustainable modern home constructed of environmentally friendly and recycled materials and designed to minimize energy use. || **Conceived as a passive solar house**, it has photovoltaic panels and solar thermal panels on the roof for domestic hot water. The photovoltaic panels generate power for the house during the day. The amount of energy produced exceeds the owner's needs and the remainder contributes to the local power grid; the house's power meter runs counterclockwise while the sun is up. || Ground-level concrete floors act as heat sinks, pulling in the sun's energy during the day and releasing it at night. They also provide radiant heating, making use of water heated on the roof. || Built as two, C-shaped rectangular bars—one two stories, one a single story over the garage—the house comprises four bedrooms and three bathrooms. The structures are separated by a courtyard that provides an opening for ocean breezes to cool the house. All rooms open on at least two sides to provide cross-ventilation. || The home faces the Pacific Ocean to take advantage of coastal breezes, solar gain, natural light, and views. Large solar-protected windows produce light-filled rooms and minimize the need for artificial lighting, which is controlled with motion-sensor light switches. || The home's landscaping mimics the surrounding sloped, rocky hillside. Rocks removed to prepare the site for construction have been recycled in the xeriscape. The inexpensive scratched-plaster exterior is painted an earthy terra cotta color to provide a natural texture that smoothes the house's introduction to its environment. The color is inspired by the hue of a soil the architect found in West Africa.

4

5

6

7

4   Malibu 5 perches on a hill with mountain and ocean views
5   Fast-growth wood floors and custom cabinets in dining room
6   Glass-enclosed living room with panoramic views
7   Skylight and windows in master bedroom capture natural light
8   Level two floor plan
9   Level one floor plan
10 Ground level floor plan

Photography: Benny Chan/Fotoworks

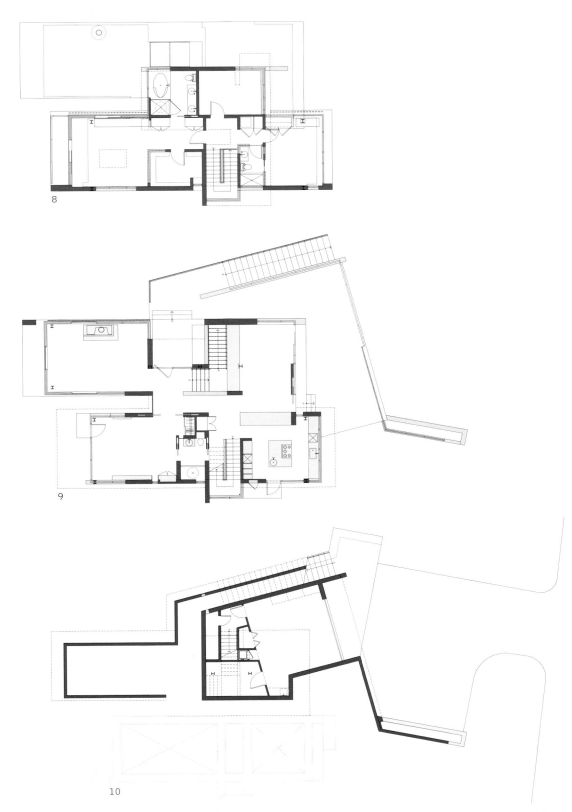

8

9

10

1 2 3

Peter Forbes, FAIA, Architects

MANIATIS HOUSE
Seal Harbor, Maine, USA

The Maniatis House defines and reinforces the edge of a rocky shelf, one of a series of giant steps dropping down the eastern slope of Mount Desert Island toward the Atlantic Ocean. The environment, though bold, is extremely fragile—there is no overburden of earth on the stone ledges, only a thin carpet of moss. ‖ The house takes its parti from the structure and organic typology of the surrounding nature. Anchored by a series of concrete walls pinned into the ledges, the house is elevated to avoid disturbing the topography or interrupting the seasonal flow of water across the site. From these walls a central core of structural steel rises 40 feet to the apex of the clerestory, forming a strong, flexible spine to withstand the severe winds that often batter the site. Longitudinal beams carry the perimeter structure of engineered wooden posts. The enclosing walls of the house, free of structural function, can be peeled away to form balconies, terraces or open the interior to light, air, and vistas of the woods and distant sea. ‖ The house is designed to be **infinitely permeable by light, air, and people**. One can pass under or through the house to paths and terraces without ever entering the building itself. Light entering the clerestory windows can filter down throughout the house, even to the ground outside. The walls, as they progress from the deeper woods to the open vista

become increasingly transparent and permeable until the house dissolves into pure glass or glass walls that can be rolled back to completely open the inside to the outdoors. ‖ Movement through the house follows a spatial path that laces the living areas together. One approaches the house along a sloping stone wall to discover the front door behind a screen of exterior wall. Upon entry, an inverted pyramid of steps leads to the living room and then up the pyramid to a landing and reading area. The path progresses between glass walls up through the house, back and forth between public and private realms until it culminates in the clerestory walkway and views to the mountains and the sea. Surrounded and directed by light, the explorer discovers rooms and balconies, terraces and bays, each unique but interrelated to the whole. ‖ Clad in cedar shingles stained to match the lichen on the rock ledges and pewter-colored lead, even those parts of the house that are not transparent blend and disappear into the environment. The undulating exterior never presents a harsh confrontation to the observer. Always yielding, masked by shadows, the building becomes elusive, ephemeral, an extension of its surroundings.

1   Southeast elevation showing the structural steel core and continuous structural glazing
2   Approach through the woods to the transparent living room and master suite above
3   Entry with glazed walls and clerestory above
4   Living room with distant panorama of the sea
5   View through dining room to the main stair
6   First floor plan
7   Second floor plan
8   Entry passage under the house to the natural landscape beyond

Photography: Wayne Fujii

4

5

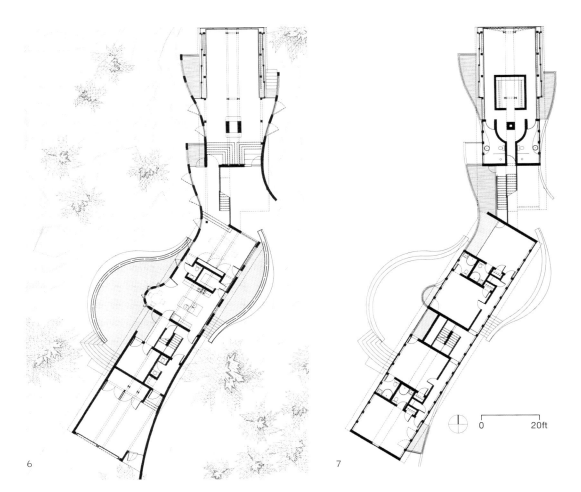

6

7

0   20ft

8

1

2

3

Klopf Architecture

MANZANITA HOUSE

Fairfield, California, USA

1   The Japanese concept of 'borrowed landscape' makes this exterior breezeway the largest 'room' in the house
2   The fireplace terminates the visual axis starting in the master suite; the ceiling beams showing are the actual structure of the house (not decorations) in order to preserve resources and express the modularity of the design
3   When lying in this bed, the owners have a view of extraordinary manzanita trees on their property
4   Floor plan
5   Indoor/outdoor living at night

Photography: © Ken Gutmaker

The owners of this house love nature and order. This warm, modern home complements the natural beauty of its wild, forested 1-acre property. The open, light-filled plan is a series of modular post-and-beam bays axially aligned to create various spaces. When inside the house one notices the openness to the natural world: plenty of daylight, moving shadows, beams of winter sunlight, changes in the weather, the movement of leaves in the wind. Moods of nature, not architectural gymnastics, animate this **clean and simple modern shed**. || As lovers of nature, it was important to the owners that the house be not only sustainable, but enduring. They intend to live in the house well into their retirement while making only a small impact on the natural site. The house was sited where very few trees would be removed, but still allow a long, almost entirely glazed, south façade. Overhangs and a light shelf properly shade the glass while bouncing daylight up onto the ceiling. In addition to functioning as passive solar heating for the winter, this overhang/light shelf system provides enough natural daylight to read a book almost any time the sun is up. || Based on the owners' lifestyle and desire for sustainability, the two-bedroom, two-bathroom house was deliberately kept small (only 1350 enclosed square feet) but it is designed to feel much larger. High, sloping ceilings

with clerestory windows at the top bring the outside in. The enclosed areas are broken into two pods, so one of the owners can rise early to work from home without disturbing the other. The exterior breezeway created by roofing between the two pods becomes the largest and most used room in the house. As an outdoor room for eating, entertaining, or relaxing, it allows for intimacy with nature while providing protection from harsh summer sunlight and rain. The owners enjoy passing through stars and moonlight when walking from the main living area to the master bedroom at night. || Air conditioning is not used, even though temperatures in the area often climb over 100 degrees Farenheit in summer. Burying the house like a bunker was not an option because of the owners' lifestyle and goals for their property. So the house remains above-ground and heavily glazed, but proper solar shading, a light-colored roof, and thick insulation prevent a good deal of heat from entering the house in the first place, while operable clerestory windows and ceiling fans flush hot air out of the house. The exposed concrete floor stores up 'coolness' overnight when temperatures drop, further cooling the space during warmer days.

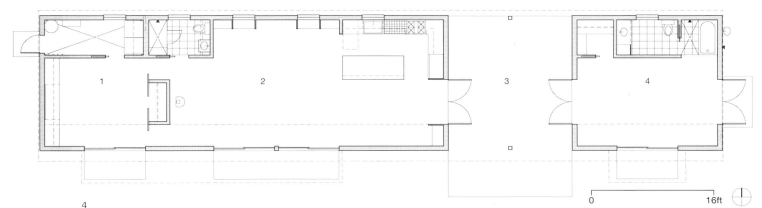

1 Guest bedroom used as an office
2 Living/kitchen/dining
3 Breezeway
4 Master bedroom suite

4

0   16ft

5

1

2

1   View from garden
2   The ceiling is raised to emphasize the space and allow light to flood the entrance
3   Ground floor plan: the spaces are organized around a courtyard
4   Quebracho wood furniture contains storage, a stove, and barbecue
5   Façades feature glass and deep red quebraco wood
6   Interior view to courtyard

Photography: Cora Surraco; Alfredo Herms

Besonías Kruk Arquitectos

MAPUCHE HOUSE

Pilar, Buenos Aires, Argentina

The lushly vegetated Mapuche Country Club, on the outskirts of Buenos Aires, is the setting for this new home. The architects worked with the clients to choose the best lot in the Mapuche Country Club estate. The selected 600-square-meter site is fronted by a row of conifers and features two old blue cedar trees, which shelter the house from direct afternoon sunlight. || The architects are proponents of **the role of the courtyard in residential architecture**. Previous projects had demonstrated the value of small courtyards, which can act as linking structures, provide additional light and views deep into the home, and can extend the plan by providing additional outdoor 'rooms.' || Accordingly, they proposed a flat-roofed, single-story house, pierced by a small courtyard. The courtyard is glazed on all sides, to let the maximum amount of light into the living areas of the house. The flat roof continues into two side walls that feature irregular cut-out windows that provide privacy from the neighboring houses. All windows and door openings are positioned to take advantage of every opportunity to frame the landscape and allow light to enter the house. As a result, a wide variety of openings give

the occupants views in unexpected locations. || Both the front and back walls of the house alternate between lengths of glass and quebracho wood with its characteristic deep red color. At the front, the glazed sections were positioned at either low levels, behind the garden greenery, or high enough to avoid glimpses in from outside. The quebracho wood is also the main material used for the external and internal walls, chimney, the grill, cupboards, and benchtops. Quebracho was specifically chosen for the contrast of its rustic appearance with the pure abstract lines of the rest of the house. Some quebracho sleepers are buried into the grassy ground surrounding the house. Furniture, specifically designed for the house, was made of Canadian pine wood. || The 14- by 10-meter base of the house is a reinforced concrete slab, framed by beams over the roof level throughout its perimeter. The slab rests on a double wall made of perforated bricks at its southeast side; on the northeast side, it rests on a concrete partition wall by means of corbels that allow light to enter the house between the partition wall and the roof.

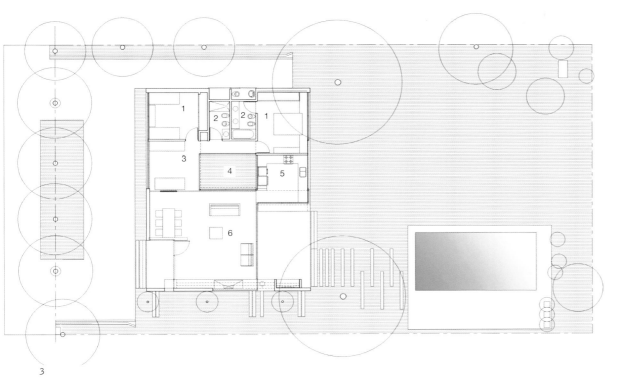

1 Bedroom
2 Bathroom
3 Study
4 Courtyard
5 Kitchen
6 Dining/living area

3

4

5

6

1

2

Avery Team Architecture Ltd

MARINE PARADE RESIDENCE
Mt Maunganui, New Zealand

The clients' brief was for a modern, spacious family home with maximum views over its unique seaside location. This necessitated a two-story home to capture the views up and down the beachfront esplanade, while maximizing privacy for the occupants. || The large site had the added benefit of rear access from the back street, which ensured that the sun could penetrate the main living rooms, which have access to generous balconies for indoor/outdoor living in shelter or sun to suit the weather. || The 505-square-meter, four-bedroom home has three-and-a-half bathrooms, garaging for four cars, lounge/dining room, kitchen/family area, rumpus room, study, games room, and a wine cellar. Most rooms open onto wide terraces or semi-enclosed decks. A fully enclosed lift is also included. || **The sun-filled home is light and airy,** and through the use of a limited palette of permanent self-finishing materials and monochromatic tones, provides a relatively timeless ambience. || Primary construction material is concrete block masonry, the exterior of which is plastered to a sponge finish and coated with an elastomeric paint system in a cement tone. Exterior joinery is a 40-millimeter commercial-style suite with a metallic powdercoat finish and glazed with Evergreen solar control glass. || Secondary exterior forms are clad in natural zinc with a traditional

standing seam detail, generally over plywood-clad timber framing. Exterior structural steel is expressed in the skillion roof forms and has a polyurethane paint system to suit the seaside locality. Clerestory glazing brings sun into interior spaces such as the family room where normal wall glazing to the northern boundary was restricted to preserve privacy. || Balconies are partially enclosed in plastered block or zinc balustrades for privacy with glazed clear panels above for views out. Naturally weathered jarrah hardwood aerofoil-shaped handrails provide a natural contrast to the other materials. || The 15-meter swimming pool, shaped for lengths and splashing, is situated to the north boundary and is accessed from the downstairs rumpus room across a flamed basalt paved terrace. The tennis court preserves a generous setback for privacy and can be overlooked from a number of vantage points. || The interior material and color palette features American white oak, which is used for floors, interior doors, and joinery fittings. The visual warmth of the timber contrasts with the honed basalt slabs on the outside terraces. The black granite bench tops and black fossil chimney fire surround similarly give a graphic contrast to the neutral color palette. || The home features a combination of under-floor heating for stone or tiled floors or under-ceiling heat pads on 24/7 controllers.

3

4

5

5   Kitchen island servery overlooks family room lit by
    clerestory windows
6   Main lounge seating area is focused on fireplace
7   First floor plan
8   Ground floor plan
9   Family room opens out to east terrace and beach
10 Master ensuite
Photography: Chris Parker Photographics

6

1	Terrace
2	Lounge
3	Dining
4	Terrace
5	Family room
6	Kitchen
7	Bathroom
8	Elevator
9	Bedroom 1
10	Dressing room
11	Ensuite
12	Bedroom 2
13	Bedroom 3
14	Barbeque

7

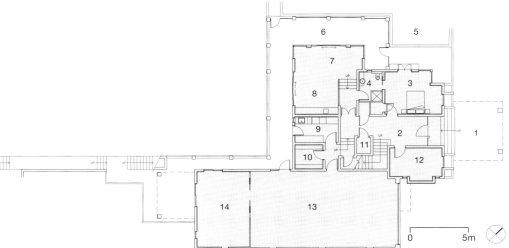

1	Porte-cochère
2	Entry
3	Guest room
4	Bathroom
5	Pool
6	Terrace
7	Gym/rumpus
8	Bar
9	Laundry
10	Cellar
11	Elevator
12	Study
13	Garage
14	Games room

0   5m

8

9

10

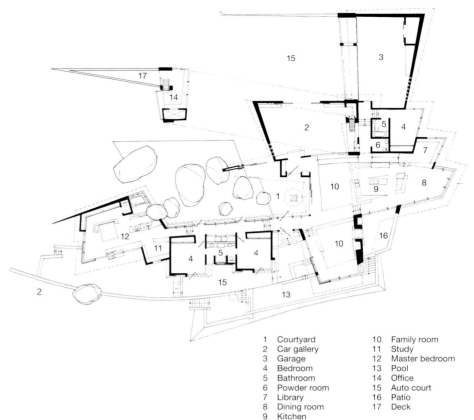

1   View from hill above displays the relationship between the dynamic topography of the surrounding canyon landscape and the arrangement of volumes and roof planes
2   Floor plan
3   Looking up at the cantilevered room projections from the hill below
4   Cantilevered dining room perched high above Mulholland Canyon
5   View showing articulation of shelving system, building system, and surrounding environment
6   The kitchen area bleeding into the dining room beyond continues the house's spatial and formal integration

Photography: Tim Street-Porter

1 Courtyard	10 Family room
2 Car gallery	11 Study
3 Garage	12 Master bedroom
4 Bedroom	13 Pool
5 Bathroom	14 Office
6 Powder room	15 Auto court
7 Library	16 Patio
8 Dining room	17 Deck
9 Kitchen	

Belzberg/Wittman Collaborative

MATAJA RESIDENCE

Malibu, California, USA

The mountainside of Mulholland Canyon is the setting for this dynamic residence. A natural sense of place is achieved through the deployment of the house's fragmented formal and organizational language, suggestive of the rocky site it inhabits. The architects sought to balance a complex program for a single-family residence on an environmentally sensitive, 32-acre site; negotiate a boulder outcropping in which the house would be nestled; and to fulfill the client's desire to create a retreat from their urban lifestyle. || Located in Malibu, two miles inland from the Pacific Coast Highway and Leo Carillo State Beach, the residence incorporates existing rock configurations into its forms and programmatic sequences. The program is wrapped 270 degrees around a boulder outcropping, utilizing the **California courtyard house type** as the genesis of its spatial progressions. Boulders contour the courtyard, provide protection from winds, and allow for privacy, and are aesthetically and experientially appropriated from every room, conceptually blending the residence into its landscape. The boulders at its nucleus anchor the residence while generating a centrifugal force manifested in projections, fragmented elements, and soaring planes. The 4500-square-foot house incorporates a 1000-square-foot gallery space, a three-car garage, a guest house, and a pool/spa. || Materiality and environmental design consciousness further allow for an integration of building and site. The butterfly roof is directed south and angled at 32 degrees to achieve maximum solar collection while it simultaneously collects and channels water for site irrigation. Trombe walls of formed concrete and an 'air floor,' created by honeycombed double concrete slabs, provide thermal massing that allows for 67 percent of the interior space to be glazed. Concrete cantilevers continue the color palette of the landscape while glass curtain walls dissolve the boundaries between inside and out. Various shades of iron oxide and mineral pigments used in cave paintings by native Chumash Indians are represented in material choices. Roof angles echo the jagged profiles of the mountains and direct expansive views. || Echoing and binding itself to the rocky surroundings, the Mataja Residence is both a perched voyeur and embedded progeny of the landscape.

3

4

5

6

1

2

Eggleston Farkas Architects

MEADOW CREEK HOUSE

Seattle, Washington, USA

This single-family residence is located on a large sloping site with western views to **Puget Sound and the Olympic Mountains**. The extensive program had to accommodate several factors, including driveway access, which was limited to its pre-existing location by the topography. The building height had to be kept to a minimum because covenants stipulated that new construction must minimize the impact upon existing views from surrounding neighbors. Similar requirements regarding trees necessitated that the building itself—not landscaping—offer privacy protection from neighbors to the north and south. || The residence facilitates indoor/outdoor living, offering direct connection to the garden while taking advantage of the dramatic view. The clients requested that the house accommodate both contemporary and Asian furnishings, as well as a handmade bubinga dining room table and chairs. || Site fit, program, construction process, and neighborhood design review were all addressed by a shallow vaulted pavilion roof under which linear service forms subdivide and direct the living spaces toward the gardens and view. The steel and PSL structure minimized structure height and was prefabricated offsite for rapid onsite assembly. Once the roof was sheathed, the pavilion served as rain protection for subsequent conventional framing work below. The primary spaces open to both the entry garden to the east and the restored meadow and views to the west. These spaces are defined by the stucco, wood rainscreen, and Corten steel-clad service forms, the northernmost of which (the master bath and closet) screens the living spaces and terraces from the adjacent neighbor.

1   West elevation from the meadow
2   Entry pool and bridge at night
3   Bedroom terrace
4   Dining terrace with rolling sunshade
5   Entry bridge, pool, and dining room

214

3

4

5

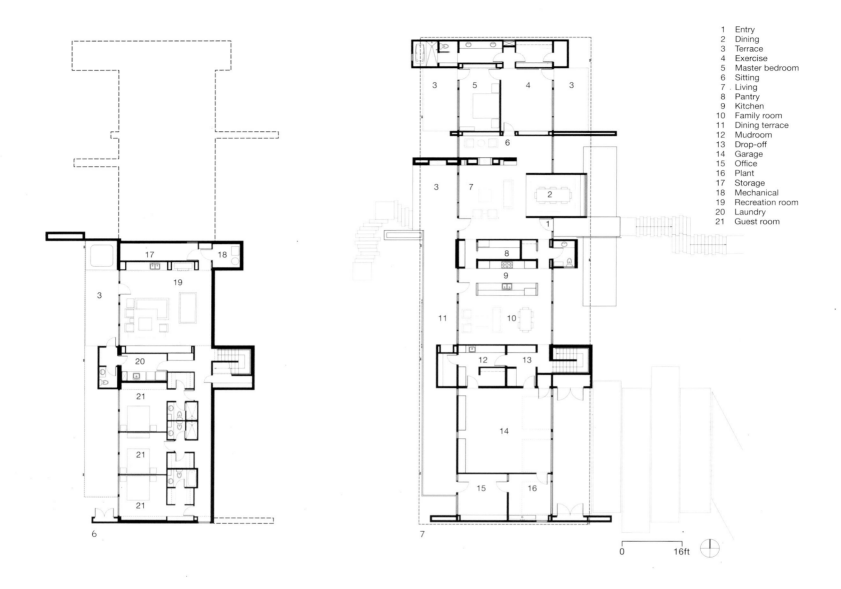

1 Entry
2 Dining
3 Terrace
4 Exercise
5 Master bedroom
6 Sitting
7 Living
8 Pantry
9 Kitchen
10 Family room
11 Dining terrace
12 Mudroom
13 Drop-off
14 Garage
15 Office
16 Plant
17 Storage
18 Mechanical
19 Recreation room
20 Laundry
21 Guest room

0   16ft

8

9

10

11

6 Main floor plan
7 Lower floor plan
8 Living room
9 Dining room
10 Kitchen
11 Bedroom

Photography: Jim Van Gundy

McIntosh Poris Associates

MELCHERS-MCINTOSH RESIDENCE

Detroit, Michigan, USA

The original, Dutch-influenced home was built and designed in 1896 by Gari Melchers for his father, celebrated Detroit-based artist and sculptor Julius Melchers. The **renovated three-story structure** includes a foyer, music room, morning room, sunroom, four new bathrooms, kitchen, dining room, master suite, three bedrooms, family room, balcony, and loft. The restoration and renovation project involved a complete overhaul of internal mechanics, restructuring of dilapidated areas, new construction, and detailed restoration based on historic photographs. || A full-scale renovation of mechanical and structural systems, as well as decorative elements, was undertaken by the homeowner, Douglas McIntosh, a principal at McIntosh Poris Associates. A new cedar and copper roof replaced three other roofs layered over the original pine roof. The exterior wood clapboard was stripped of 20 layers of paint; rotted perimeter eaves and inverted soffits were rebuilt. A meticulous restoration of the original Melchers hand-carved details was achieved by consulting historic photos of the house. || Interior construction required establishing sectional relief where there originally was none. Three bedrooms evolved into the master suite on the second floor. A revision of the original sunroom created a two-story sunroom with views of the newly created courtyard and carriage house. A large family room was created on the third floor and a new third-floor balcony replaced unfinished attic space. A fourth-level loft overlooks the third-floor space and completes the complex relationship within the restored structure. || The foyer, music room, and dining room were designed to maintain original tones set in the 19th century. An Art Moderne prismatic light fixture from the 1930s graces the entry foyer, while pocket doors cordon off the music room and sitting room. Off the stair hall is the original, restored marble butler's sink. || The dining room's design includes the restoration of the original corner cupboards and 400-year-old Delft tile imported from Holland. A century of paint was stripped from the ceiling, walls, and ornamentations to reveal original, hand-carved details. A blue porcelain finish completes the walls above the wainscoting, accentuating the hues of the Delft tile surrounding the fireplace. || Outside, a new carriage house functions as garage, courtyard, and storage facility, taking advantage of the alley access to the home. The space comprises two symmetrical wings flanking a sunken courtyard. Each wing accommodates one car, with a storage loft located above. The connecting space between the two garages was designed to be a summer kitchen that can extend to the courtyard, which doubles as an alfresco dining room.

3

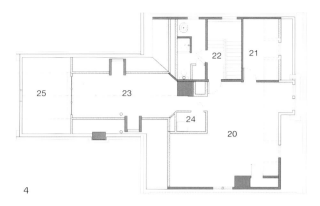

4

5

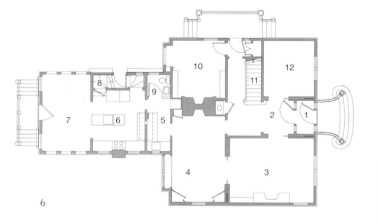

6

7

8

1	Vestibule	9	Powder room	17	Mechanical room
2	Lobby	10	Library	18	Open to sitting room below
3	Living room	11	Front stair	19	Sitting room
4	Dining room	12	Music room	20	Master bedroom
5	Butler's pantry	13	Great room	21	Guest bedroom
6	Kitchen	14	Archive room	22	Dressing room
7	Sunroom	15	Loft above stair, open	23	Master bathroom
8	Rear stair		to great room below	24	Card room
		16	Sitting room	25	Sunroom

9

4 Third floor plan
5 Second floor plan
6 First floor plan
7 An Art Moderne prismatic light fixture from the 1930s graces the entry foyer
8 A 17th-century chest stores piano rolls for the baby grand piano
9 Highly functional kitchen maintains historic appeal
10 Antique Delft tiles are used as accents throughout the house

Photography: Kevin Bauman (2,3,7); Justin Maconochie (1,8,9,10)

10

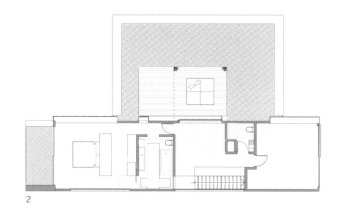

1   Rear of house
2   Second floor plan
3   First floor plan
4   Side view from second-floor balcony
5   Kitchen island chairs
6   First floor view

Photography: Ralf Seeburger (1,4,5); Bragi Josefsson (6)

Minarc

MINARC HOUSE

Los Angeles, California, USA

The architects' objective was to create a healthy home, designed for modern, environmentally conscious individuals. The fundamental thought behind the design was to strategically create a home that was high-tech, but in an effortless, almost invisible, fashion. || The core, or heart, of the home is reached as soon as one enters the house. The first floor features an open, flowing plan that combines the kitchen and living room into one space; a large, orange kitchen island is the focal point. The color orange was deliberately chosen for its creative and spiritual powers. The kitchen cabinetry is clad with recycled tires—the result is a kitchen that retains its elegance but which is unaffected by wear and tear. || Access to the garden is through movable sliding glass door panels that constitute a disappearing wall leading to the outdoor dining room, which instantly becomes a part of the open floor plan. The dining room has a heated wooden floor and additional roof heating for cold winter nights. || Other spaces on the first floor include two bedrooms, two bathrooms, and a family/TV room secluded from the bustling main room. || The second floor is a private world on its own, a creative

sanctuary designed to cater to the complexities of modern living. The needs for privacy, rest, and rejuvenation are addressed by a master bedroom with a spa/bathroom, a walk-in closet, and a balcony intended for relaxing and outdoor sleeping. || A generous, bright office/den for creative home living/working is also on the second floor. Like an enclosed nest, it is a sanctuary from the ever-demanding outside world. || Radiant floor heating throughout the house keeps the heating balanced. Natural breezes are used as an environmentally responsible cooling system—no mechanical air conditioning is used. A central audio and visual system is built into the walls, so no cables are visible. The lighting takes advantage of maximum use of daylight; natural sunlight reflects throughout the house through glass on doors and windows. || In designing the house there was a **conscious effort to use only materials in their most organic form** and to use recycled material wherever possible. Paint, chemicals, carpets, and tiles were avoided, resulting in a low-maintenance, environmentally responsible family home.

4

5

6

223

1

Graham Jones Design

MORNINGTON RESIDENCE
Mornington, Victoria, Australia

The architect's passion for **minimalist contemporary design** and a love for warehouse styling are reflected in the layout and finishes to this new house on the picturesque Mornington Peninsula, a one-hour drive south of Melbourne. || The integration of Corten steel with compressed cement sheet, battened out with anodized aluminum, results in a hard-edged 'industrial' approach to the façade of this building. Exposed galvanized steel awnings and polished rendered boxes finished in clear lacquer provide three-dimensional styling to selected windows. Building massing is visually powerful, softened only by staggered galvanized steel and timber fencing, designed as an integral part of the total building to provide depth and articulation. || Imported slabs of bluestone adorn the ground floor and al fresco entertaining area, creating seamless access via large bi-folding doors from the principal living room. Aluminum louver blades angled over part of this space provide protection from the hot summer sun while allowing winter solar access into the room. A methylated spirits-fuelled 'Eco-fire' epitomizes the minimalist design as it disappears into the exposed galvanized steel hearth that wraps around an entertainment system totally integrated into a feature black-painted bulkhead. Color is introduced by accessorizing with contemporary art works specifically created by leading Melbourne artist Bill Sayers. || The double-volume entry draws light in from the rooms above, while a 5-metre-high narrow window slices through the entry porch in search of additional natural light. || Restaurant-style banquette seating around a polished concrete dining table is adorned by painted MDF panels that delineate the dining space from the living room and create a more commercial restaurant feel. A built-in bar with wine and glasses on display continues the commercial theme, which flows on into the kitchen. A large butler's pantry houses the refrigerator, freezer, microwave, and additional sink, allowing the kitchen to remain uncluttered and minimal. || Lime-washed Tasmanian oak stair treads are open and fixed directly to the wall on one side, the other being fixed to a steel stringer and filled in with glass panels attached to stainless steel patch fittings. The stair opens into a large void over the entry; this space is also utilized by the adjoining sitting room, extending the spaciousness of the home. Three bedrooms and a bathroom occupy the remainder of the upper floor of the building. Bathrooms are creative and well-detailed; the principal ensuite features a 1.2-meter-wide shower with a floor-to-ceiling window overlooking a stone garden constructed on the roof of the laundry below.

3

4

5

3   Built-in bar flows into the kitchen
4   Upper sitting room
5   Entertaining system and fireplace detail
6   First floor plan
7   Ground floor plan
8   Principal ensuite overlooks a stone garden on the second level
9   Main entry featuring computer art printed onto canvas
10   Kitchen is uncluttered and minimal

Photography: Chris Groenhout

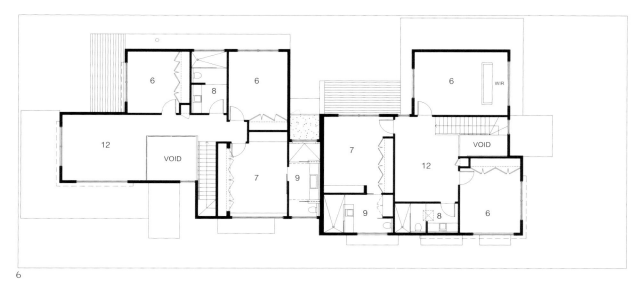

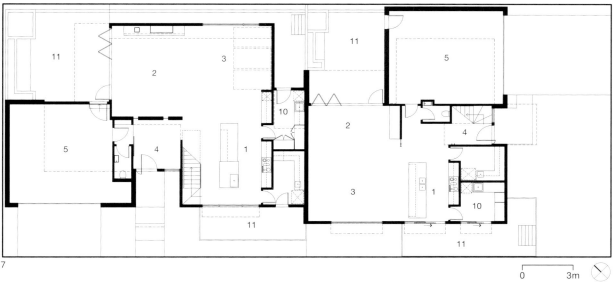

1 Kitchen
2 Living
3 Dining
4 Entry
5 Garage
6 Bedroom
7 Master bedroom
8 Bathroom
9 Ensuite
10 Laundry
11 Courtyard
12 Sitting room

0   3m

1

2

Inarc Architects

MOUNT MACEDON RESIDENCE

Mount Macedon, Victoria, Australia

This house is sited in the center of a 12-hectare rural site that borders native state forest and small farm allotments, which gradually spread out to larger land holdings. The high point of the site offers magnificent valley views and towering messmate trees close to the house frame the long-range view. || The external composition is that of a long, low, crafted timber sculpture composed of **overlaps, cantilevers, decks, and voids**. The rustic palette of external materials consists of stained recycled ironbark, local basalt boulders, rusted steel panels, and glass. || To accommodate family and friends, the house is planned in three compartmentalized zones that allow for isolated or integrated use. The individual compartments contribute to efficiencies of heating and cleaning and concealed sliding doors allow the three zones to be isolated thermally and acoustically from each other. || The living areas are as long and vast as the views, with continuous decks running along all sides to entice the occupants onto these traditional Australian veranda spaces. || The simplicity of the architectural expression belies the technology embedded in the house. Mount Macedon has a long cool season with bitter winters. Double glazing and a highly insulated shell minimize heat loss. An environmentally and energy efficient geothermal heating/cooling system utilizes 500 meters of underground water pipes, which use the stable median temperature of the earth to act as a heat source or sink. || This area is prone to extreme bushfires. Defences employed include roofs connected to rainwater tanks, topped up by naturally occurring bores. The water tanks act as fire-fighting support as well as a source of irrigation of the immediate garden surrounds. || The use of recycled and naturally occurring materials minimizes the embodied energy used in the construction of the building. The exterior palette of materials flows to the interior. Recycled ironbark has also been used as flooring, wall lining boards, and as the main component in the joinery. The rough hewn local basalt external buttress extends to the interior in the form of a fireplace wall with niches cut out of its mass to accommodate wood storage and the television. Lighting has been kept discreet with recessed ceiling lights washing walls and providing a soft reflected light to living and bedroom areas. Furnishing and artwork have been kept simple and to a minimum to reveal an interior that is open and uncluttered, and which forms a seamless whole with the exterior. || This house exudes a warmth and rustic charm not normally associated with contemporary buildings, and represents a leap forward for the integration of architecture and the rural idyll.

1. Basalt boulders are used as retaining walls around existing trees; the surrounding terrain rises to meet the decks
2. At dusk the valley views are replaced by floodlit gum trees
3. Rear of house as seen from motor court; a bluestone buttress wall signals the front door entry

3

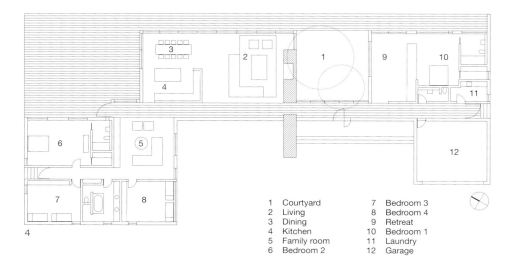

1	Courtyard	7	Bedroom 3
2	Living	8	Bedroom 4
3	Dining	9	Retreat
4	Kitchen	10	Bedroom 1
5	Family room	11	Laundry
6	Bedroom 2	12	Garage

4 Floor plan
5 Ensuite bathroom with glazed wall to paddock beyond; earthy colors complement the exterior
6 Drystone Kyneton basalt fireplace wall with axial circulation space either side of front door
7 Fully glazed front of house faces the countryside views and surrounding verandas
8 Transverse section
9 The entry courtyard frames the valley view via the cantilevered fascia and veranda

Photography: Peter Clarke – Latitude

7

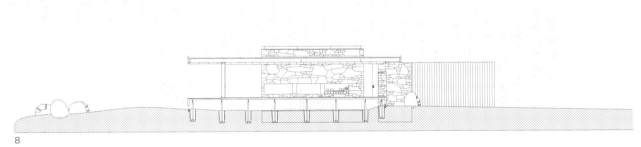

8

9

Robert M. Gurney, FAIA, Architect

NICHOLS RESIDENCE
Great Falls, Virginia, USA

This house differs immensely from the red brick colonial houses typically being built in the surrounding Virginia countryside. The sloping, 12-acre site is heavily forested with mature hardwoods. The strategy was to locate the house on a ridge and take advantage of the most desirable wooded views and sloping topography from a high vantage point. || The house is organized around a **24-foot diameter cylinder clad in Corten steel**. This cylinder contains the stairs and a series of bridges that connect spaces in different volumes. Two linear, ground-faced block bars engage the cylinder. One of the bars is rotated 10 degrees toward the optimal views. A pair of shed-roofed structures, clad in corrugated galvalume, emerge from the ground-faced block bars. || An indoor tennis court occupies 8000 square feet and is 40 feet high at the net. This is a large structure, even on the 12-acre site. The tennis court is set into the heavily wooded hillside to reduce its visibility, and is sited so that it is not visible from inside the main house, except from a viewing space adjacent to the main living room. To integrate the tennis court and the house, the tennis court structure employs sloping shed roofs, similar to those on the main house, corrugated galvalume, ground-faced block, and standing seam metal siding and roofing. || Materials were selected to ensure the house fits comfortably into its wooded environment and will not require extended maintenance. The ground-faced block and galvalume are soft gray in color, similar to the bark on adjacent trees. The Corten steel is reddish brown and is constantly changing in color; the concrete retaining walls and bluestone terraces continue the palette of materials that are harmonious with the landscape.

4

5

6

7

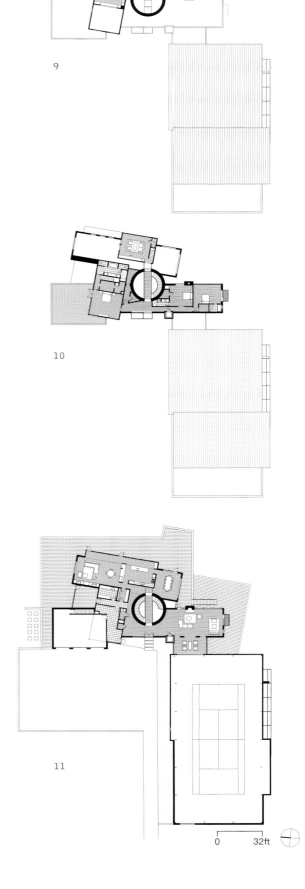

9

10

11

4 Stair at ground floor in central cylinder
5 Bridge at first floor with central stair beyond
6 Bridges and stairs viewed from below
7 Living room
8 Family room with kitchen beyond
9 Third floor plan
10 Second floor plan
11 First floor plan

Photography: Anice Hoachlander/HDphoto

0   32ft

8

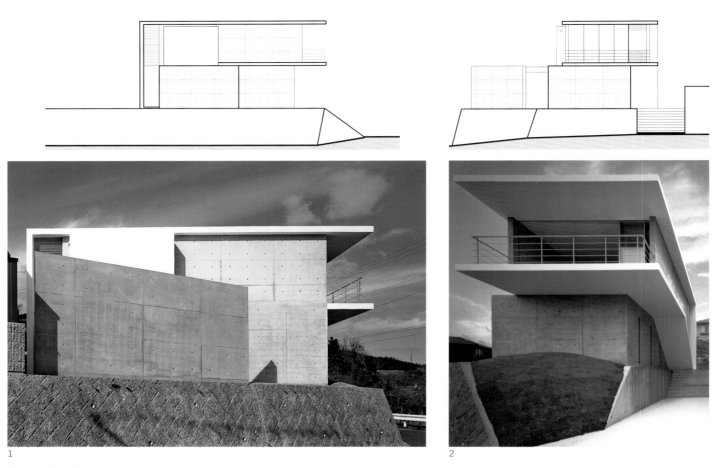

1

2

Katsufumi Kubota/Kubota Architect Atelier

NK HOUSE

Hiroshima, Japan

This single-family house, designed for a couple with young twins, is in a suburb of Hiroshima. The hillside site is close to a new housing development and overlooks a small town at the bottom of the hill. The town provides a bright, green outlook during the day and a glittering canvas at night. || The site conditions imposed some difficulties: its small area (172 square meters), triangular shape, and proximity to neighbors all had to be taken into account in the design. || Although the ground level had been raised from the street level to provide privacy, it was not a sufficient barrier, so an upper living level was added above the ground level. A cantilever above the parking area proved to be the solution to many difficulties. The white concrete slab rises up high to capture the spectacular views of the hillside. The architects liken the slab to **a 'warm carpet,' floating in the air**, filled with a feeling of freedom. || Windows on the sleeping floor were kept as small as possible; larger windows on the living floor provide the most privacy from neighbors. The primary entry into the 110-square-meter house is double-height and emphasizes the white concrete bent slab. || Ducts, plumbing, and air conditioners are all hidden in this streamlined house. Chestnut wood was chosen as the primary flooring because of its dimensional stability after exposure to the heat of the floor heating system in winter. It was also chosen for its under-foot comfort.

3

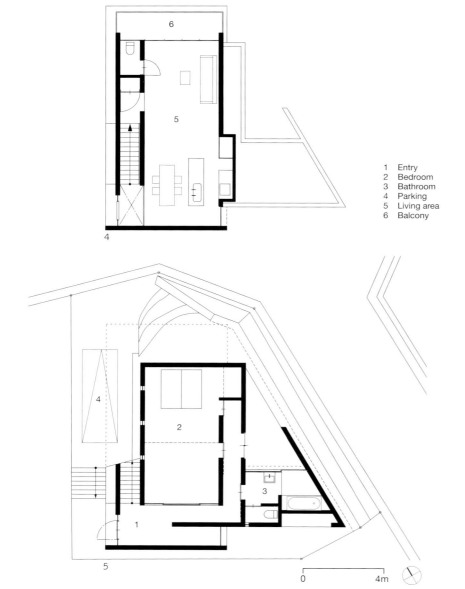

1 Entry
2 Bedroom
3 Bathroom
4 Parking
5 Living area
6 Balcony

6

7

8

9

Photography: Hiroshi Ueda

10

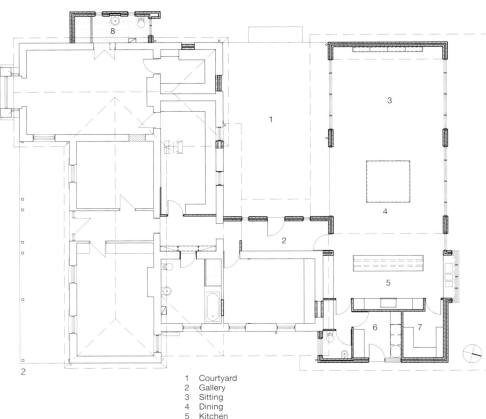

1 Courtyard
2 Gallery
3 Sitting
4 Dining
5 Kitchen
6 Laundry
7 Pantry
8 Ensuite

Studio 9 Architects

NORTHCOTE

Salisbury, South Australia, Australia

The original portion of this home, built circa 1870, was a simple cottage to the rear; a grander 1910 addition faced the street and featured detailing common to villas of the late 19th century. Later lean-to structures and veranda enclosures presented a 'rambling' villa with problems such as land-locked rooms, lack of natural light, and a number of differing floor levels. || In general terms, the area of demolition exceeded that added. The new addition is designed to complement, but not replicate a turn-of-the-century villa and to **reflect contemporary Australian lifestyle** with indoor–outdoor living for a family of four. || The grand original front part of the house was maintained as the sleeping zone, as the rooms can be quite dark during the day and offer little opportunity for indoor–outdoor flexibility. An ensuite was added, the room uses were changed, the 130-year-old, 350-millimetre-thick pug and stonewalls were reused, floor levels were raised, the cellar was re-opened, and new roofing and new ceilings were installed. || The new elements provide a large flexible, open, and 'clean' living area—

effectively a pavilion oriented to the north and taking advantage of a direct outlook onto a river and linear park. The new areas are separated from the original structure by a courtyard with a raised deck (or external room) that promotes indoor–outdoor interaction. While the formal front door facing the street was maintained, the external deck also acts as the primary entrance for informal visitors. || The simple linear form with a skillion roof, rising to the north and the sun, defines the positioning and orientation of the living spaces. Living areas are arranged with direct access to the outdoor living arrangements. Service areas are discreetly located to one end of the addition. To promote the flow between internal and external spaces, large windows to the north provide views of the park, light, and winter solar heat gain, while the large-expanse café door provides access to the deck and outdoor living. || Hard-wearing, long-lasting, and low-maintenance materials such as galvanized steel, aluminum, glass, Australian hardwood decking, and highly polished concrete floors make up the palette of materials.

1   The courtyard separating old and new
2   Floor plan
3   View of relationships: outdoor living–dining–kitchen
4   Outdoor living link to indoors
5   North-facing pavilion windows
Photography: James Knowler

240

3

4

5

1. A bespoke cantilevered glass and timber staircase rises through a triple-height volume at the front of the house
2. A second stair leads from the hall into a double-height lower-ground reception area featuring a chandelier by Verner Panton
3. The master bedroom features floating oversized bespoke closets with sliding doors and concealed lighting
4. An opal acrylic light wall runs from the breakfast bar to the garden elevation, illuminating the lower-ground living space
5. Living room features a sofa from Living Divani upholstered with brushed velvet fabric and a bespoke mocca oak coffee table

Photography: Keith Collie

1

2

Turner Castle

OPAL HOUSE

London, UK

This property in northwest London is a four-story semi-detached Victorian townhouse, which has been stripped back to its load-bearing walls and completely remodeled inside. Externally the original brickwork and window surrounds have been retained and restored; a modern glazed pavilion added to the rear provides a terrace at upper-ground level. The real transformation reveals itself inside in an assembly of spacious volumes carved out of the original architecture. ‖ **The concept for the house was like a well-tailored suit**: elegant and restrained on the outside, and distinguished by flashes of color and sumptuous materiality in the lining. ‖ At the front of the house a cantilevered wood-and-glass open-tread staircase rises through a stupendous triple-height volume. The reception area is a double-height open-plan space with a polished concrete floor, which runs the full length of the extended lower ground floor, and is accessed from a second stair at entrance level. This floor is the main entertaining space and features the living room, dining area, and kitchen. Toward the glazed garden elevation the floor is reduced to single height by a study and library above with access onto a new timber-boarded terrace. ‖ A palette of muted neutral colors (pinks, grays, and corals) and rich natural materials was chosen to enhance the flow of interconnected spaces. The study room shelving and cupboards, cantilevered stair treads, and kitchen island unit are all finished in dark oak, which is used for the flooring throughout. Every effort was made to retain the integrity of form. Lighting is concealed in the fabric of the building and doors are floor-to-ceiling slices of the volume of the room they open into. ‖ The upper floor is reserved for the principal bedroom, which features a series of oversized floating closets that are cantilevered from the wall, finished in dusty pink, and lined with a deep aubergine.

3

4

5

Swatt Architects

ORR HOUSE

Saratoga, California, USA

This 5080-square-foot house is located on a steep, west-facing down-slope lot in semi-rural Saratoga, California. Surrounded by mature oak trees and groves of maple and redwood trees, the site enjoys spectacular valley views to the north, west, and south. || This program called for an addition and remodel to a 1970's stucco-clad two-story home. Although the original home was built well, it had major deficiencies: a long and narrow living room not conducive to entertaining, a formal dining room that did not fit the owner's casual lifestyle, inadequate parking, a severe and uninviting exterior entry, and tired and outdated interiors throughout. The design program was to address all of the deficiencies in a creative, modern way. Additionally, the owner requested that the project be sensitive to sustainability, with major portions of the existing framing and skin of the building either retained or recycled into the new design. || Because of the almost square proportions of the existing building, affectionately called a 'wide body' by the architects, **the first strategy was to cut an atrium into the center of the building** to maximize natural daylight. Bathed in light from a skylight above, the new atrium brings natural light

to the entry, the living room, and a lower-level tatami room and home office. The atrium also dramatically illuminates the stairs to the lower level, and a beautiful mahogany bridge that spans the two-story space. || The kitchen was planned as a large multipurpose space, which includes an informal dining area. The kitchen/dining area and the living area share a new stone terrace, bordered by a cantilevered reflecting pool that extends vistas to the south horizon while minimizing views of the expanded driveway below. || The new design introduces a series of overlapping horizontal cedar-clad planes, which protect the glazing and visually extend interior space to the exterior. Two of the four pre-existing sloped roofs were retained in the new design. One of these roofs is used to support new photovoltaic panels, while the other serves to reduce the scale of the north side of the building, adjacent to a Japanese-inspired garden. One of the most successful aspects of this project is the sensitive combination of new and old elements to create a contemporary design that is fresh, unique, beautiful to look at, and a delight to live in.

3

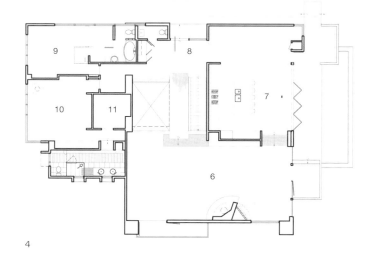

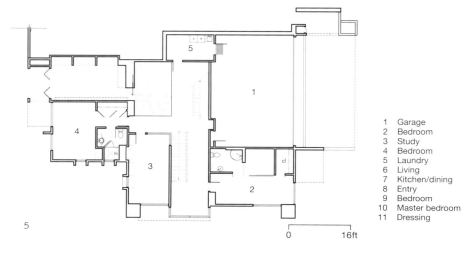

4

5

1 Garage
2 Bedroom
3 Study
4 Bedroom
5 Laundry
6 Living
7 Kitchen/dining
8 Entry
9 Bedroom
10 Master bedroom
11 Dressing

0   16ft

6

7

8

9

4 Upper level floor plan
5 Lower level floor plan
6 Kitchen/dining room
7 Kitchen
8 Tatami room
9 Living room with atrium skylight beyond

Photography: Cesar Rubio

paastudio

PACIFIC PALISADES RESIDENCE 2

Pacific Palisades, California, USA

The extraordinary views and topography of the site dictated the design approach of this house. While a harmonious presence was sought for the exterior, terrain integration, lucidity and tranquility of shapes, and preserving nature as the focal point of the house were also strong design objectives. The design also considers local geological and municipal restrictions, including dual coastal jurisdiction, hillside ordinance, and landslide hazard—the building stands on 37 concrete piles up to 70 feet deep. || The house features **passive solar elements** including stationary exterior wood louvers to the south, motorized blinds, skylight ventilation with natural draw, and operable low air intakes. Well-designed cross ventilation practically eliminates use of forced air cooling, while the rear underground portion of the house provides a steady volume of evenly tempered atmosphere. While the dining room and kitchen are completely underground, the continued flow and scale of space eliminate any visual relation to the fact. The delicate definition of space with suspended ceilings creates distinctive parts of the overall unified living area. || The living room deck and barbeque area are naturally sheltered from the sun to the north, while the 'winter' bedroom top-floor terrace extends to the west. A service dumbwaiter from the garage stops at every level, and has double access in the master bedroom/exterior deck. It can be used to either lift groceries to the kitchen level or even shoot up martinis from the bar area to the deck. The architects describe their interior approach as 'controlled transparency,' with 'livable minimalism' the aim. This approach is reflected in the material selection, with Brazilian slate floors in slab-on-grade application, as well as at entry level, and maple wood finish for framed floors. Custom-built birch plywood millwork and cabinetry feature throughout and reflect the overall natural design and logic of interlocking L and U shapes, while bringing exterior elements to the interior.

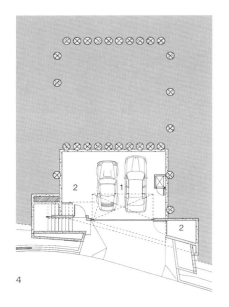
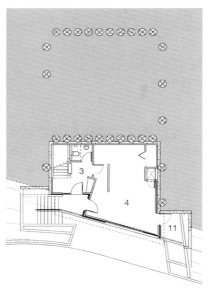
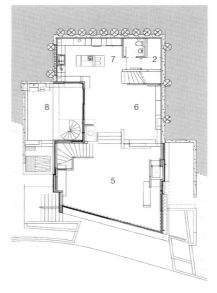
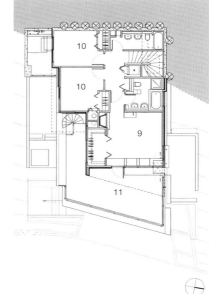

4

1 Garage
2 Utility
3 Entry
4 Studio
5 Living
6 Dining
7 Kitchen
8 Patio
9 Master bedroom
10 Bedroom
11 Exterior deck

5

7

4   Left to right: level one, level two, level three, level four floor plans
5   View of living area through to dining room
6   Dining and living room
7   Cleverly placed windows provide surprising exterior transparency
8   Master bedroom and view at dusk
9   Guest bathroom

Photography: Klaus Knoll

6

8

9

1   View from west
2   East façade with garden
3   Floor plan
4   East façade
5   View of main upper access/entrance to the top floor of
    the house
6   View from veranda to the east
7   Main veranda with bougainvillea-covered pergola
Photography: Filipe Branquinho; Jorge Campos

1

2

José Forjaz Arquitectos

PAULINO RESIDENCE

Maputo, Mozambique

Located in a steep slope overlooking the magnificent bay of Maputo, the capital of Mozambique, this residence was designed to ensure that views from the upper access road would continue to be enjoyed by the public. || The house is arranged as a double-story building with the bedrooms above and the lounge–dining areas at lower ground level. The living areas adjoin a generous veranda–belvedere under a bougainvillea-covered pergola. || The character of the building comes from the use of vaulted roofs, realized in hollow brickwork contained by reinforced concrete gutter beams. The relationship of the different internal spaces with the exterior levels creates **a rich variety of living environments that negotiate the steep slope of the site**. || The treatment of the garden slopes and platforms was an essential part of the architectural concept; the client was heavily involved in the creation of the rich green backdrop, achieved exclusively with local flora. || The splendid color of the building was the result of a long debate with the owners. The result is a striking presence, both complementary to and in contrast with its surroundings. The play of retaining walls and greenery creates a joyful sculptural effect.

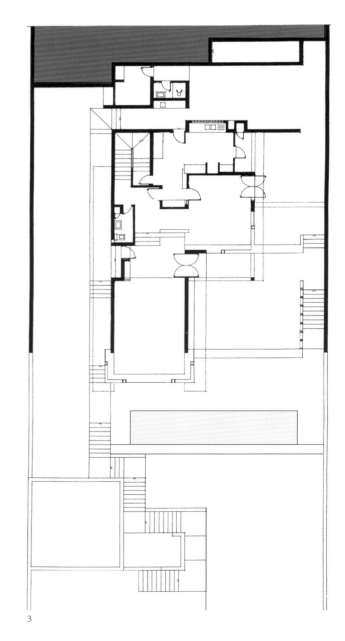

3

4

5

6

7

1

2

1 Kitchen
2 Living room and terrace from kitchen
3 North elevation in late afternoon light
4 Stairs from mezzanine to living room
5 Architect's studio
6 Second floor plan
7 First floor plan

Photography: Doug R. Fogelson (1,3–5); Roland Halbe (2)

Zoka Zola architecture + urban design

PFANNER HOUSE

Chicago, Illinois, USA

This house suggests ways of urbanizing residential planning in Chicago. It is placed on its undersized (180-square-meter) corner lot in a way that articulates the yard spaces around it. The side yard is wide enough to form a defined space between the two buildings and to plant four cottonwood trees, which provide shade and privacy to the southern windows. The back yard is the site for a future office extension. Other means of urbanizing this lot include opening the interior of the house to the street through its balconies, terraces, and windows. ‖ The 300-square-meter house explores the architectural concept of 'opening.' Not an opening that merely extends the space, or a continuously transitioning space; instead, an opening of one space to another space. These openings are smooth, unhindered, non-fretful, openings of one space to the other—openings that are formed like breathing channels in healthy lungs where movements are long and smooth. ‖ The views that one sees through the windows of

the house are not purely visual and not framed selectively according to ideas of a good view. Instead, they are reminders of what exists outside. The ability to see the sky is an important feature. ‖ The house is clad in red brick, the same color as most of the buildings surrounding it. The common material, though, emphasizes the main difference—its degree of openness—between it and the other buildings. ‖ **The house embodies the pleasure of being alive.** The terrace is the main source of pleasure—allowing bodily pleasure, social pleasure, pleasures with the passage of time, pleasure with air, sun, and trees. The kitchen counter, the balcony, and the bathrooms are the places where daily activity is enjoyed. All the exits from the house, the entrances, balcony extension, terrace, and the bedroom extension are the places where the daily pleasures of being with the house are experienced.

3

4

5

6

1 Bathroom
2 Terrace
3 Living room
4 Kitchen
5 Balcony
6 Closet
7 Bedroom
8 Laundry

7

0   10ft

1

2

Stuart Tanner Architects

PIRATES BAY HOUSE

Eaglehawk Neck, Tasmania, Australia

This house is a coastal retreat near Eaglehawk Neck on Tasmania's Tasman Peninsula. The clients requested a contemporary, steel-framed building that made best use of an awkward site and brought the coastal aspect of its location into the living spaces. ‖ Expressed structure and engineering are integral to the architecture, correlating with the notion of the building as a hovering platform from which to experience nature. Architect, engineer, and contractor worked closely to craft a place where **landscape, structure, and space combine in an exhilarating experience**. The structure is predominantly a prefabricated steel frame that rests on a core-filled block wall. The main platform is connected to the site at the rear, suspended approximately midway by two steel straps and the entire structure is stiffened beneath by thin steel rods to footings. Materials include blackwood exterior cladding, ship lapped, with each screw fixing countersunk and plugged with myrtle. Significant pieces of joinery are solid blackwood. The timber louvers are cedar. ‖ Entrance to the building is intentionally at the rear to avoid the insertion of a stair and, more importantly, to reinforce the experience of a 'bridge journey' upon arrival. Visitors experience the bush as they approach the building entry, then Pirates Bay reveals itself both in sight and sound as one proceeds along the platform.

Internal spaces invite the user to engage with both intimate and distant vistas, thus dismissing the need for a complex plan. ‖ The brief required that the building, a coastal getaway, should connect with the environment both visually and thermally, rather than being 'sealed off from outside.' The glass of the main panels was intentionally specified as clear single skin, to reduce overall cost and ensure maximum visual connection from inside to the surrounding landscape. The glazing permits year-round solar gain with passive ventilation harnessed by the louver system. Careful attention to insulation in the floor, ceiling, and walls, coupled with louver systems and exterior sunscreens, assist in keeping interior temperatures ambient. Little supplementary heating is required. ‖ Interior spaces are flexible, and the circulation arrangement generates privacy for sleeping areas. The main corridor serves as entry circulation and two equally sided bedrooms are set on the southern, 'quiet' edge of the building. Wet areas are consolidated to one zone. The kitchen was designed to be a place of entertainment as well as a work area. Decks surround three sides of the building to enhance the feeling of space and the sense of a 'floating platform for living.'

3

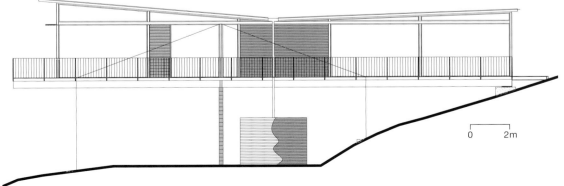

1   Slender frame suspends the platform
2   Entry
3   Living space floats over the sea
4   Elevation

4

0   2m

5

6

7

5   Structure is the external focus
6   Rainwater tanks as integrated element
7   Landscape is part of the interior experience
8   Walls retract to reveal living spaces
9   Floor plan
10 A platform for living

Photography: Brett Boardman

8

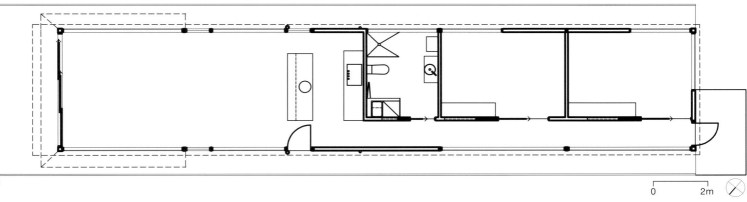

9

0   2m

10

1

2

Keith Pike Associates

PITTWATER HOUSE
Pittwater, New South Wales, Australia

The site is a sloping, elevated block with northerly aspect and panoramic views over Pittwater, a beautiful inlet about 45 minutes' drive north of Sydney. || The house is configured around a central circulation stair and lift and connects a basement six-car garage with three accommodation levels above. Cut into the side of the hill, the main body of the house is essentially buried, with only the top floor visible and accessible to the rear south garden. || All principal rooms are on the northern face and are attached to **extensive cantilevered terrace structures** that enjoy ideal solar aspect and magnificent water views. The ground floor level is built as a podium over the garage and contains the principal entry, connected via a staircase to the street below. A glass-fronted plunge pool and a fishpond located either side of the entrance pathway extend the visual connection between the house and its water features with Pittwater beyond. Both bedrooms at this level enjoy extensive views, both man-made and natural. || The living and dining areas occupy the level above. The dining room, housed in a zinc-clad pavilion, projects out over the driveway below. The main bedroom suite and home office/gym occupy the entire top floor. Designed as the owners' retreat, the top floor also has an extensive external terrace from which aerial views north to Barrenjoey Headland can be enjoyed. || Despite being buried into the hillside, all rooms are naturally ventilated and all north-facing glazing is protected from summer sun by overhanging roofs. The upper levels of the house are constructed in zinc-paneled reverse brick veneer for better thermal performance and low maintenance.

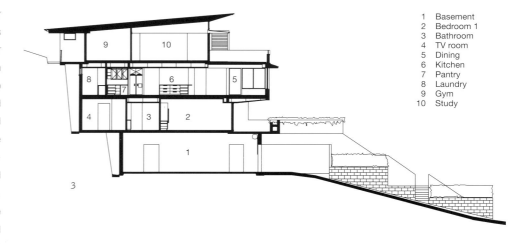

1	Basement
2	Bedroom 1
3	Bathroom
4	TV room
5	Dining
6	Kitchen
7	Pantry
8	Laundry
9	Gym
10	Study

1   Upper terrace
2   Elevation from road
3   Section
4   Detail of north elevation

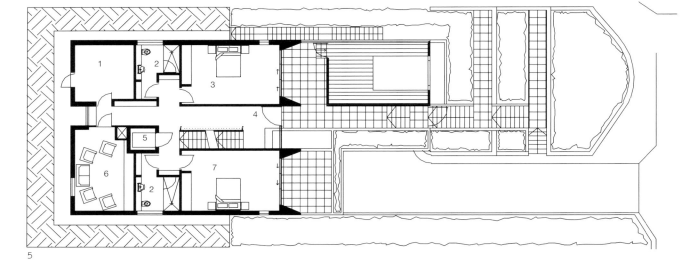

1 Storage
2 Bathroom
3 Bedroom 2
4 Entry
5 Lift
6 TV room
7 Bedroom 1

5

6

7

8

9

5   Entry level floor plan
6   View from living room into dining room
7   Pool terrace
8   Entry level fish pond
9   Zinc cladding on east elevation

Photography: Adrian Boddy

263

1

Abramson Teiger Architects

PLATEAU HEIGHTS RESIDENCE
Los Angeles, California, USA

Perched high in the Hollywood Hills above Sunset Boulevard, this house is designed with a procession of spaces that move one through the project with a continued anticipation of the view to come. The first event in this sequence is the motor court. Here, solid, embracing concrete walls shield the house from the street. The concrete is dynamically cut to reveal the front door, which in itself is a living sculpture enveloping the visitor. To the left of the front door is a children's playroom where translucent glass beckons a constant flow of soft light without being exposed to the motor court. || The sweeping views of the west Los Angeles Basin are majestically revealed from all the living spaces in the house. The house is **a compound of buildings** around a rectangular stretch of lawn that flanks an infinity-edge swimming pool. Patios hug the edge of the hill and showcase the swimming pool, creating an entertainment environment that embraces both the interior and the exterior areas. The new pool house on the west of the lawn was designed as a series of rotated objects, addressing the magnificent 360-degree views while celebrating the stylistic theme of the house. || In the main house, high wood ceilings thrust outward and tall sliding doors open to create an ideal entertaining environment, which flows from the interior to the exterior. The residence is the resort, a destination point for both rest and play. Its luxurious master bath overlooks the jet liner views; the spa is tranquil, serene, and bathed in soft light.

2

3

3   Kitchen with cabinets by Bulthaup
4   Living room
5   Breakfast room
6   Second floor plan
7   First floor plan
8   The master bathroom creates a spa resort at home

Photography: David Lena Photography

4

6

1 Entry
2 Living room
3 Dining room
4 Breakfast room
5 Kitchen
6 Media room
7 Bedroom
8 Garage
9 Playroom
10 Master bedroom
11 Master bathroom
12 Master closet
13 Study

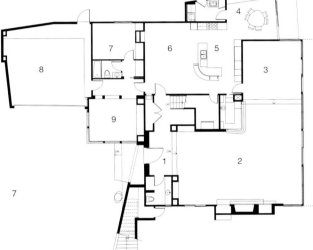

7

1

2

Dirk Denison Architects

PRIVATE RESIDENCE
Midwest, USA

This renovation and addition to a country house provides generous and contemporary living spaces to accommodate both large and small family gatherings within the context of the existing traditional structure. The renovation allows for clear and open circulation throughout the main living spaces, while several new volumes add space and light while connecting the house with its surrounding landscape. A series of windows overlooking a central courtyard establishes **a rhythm of opacity and transparency** that connects the new and old sections of the house. || At the back of the house, a new structure extends beyond the main volumes into the courtyard and surrounding landscape. Open in varying degrees to the outdoors, this structure provides alternate possibilities for circulation and encourages the use of both indoor and outdoor spaces.

3

1 The new sections of the house extend out into the landscape
2 The structure extends beyond the main volume of the house into the courtyard
3 In the evening, the open-air structures are lit to extend spaces for living and circulation to the outdoors
4 A series of windows overlooking a central courtyard establishes a rhythm of opacity and transparency
5 The new additions are visible from the back of the house

4

5

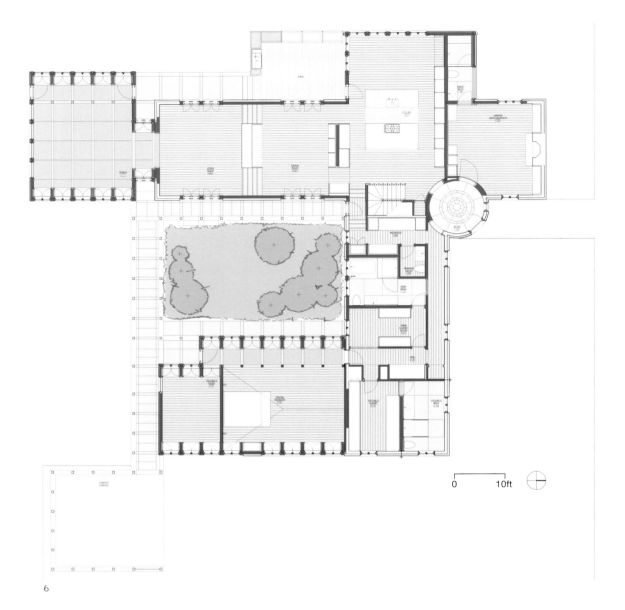

6   First floor plan
7   The large open kitchen is part of the new plan for the
      existing structure of the house
8   The new addition adds light and space to the existing plan
9   The dining room is part of a large open living space
10   Set at the end of the main living space, the living room is
      sunk below the level of the dining room and kitchen and
      opens onto the courtyard
11   The new structure can be closed and opened in varying
      degrees to the outdoors

Photography: Scott Shigley

0   10ft

6

7

8

9

10

11

1   Detail of street façade
2   Oblique view of street façade
3   Projected dining room with decorated ceiling and rear garden beyond
4   Third floor bathroom interior
5   Third floor plan
6   First floor plan
7   Ground floor plan

Photography: Hélène Binet

Tony Fretton Architects

THE RED HOUSE

Chelsea, London, UK

This London town house was commissioned as a place in which to live and work, initially for a single young man and eventually for a family. The client also wanted the building to not only house his significant collection of contemporary art, but to appear as a work of art in its own right. || The project attempts to reconcile a new London house type within a heritage site by drawing on the arrangement of existing classic buildings in the street to arrive at **a unique design that sustains the urbanity and culture of its location.** || The build was proposed as a replacement of two existing 1950's neo-vernacular cottages on the site, which overlooks Christopher Wren's Royal Hospital and Westminster Cathedral beyond. The house is a new construction, made of reinforced concrete and clad with an insulating rain screen of sumptuous French red limestone, punctuated with windows made of bronze drawn onto wood. The house is set back to align with the house to the left, making the two houses an ensemble at the point where the street widens and curves. || The entrance features a red stone door that slides into the garage on the ground floor. Access to the house is via an entrance court to the

right of the garage doors, which leads into a double-height entrance hall with views into the garden. In contrast to the stark stone façade and paving of the street, the entry space is permeated with views of the greenery. || The project included a complex interior, which was designed in partnership with Studio Mark Pimlott, to invite use without delineating purpose. The spatial qualities and character of each floor are different. The ground floor has a horizontal emphasis reminiscent of early modernism and terminates in a glazed dining pavilion within the garden. The first floor is an Italianate room of some scale and accommodates a collection of large canvases and sculpture. This room looks out across a balcony to the grounds of the Royal Hospital and has a more intimately scaled room next to it. A long and narrow study is on the mezzanine floor. The top floor has bedrooms arranged around a planted court. A principal stairwell links the entrance hall to the lounge and the light spaces of the top floor. || Materials were chosen for their intrinsic beauty and longevity. They include stone for the façade, bronze drawn onto wood for the windows, and frameless glass for the window balustrades.

3

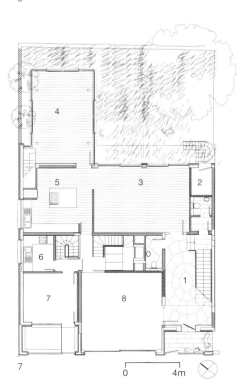

4

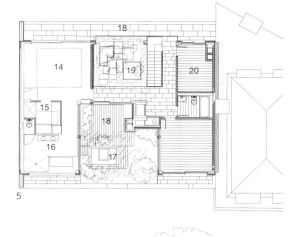

5

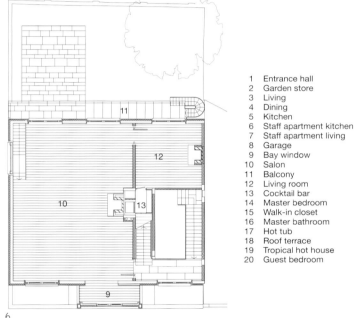

6

1 Entrance hall
2 Garden store
3 Living
4 Dining
5 Kitchen
6 Staff apartment kitchen
7 Staff apartment living
8 Garage
9 Bay window
10 Salon
11 Balcony
12 Living room
13 Cocktail bar
14 Master bedroom
15 Walk-in closet
16 Master bathroom
17 Hot tub
18 Roof terrace
19 Tropical hot house
20 Guest bedroom

7

0   4m

273

1

FMSA Architects

REDBANK PLAIN HOUSE

Redbank Plain, Victoria, Australia

The house is located in rural Victoria's High Country, between Dinner Plain and Mount Hotham Airport. The 40-hectare site is isolated, cannot be seen from the road, and is not connected to any services. || The clients requested an original house with a unique form that engaged the panoramic views surrounding Redbank Plain. The house is used recreationally throughout the year to enjoy the four seasons on this alpine plain. The house needed to provide accommodation and living spaces to allow two family groups to be self contained. It was also required that the house be **environmentally sustainable and minimize energy consumption** while managing the climate extremes of the alpine environment. The design creates a simple form, sitting in balance with the surrounding eucalypt snow gums and offering panoramic alpine views. The building responds to the evocative image of the simple cattlemen's hut but offers the comforts of a 21st-century lifestyle. || Issues of sustainability and self-sufficiency were

resolved to provide a five-star amenity in a building that is legible and easy to use by visitors and guests. The house is powered by 12 photovoltaic cells and a battery supplying 240 volts via an inverter. A back-up gas-powered generator, as a failsafe precaution, is necessary in this isolated location. The house, designed principally to operate on glasshouse solar heating with internal mass storage, has minimized heating running costs. Solar gain is stored by the dark concrete floor slab and re-emitted during the night. The north elevation maximizes the opportunity for solar penetration. Balcony sun shading is formed from the row of solar panels positioned so that snow damage from the roof is not possible. A simple layered skillion roof provides trouble-free snow management. || Water supply is from a 90-meter-deep bore. The bore provides clear drinking water, effectively tapping ground water stored across the locality; roof gutters are not practical in snow areas, so cannot be used to channel additional rainwater.

2

3

275

4

4   The layout is efficient, minimizing circulation and service areas
5   First-floor rooms open onto a linear north-facing balcony
6   First floor plan
7   Ground floor plan
8   Building materials and colors are from the natural palette
9   Durable materials withstand the harshness of the environment

Photography: Mark Munro

5

6

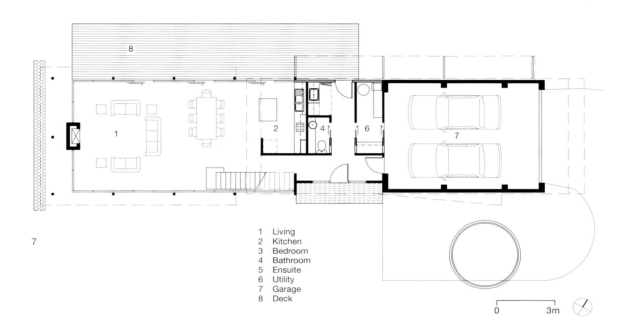

7

1 Living
2 Kitchen
3 Bedroom
4 Bathroom
5 Ensuite
6 Utility
7 Garage
8 Deck

0   3m

8

9

1 View from breezeway to living space below
2 Living room, with dining area beyond
Opposite:
    Front façade, viewed from the street

Pugh + Scarpa Architects

REDELCO RESIDENCE
Studio City, California, USA

This 4700-square-foot house remodel and addition was more than a decade in the making. The architects began work on the project in early 1994, but all construction ceased due to circumstances beyond the owner's control. Seven years later, the owner asked the architects to complete the partially constructed house, but due to code changes, city ordinances, and a wide variety of obstacles, it was determined that the house could not be completed as originally designed. || After much consideration the client asked the architect if it were possible to alter/remodel the partially constructed house—which was a remodel/addition to a 1970's ranch-style house—into a project that would fit into current zoning and structural codes. The owner also requested that the house's footprint and partially constructed foundations remain to avoid the need for further entitlements and delays on an already long-overdue project and difficult hillside site. || The architects' main challenge was how to alter the design that reflected an outdated philosophical approach to architecture. How could the house be re-conceived, reflecting the architects' and client's maturity on a ten-year-old footprint? ||

The answer was to remove almost all of the previously proposed existing interior walls and transform the existing footprint into a pavilion-like structure that allows the site to, in a sense, 'pass through the house.' This allowed better use of a limited and restricted building area while **capturing extraordinary panoramic views** of the San Fernando Valley and Hollywood Hills. Large, 22-foot-high custom sliding glass doors allow the interior and exterior to become one. Even the studio is separated from the house and connected only by an exterior bridge. || Limestone floors extend from inside to outside and into the lap pool that runs the entire length of the house, creating a horizon line at the edge of the view. Other natural materials such as board-formed concrete, copper, steel, and cherry provide softness to the objects that seem to float within the interior volume. By placing objects and materials 'outside the frame,' a new frame of reference deepens our sense of perception. Art does not reproduce what we see; rather it makes us see.

Photography: Marvin Rand

4

5

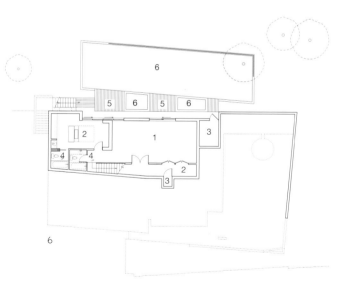

6

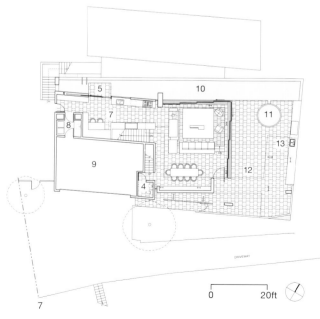

7

0   20ft

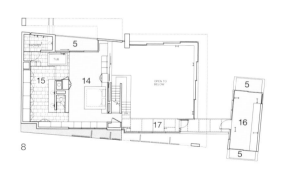

8

1	Gym	9	Garage
2	Closet/storage	10	Pool
3	Mechanical	11	Jacuzzi
4	Bathroom	12	Entry patio
5	Balcony/deck	13	Outdoor kitchen
6	Lawn	14	Master bedroom
7	Kitchen/breakfast area	15	Master bathroom
8	Laundry	16	Studio
		17	Bridge

9

1

2

De Maria Design Associates

REDONDO BEACH RESIDENCE
Redondo Beach, California, USA

This single-family custom residence utilizes **recycled ISO cargo containers**. These redeployed containers are a critical element of the transportation infrastructure that facilitates global trade; with the ongoing trade imbalance, millions of containers remain in ports around the USA. Combined with technologies from the neighboring aerospace industry, the containers have been brought together with traditional stick-frame construction to create a 'hybrid' home. || The use of materials and methods from other industries, unrelated to residential construction, is part of the architect's philosophical approach. Airplane hangar doors open the family room to the courtyard where a subterranean cargo container swimming pool is located. Features including the recycled containers, the ceramic-based insulation (as used on NASA's space shuttle), the prefabricated metal roof panels, the multi-skinned acrylic sheets employed on greenhouses, the formaldehyde-free plywood, and the tank-less hot water heaters, all add up to a home that is innovative, affordable, and environmentally conscious. || The house consists of eight containers, of various sizes, stacked two high, some perpendicular to the others. Four of the largest containers sit perpendicular to the street

above a concrete garage, two stacked on the right, two on the left. The lower boxes serve as hallways and open-air porches; the upper boxes house the master bath and walk-in closet, and a library-guestroom. The four smaller, 20-foot containers are joined to the rear of the right-side front containers and house bedrooms, kitchen, and a utility room. Door and window openings have been cut to provide daylight and the main stair is enclosed in translucent, lightweight acrylic panels, extending the industrial aesthetic. Larger spaces between the containers are framed in wood and steel, and house an artist's studio, master bedroom, and a double-height living room with a 20-foot ceiling. || The containers are virtually mold-proof, termite-proof, and fire-proof, and nearly indestructible. Their sturdiness has great appeal in this area, which is vulnerable to earthquakes and mudslides. Those features, combined with the affordability of the building system, will assist many people to realize the dream of creating a quality custom home at an affordable price. This project is the torch bearer for a new, more affordable, method of design and construction—architecture as a product.

1 Stairs leading to entrance porch
2 Evening view of street elevation
3 Artist studio framed by ISO cargo container
4 Detail of interior plywood finish and translucent acrylic panel
5 Cube-skylight of artist studio
6 Detail of stacked cargo container
7 Top to bottom: second floor, first floor, and basement plans

Photography: Andre Movsesyan; Christian Kienapfel

1 Library/guest
2 Laundry
3 Balcony
4 Bathroom
5 Bedroom
6 Hallway
7 His closet
8 Master bedroom
9 Her closet
10 Master bathroom

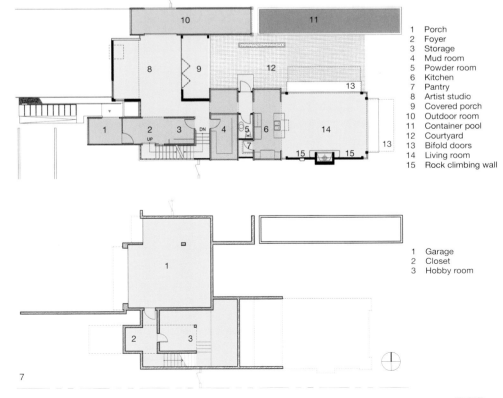

1 Porch
2 Foyer
3 Storage
4 Mud room
5 Powder room
6 Kitchen
7 Pantry
8 Artist studio
9 Covered porch
10 Outdoor room
11 Container pool
12 Courtyard
13 Bifold doors
14 Living room
15 Rock climbing wall

1 Garage
2 Closet
3 Hobby room

Atelier Tekuto

REFLECTION OF MINERAL HOUSE
Nakano-ku, Tokyo, Japan

The remarkable shape of the Reflection of Mineral house was the result of a combination of a very limited building site (only 45 square meters); local building regulations; and the client's desire for a fun design that maximized site use and incorporated undercover parking. After creating dozens of models, the architects arrived at the ultimate design that has the cut of a precious stone. ǁ The house is one of Atelier Tekuto's 'Reflection' series, in which experimental designs for small houses have been developed around **the theme of shifting perspectives**. This polyhedron, constructed from reinforced concrete, comprises a variety of interior surfaces that create optical illusions: for example, light that passes through a very narrow glass window reflects on the mass of polygonal surfaces, directing the light back up through and distorting the occupant's sense of the actual size of the building. ǁ The four-level, 86-square-meter family home features an unusual distribution of living spaces. Bedrooms are in the basement; kitchen, living, and dining rooms are on the first floor, and the bathroom is on the second floor. Sharply defined concrete surfaces and angular windows contribute to the overall feeling of spaciousness. ǁ The Reflection of Mineral house has even had a positive effect on the neighborhood, providing improved visibility for drivers at the corner—the set-back, acute angle on the corner opens it up and provides open space, like a piazza.

1   House in its neighborhood context
2   The house's setback increases visibility for drivers at the corner
Opposite:
    The fun design maximizes site usage

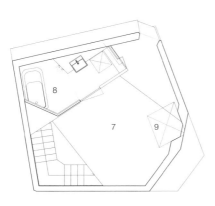

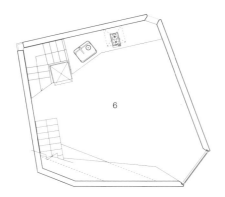

1 Bedroom
2 Closet
3 Parking
4 Hall
5 Porch
6 Living/dining/kitchen
7 Utility
8 Bathroom
9 Skylight

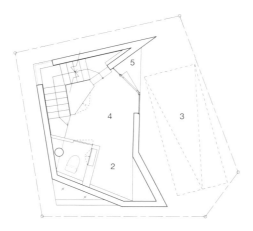

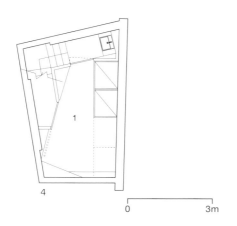

4

0   3m

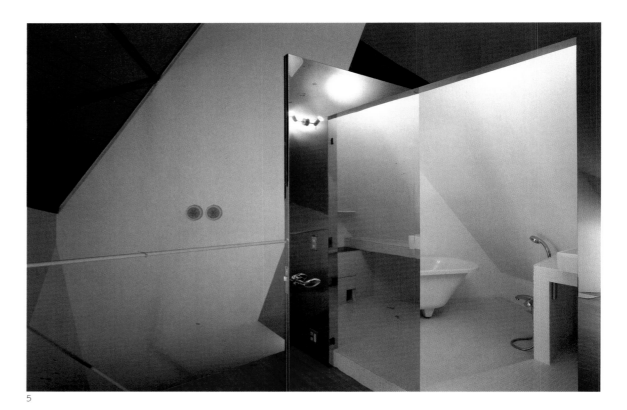

5

6

4 Floor plans, from top to bottom: second floor, first floor, ground floor, basement
5 Bathroom
6 Kitchen
7 Living room

Photography: Makoto Yoshida

7

1   Open communal living space flanked by more solid
    wings, which include media room on one side and the
    master suite on the other
2   Open kitchen with cherry cabinets looking through the
    living room into the office
3   The clerestory windows provide light and ventilation to
    the double-height living room and kitchen
4   Floor plan
5   Indoor/outdoor feel for the master bathroom with
    access to a private patio
Photography: David Lena Photography

1

William Hefner Architecture

ROSCOMARE RESIDENCE
Bel Air, California, USA

On a wooded site in upper Bel Air, this new 3000-square-foot home for a family of four
is **a private haven among the pine trees**. ‖ The kitchen, dining, and living areas are
open and flowing in this two-story space. Large expanses of glass take advantage of
privacy, views, and the pool beyond. The communal space is bordered by private
spaces, which include the office, media room, and bedrooms with full privacy. ‖ All of
the materials impart warmth: oak floors, cherry cabinets, and Douglas fir doors, windows
and trim, which work well with the warm color of stucco and interior plaster.

2

3

4

5

Johnston Marklee & Associates

SALE HOUSE
Venice, California, USA

The Sale House replaces a 1920's bungalow that was destroyed by fire, which left behind an annex building at the rear of the lot. The annex, commonly known as the 2-4-6-8 House, is a two-story studio and garage designed by Morphosis in 1978. Taking 2-4-6-8 as a starting point for a new host structure, the Sale House acknowledges the historical pedigree of its esteemed neighbor while reversing the process by which it was generated. The new design repeats and integrates the historical structure, preserving the original function of 2-4-6-8 and producing new variations on a Los Angeles classic. || The massing concept of the 3600-square-foot Sale House originated from a Morphosis drawing that multiplied 2-4-6-8 as identical quadruplets. Repeating and transforming the original volume of 2-4-6-8, a 'condensed mass' for the master bedroom mirrors the Morphosis pavilion across the 'excavated void' of the courtyard. The original element and these two serialized variations are anchored to a rectangular base that contains the main living areas and joins the new and existing structures. By redistributing the outdoor spaces typically devoted to driveways and front and side yards to the internal courtyard, **the overall design turns the typical single-family house inside out.** || The geometry and primary colors of 2-4-6-8 are reflected in the new design. Private rooms in bright pink, turquoise, and yellow-orange are conceived as shaped volumes—serial deviations from the red, blue, and yellow of the studio windows. The white walls of the main living spaces reflect these vibrant colors. The exterior contrasts this vivid palette with the most neutral color available—that of the photographic gray card. || The apertures in the new house are sized to match those of 2-4-6-8. Shifted to the volume edges to accommodate circulation and services, these openings reinforce the outward orientation and rotational quality of the new intervention. Within, a wall of sliding glass doors renders the shared living space continuous with the glass box of the interior courtyard, and the glazed lower-level street façade visually links both spaces with the pedestrian street beyond. Taken together, the courtyard and apertures comprise an ideal passive cooling configuration: the courtyard draws fresh air into the base of the house, while the upper windows, puncturing each face of the new volume, expel warm air and promote cross ventilation.

3

1 Exterior view of 2-4-6-8 House from alley
2 Exterior view of Sale House from street
3 Exterior view with 2-4-6-8 House

4 Upper level floor plan
5 Ground floor plan
6 Exterior view showing the relationship between Sale House and 2-4-6-8 House
7 Bedroom shows interplay of color and materiality
8 Staircase is lined with a bold hue
9 Exterior view from courtyard into living space

Photography: Eric Staudenmaier

1 Entry
2 Living room
3 Patio
4 Storage
5 Laundry
6 Existing garage with studio above
7 Pantry
8 Parking
9 Kitchen
10 Dining
11 Skylight above
12 Toilet
13 Closet
14 Bedroom/study
15 Hall
16 Closet
17 Master bedroom
18 Bathroom
19 Roof deck
20 Open to courtyard below
21 Roof deck
22 Existing studio

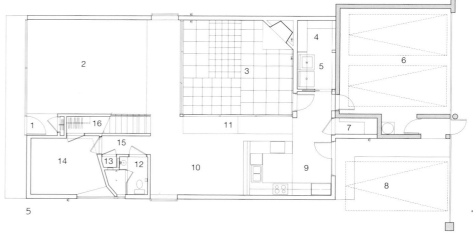

6

7

8

9

1

Mojo Stumer Associates

SALEM RESIDENCE

North Salem, New York, USA

The site for this house is on top of a mountain overlooking the entire valley in North
Salem. In the architect's words it is, '... **the most beautiful site we had ever seen.**
It's absolutely breathtaking, with the most amazing views.' || The program called for an
11,000-square-foot main structure and four additional outbuildings: a guesthouse, a
six-horse barn, a storage facility, and a pool and cabana. The total project, including the
outbuildings is approximately 15,000 square feet. || The site plan was the first major
design problem that needed solving. The site had very demanding design constraints,
restricting height, mass, and materials. The owner of an adjacent property had originally
owned the land and had control over what could be built on it. || The design direction
began by angling the house and garage to create a courtyard and using the guesthouse
to help frame the magnificent views from the entry court. The barn and storage structure
was located higher on the site so as not to interfere with the view, while the pool and
cabana are on a lower level, again, not restricting any view. || The design philosophy was
to create a barn-like structure but still embrace the necessary residential qualities for the
elevations. All primary rooms face the view with access to the outside via decks and
terraces. || Materials used include stone, cedar, and old barn beams. Lead-coated
copper is used at the silo, main front entrance, and for all scupper and flashing details.

2

3

4

5

6

Photography: Scott Frances

7

1

2

Shubin + Donaldson Architects

SANTA BARBARA RIVIERA

Santa Barbara, California, USA

Though not immediately obvious, this is **an environmentally sustainable house** on many levels: relationship to the site, reuse of foundation, built-in devices, photovoltaic heat capture, radiant floor heating, and use of natural and sustainable materials. The relatively small house has all the elements of a 5000- or 6000-square-foot house in a tidy, 3200-square-foot package. || The client wanted to take advantage of a classic Santa Barbara site on what is known as 'The Riviera.' Situated on a ridge, the near-perfect location commands a 270-degree view of the Pacific Ocean below and a view to the Santa Barbara mountains above. Each room affords great vistas in every direction, as well as stunning natural light throughout the day. || The three-level home and garage incorporate an open living/dining area, kitchen, master bedroom, master bath, guest bedroom and bath, powder room, home office, outdoor dining area, outdoor lounge area, and swimming pool/spa. || A monumental feeling is emphasized because the house constantly opens up to the outdoors. The colors of nature are the predominant palette and are a perfectly complementary color scheme. An infinity pool just outside the living room furthers the idea of expanse. || A dramatic glass canopy ceremoniously marks the entrance, bisecting the ground-to-roof planes of glass that form sidelights and clerestories. Walls intersect with glass throughout in a play of solidity and transparency. Floor-to-ceiling bookshelves complement an imposing monolith of mahogany on the living room wall that houses an entertainment center. Set into the wall, and surrounded by floor-to-ceiling glass, it appears as an extension of the outdoors. Doorways in general—even in the limestone-clad bathrooms—are taller than usual and lead the eye upward to be rewarded by either natural light or a beautiful vista. Dark wood floors and softly minimalist furniture are sophisticated and inviting. || A terrace surrounds the house, continuing the indoor/outdoor feeling and accessibility. Bedrooms and bathrooms look out to the ocean. The kitchen faces the hillside, emphasizing the connection with nature. By taking up minimal space, the house also takes up minimal resources. During construction, whatever could be reused was incorporated into the building. Finally, there is a certain efficiency of design in the layout, yet it provides all of the amenities so that the house looks and feels like a five-star private residential club. Making concessions to nature reaps great rewards.

1 The near-perfect location commands a 270-degree Pacific
   Ocean view
2 A dramatic glass canopy ceremoniously marks the entrance
3 The design strategy is to site the house based on solar
   orientation

3

4

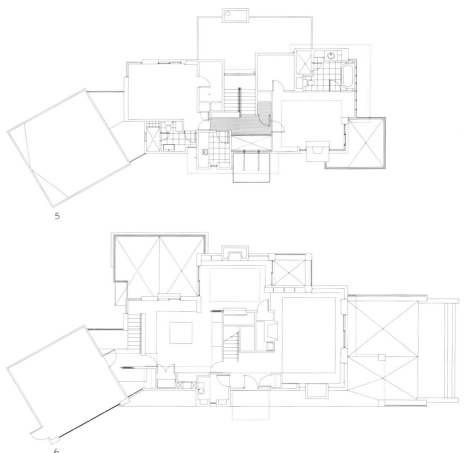

5

6

7

Photography: Ciro Coelho

8

9

10

11

301

1

Mark English Architects

SHAW RESIDENCE
Los Gatos, California, USA

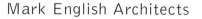

2

1	Master bedroom
2	Master bathroom
3	Bedroom
4	Bathroom
5	Laundry
6	Hall
7	Open to below

3

0   16ft

1	Entry	8	Office
2	Bridge	9	Media
3	Family room	10	Library
4	Kitchen	11	Utility
5	Dining	12	Garage
6	Living	13	Bathroom
7	Studio		

The design goal for this project was to create **an elegant urban home for a young family** with three boys who needed room to run. The interiors are comfortable and playful, and the exterior façades are informed by the unique characteristics found in each cardinal direction. || The hillside site is unique in size and shape. Nearly a quarter of a mile long, it is oriented north–south. The east boundary is on the ridge of a hill and the west boundary follows a small perennial creek. The vegetation is grassland with large, scattered oak trees. The site had been undeveloped for years because of the steepness of the slope and the resistance of neighbors. || The design concept is based upon a careful reading of the topography, orientation, and neighbor's views. The 4600-square-foot building is designed to inhabit a series of terraces that curve to follow the bend in the hillside. Some terraces extend out from the conditioned space and become bridges, driveways, and exterior terraces. Others provide for varying levels of privacy

within the home itself. The structural logic has the majority of the bearing members resting upon walls parallel with the topographic lines, leaving the north and south walls open for great amounts of glazing. The resulting fairly solid east and west walls provide for protection from the neighbors above and from the western sun at the creek's edge. The segmented gabled roof sequentially segments as the building curves in plan, and reduces in height as the footprint diminishes in width. The dining room is suspended as a complete circle in the gently bending matrix of the plan. || Interior materials include maple floors with radiant heating, maple cabinets and built-ins, custom stainless sink and hood, and marble countertops. The exterior is finished with natural copper sheathing at the façade and roof edges, wood siding, China jade slate terrace paving, and Trex decking.

4

5

6

1   Kitchen
2   Second floor plan
3   First floor plan
4   South elevation at dusk
5   Interior view from living room
6   Dining room

Photography: Mark Luthringer

1   Lakeside elevation
2   Lakeside deck
3   Main entrance

Charles R. Stinson Architects

SIEGEL RESIDENCE

Excelsior, Minnesota, USA

This lake-view house in Minnesota was designed as a summer retreat. The site is a hilly, wooded lot, with easy access to the quaint downtown of cozy, beachside Excelsior. || To take advantage of the property's unobstructed lake views, the architect designed what he calls an **'urban tree house,'** with a main floor that rises above the split-level entry to capture choice views, yet maintain the feeling of being nestled in the trees. || Most of the activity in the home, which measures a relatively modest 3300 square feet, is centered on the raised main level. The sleek, modern kitchen, outfitted in stainless steel with maple accents, boasts a custom-designed breakfast nook for two. A streamlined snack bar mirrors the home's exterior and provides a subtle separation between the kitchen and the larger dining room, which flows effortlessly into the bamboo-floored great room. The master bed and bath, as well as a guest suite (which doubles as a yoga studio) complete the main level. || A highlight of the house is the open, geometric great room, which features high ceilings and a large floating fireplace made of sculptural, burnished concrete block. The room's lake-facing walls are glass, while higher transoms on the opposite wall let in warm rays of southern light. Architecture is skillfully manipulated to bring natural light into the house from sunrise to sunset. || Furnishings and accents create a spiritual, Asian feel, to suit the client's request for the 'zen' atmosphere of a very peaceful, modern home. || The home's lower level includes another guest suite, a sauna, a media room, a raised study, and an artist's studio with a blue concrete floor. || To further enhance the tree house feel, a 12-foot-tall charcoal-colored planter runs the length of the great room, balancing the front entrance. It is filled with small trees that dapple the light entering through the great room's mid-height ribbon of windows. The planter brings in nature; it balances, creates calm, and promotes relaxation. || This new home was such a success that the owners sold their Florida condominium and now spend their winters at home in Minnesota, watching the theater of seasons play out on the nearby lake.

4

5

6

7

8

9

10

4 Foyer and stairs
5 Main level floor plan
6 Art studio with blue concrete floor
7 Kitchen view
8 View of kitchen and great room from breakfast nook
9 View of great room from kitchen
10 Guest suite bathroom

Photography: Peter Bastianelli-Kerze

1

Preston Lane Architects

ST CANICE RESIDENCE

Sandy Bay, Tasmania, Australia

This project involved a major alteration and extension to an existing 1920's house in Sandy Bay, close to the center of Hobart. It presented a unique opportunity to provide two separate additions: an inward-focused rear extension containing a gallery, bedrooms, and services, and a projecting living addition to the front of the house responding to the panoramic views of the Derwent River. || A key feature of the original house is the sandstone retaining wall that originally housed stables and over the years had been built in with a series of ad hoc extensions. The architects identified the key original elements—the sandstone wall and the majority of the original double brick house—and then inserted a new contemporary extension that contrasts with and highlights the original features. || The rear extension focuses on **revealing and highlighting sections of the original sandstone wall** and its unique deep reveal highlight windows. The light-filled gallery space to the west provides a secondary entry into the house and access to the rear bedrooms as well as a cellar in the south corner and a laundry extending onto a new deck to the southeast. A singular sliding door track provides neat concealment of the bedrooms; feature joinery and natural off-form concrete provide highlights down the hallway. || The original entry to the house has been maintained and a concealed sliding door to the dining room ensures this space feels light and open, but provides the flexibility to close the living spaces from the rest of the house. The living room extension projects from the line of the original house and is composed of a series of different-height windows that frame specific views from within and control views from close neighboring houses. Some major steel beams were required where the old meets the new and the resultant bulkheads were visually simplified by the insertion of a suspended timber ceiling lining over this area. A large deck opens up from the living room to the northeast and bifold doors allow the space to nearly double in size. Through careful detailing of concealed retractable blinds, and a television screen that rises from the crafted joinery unit, the expansive living room view can be closed off and is easily converted into a home theater. || Externally, a simple palette of materials provides a contrast with the original house. Most of the new walls are clad with painted cement sheet; oiled Tasmanian oak shiplapped timber boards provide a textural highlight and contrast with black aluminum window framing.

3

4

3   Rear hallway
4   Exterior view of living room deck
5   Interior view of gallery
6   Bathroom detail
7   Ground floor plan
8   New living room and views beyond

Photography: Ralph Alphonso (1–5,7); Daniel Lane (6)

5

6

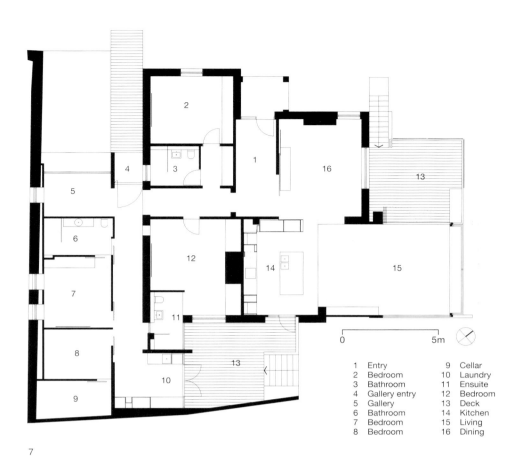

7

1 Entry
2 Bedroom
3 Bathroom
4 Gallery entry
5 Gallery
6 Bathroom
7 Bedroom
8 Bedroom
9 Cellar
10 Laundry
11 Ensuite
12 Bedroom
13 Deck
14 Kitchen
15 Living
16 Dining

8

1 The impressive double-height chimney is finished in Italian split-face marble
2 A large pivoting door is the focal point of the entrance
3 Extensive glazing maximizes the sea views
4 The open-plan kitchen and living area is light and spacious
5 Calming neutral tones complement the stained oak floors

Photography: Kallan MacLeod

Hulena Architects Ltd

TAKAPUNA BEACH HOUSE
Auckland, New Zealand

The owners of this new beachfront residence on Auckland's North Shore requested a sophisticated family home that would provide a private retreat from their busy working life. A number of factors served to complicate this simple brief. The first was the long, narrow shape of the 800-square-meter site, tucked away down a right-of-way with a narrow beach frontage. In addition, a number of development covenants in place set limits on the height, mass, and bulk of the building, as well as the number of levels allowed. Another important consideration was the need to retain a stand of native pohutukawa trees planted along the site's boundary abutting the beach. || The design of the house focuses on creating private, informal living spaces that take full advantage of the spectacular seaside location. Natural, textural materials soften the slick, modern form of the house, which covers approximately 400 square meters. Built from concrete clad with plaster, it also features Italian split-face marble feature walls, zinc fascias, and louvered timber shutters. || The scheme centers around a sunny, sheltered courtyard

featuring a rectangular swimming pool and a fireplace, which offers relaxed outdoor living and also ensures there is a water view from every room. A large pivoting door is the focal point of the entrance, with visitors proceeding along a gallery bordering the courtyard to the spacious, open-plan kitchen, dining, and living area adjacent to the media room. || The upper level contains four bedrooms, two of which have ensuite bathrooms. A large terrace off the master bedroom offers views over the patio and lawn out to the beach beyond. || The home's interior scheme is characterized by calming neutral tones enhanced by a palette of natural materials. Limestone and dark-stained oak are used on the floors, while the doors, skirtings, and the ceiling in the double-height living room are in dark-stained, paneled timber. Extensive glazing allows the owners to enjoy light and sea views. This transparency is juxtaposed with the solidity of the construction, resulting in **a constant play of light and shade**, and complementing the overall palette of textures and materials.

3

4

5

1

Studio 9 one 2 Architecture

TUCKER/VOLZ RESIDENCE

Manhattan Beach, California, USA

This residence stands on a 30- by 80-foot lot. The constraints posed by the lot and the clients' request for an ocean view challenged the architectural detailing of the building. || The composition of rectangular shapes intermixed with a 12-degree angle through the building creates the **dynamic interlocking geometry**. The wave shape and blue glass celebrate the nearby ocean, while the metal detailing reflects the often-lingering gray skies of the area. || A large window wall shields the entry and staircase from the street. This space is small due to the constraints of the lot, yet needed to be exciting because of its repeated use by the residents. Curving open metal stairs, which hover over a water element, make the vertical circulation a dynamic experience. || The large, open plan of the top level looks over neighboring structures and invites in the 180-degree ocean view that extends from Malibu to Palos Verdes. The desire for such a view drove the design scheme to minimize the roof structure, which is 9 inches thick, to maximize the height of the viewing platform but not exceed the requisite height limit.

2

3

1 Dining/living room with ocean view beyond
2 East and north elevation
3 South and east elevation
4 Entry with ball suspended in glass wall

4

5

7

6

5   Kitchen and glass wall beyond
6   Main stair and gallery space
7   Gallery middle level
8   Built-in flat-screen TV and fireplace in master bedroom
9   Powder room
10 Second floor plan
11 First floor plan

Photography: Dean Pappas Photography

8

9

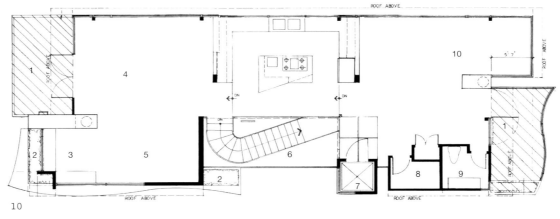

1 Deck
2 Planter box
3 Sitting area
4 Living room
5 Dining room
6 Open to below
7 Elevator
8 Pantry
9 Powder room
10 Family room

10

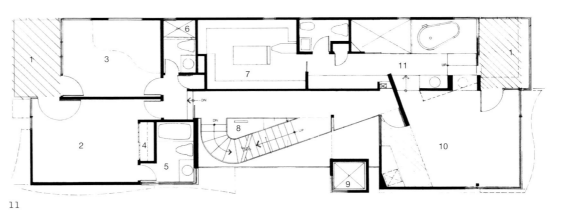

1 Deck
2 Bedroom 1
3 Bedroom 2
4 Closet
5 Bathroom 1
6 Shower
7 Walk-in closet
8 Open to below
9 Elevator
10 Master bedroom
11 Master bathroom

11

1

2

studio**piperov**

VILLA DUVARA
Varvara, Bulgaria

1　View from the sea
2　Exterior fragment at dusk
3　Exterior view at dusk
4　Dining area overlooking the sea
5　View at atrium and living area
6　Lower level floor plan
7　Upper level floor plan

Photography: Julian Piperov (1); Bogdanov and Misirkov (2–5)

The site for this house is on the outskirts of the tiny village of Varvara on the Bulgarian Black Sea coast. The long and narrow geometry of the gradually sloping plot defines the linear organization of the house. || A long, rustic masonry spine ('duvar' in Bulgarian) runs along the entire structure, merging interior and exterior. It enters into the double-height living room space and serves as a natural backdrop for the gray steel stair. The occupants of the house are constantly aware of its presence as they are guided in their everyday routine to walk along and through it. The spine also serves as a basis for both horizontal and vertical circulation in the house and the living spaces are organized along it. Niches are cut out of its mass to house the rusty remnants from a shipwreck found nearby by local fishermen. || The connection with the sea is never lost as fragments of the horizon are carefully framed in the window openings. Entering the house, the space dramatically expands into the glazed double-height atrium, which acts as a vertical

counterpoint to the general horizontality of the house. || A home office is located in a loft suspended in the atrium space. Its metal structure is clad in the same hardwood flooring as the living room. The wood finish intentionally reduces the contrast between floor and ceiling. The polished concrete recessed floor of the kitchen and dining rooms fluidly extends over the covered patio and the outdoor terraces. The metal sculptural fireplace on a concrete base is the focal point in the living room area and its black chimney runs vertically through the double-height atrium. || Villa Duvara was intended to be **a subtle intrusion into the natural environment**. The material palette used both for the interior and exterior is derived from the surrounding nature: sea rocks in shades of black and gray, warm beige sandstone, and white stucco. Materials include concrete, exposed stone masonry, white plaster, polished concrete floors, oak hardwood flooring, limestone cladding, and perforated steel mesh.

3

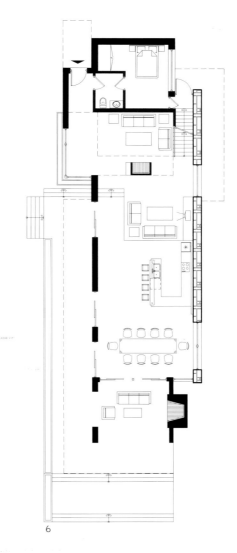

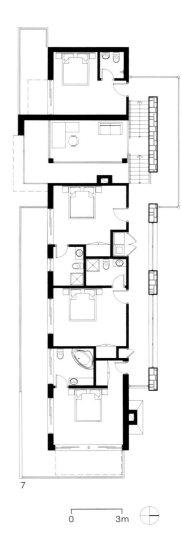

6

7

0   3m

4

5

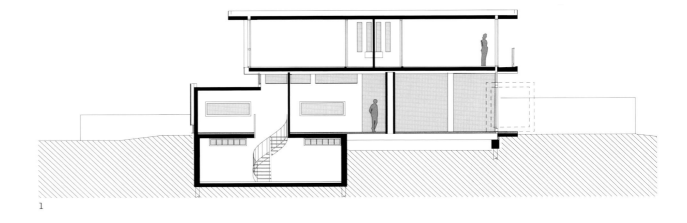

1

HM Architecten

VILLA OUBORG

Amsterdam, The Netherlands

This private home in Amsterdam was designed for Leontine and Eric Eggink, and their two daughters. In keeping with its neighbors, the house embodies the principles of the International Style: **light, air, and space**. These qualities are especially apparent in the main living area, which encompasses the living room, kitchen, and dining room, and features floor-to-ceiling glazing and an open floor plan. The floor plan includes both inside and outside spaces to create a dramatic spatial impact. ‖ The garden is an integral part of the house and has an impact even from the front door. Lower-level screens and garden plantings were designed in association with a sound consultant to achieve maximum sound absorption. Outdoor living and dining in the garden is accompanied by views over the adjacent canal. ‖ The main living area is rather closed toward the street frontage. A bluestone wall shields the front door and hallway from view when entering the house. The wall is elevated from the street level, allowing it to 'float.' ‖ Two abstract plastered volumes hover above the open floor plan. The bedroom volumes are more enclosed and private to reduce sound and heat from the sun. At the garden façade, deep overhangs and a brise soleil above keep the interiors cool and protected.

2

3

4

5

6

5   Living room
6   Terrace
7   Hallway
8   First floor plan
9   Ground floor plan
10   Basement plan

Photography: Luuk Kramer fotografie

7

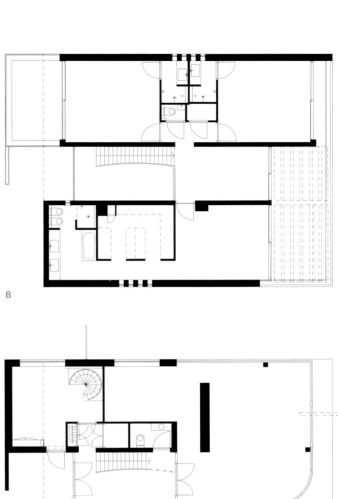

8

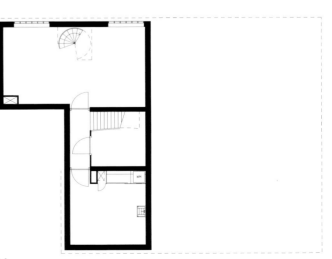

9

10

323

1

2

Irving Smith Jack Architects Ltd

VINEYARD HOUSE
Marlborough, New Zealand

Marlborough's Wairau Valley lies at the top of the South Island, New Zealand's premier wine region. High sunshine hours and stony river soils are perfect for growing grapes, and the region offers a wonderful lifestyle opportunity. || This vineyard house meets a balance of demands. It combines a relaxed rural home and year-round outdoor living with the practical requirements of managing a grape-growing enterprise. It also independently caters for visiting family and guests. || The two wings of the house are set to capture north views and sun. Of differing heights, and separated to create a sheltered courtyard between, they are nevertheless related by a continuity of roof line that links them as a pair. || From the approach, the weatherboard-clad two-story wing presents as a **simple utilitarian building**, incised by a central entrance. Above garaging and utility spaces, this higher form contains a master suite and separately accessed guest accommodation. Cement bagged concrete masonry walls to the lower level give a feeling of substance and extend outward to shape the arrival space and connect the house and landscape. || In parallel, but set apart, the living wing commands expansive views north across gently undulating vines and opens opposite to the roofed

courtyard for outdoor living in all weathers. Circulation is defined by a glass-roofed gallery that links the lounge and courtyard. Beneath an external glazed roof, spaced battens admit filtered sun to the courtyard, which is protected from wind by the surrounding house. || Connecting the two wings is a counter-axial walkway, announced at the point of arrival by a penetration of the facing wall, and leading beneath the upper level to the entrance, linking en-route with the garage, laundry, guest suite, and courtyard. The walkway is a functional space—the transition from vineyard to house—where working clothes are shed, hands washed, and visitors diverted to their quarters. || Broad eaves and sheltering roofs protect the perimeter, yet natural light permeates throughout the interior. Roof glazing admits controlled sunlight onto tiled floors that act as thermal collectors, releasing heat back into the house. Expansive glass gives a strong sense of living among the vines, and captures contrasting views through the gallery, courtyard, and walkway. In shaping space for outdoor living, the simple forms create a rich sense of complexity, textured by the patterning of light through sun filters and screens.

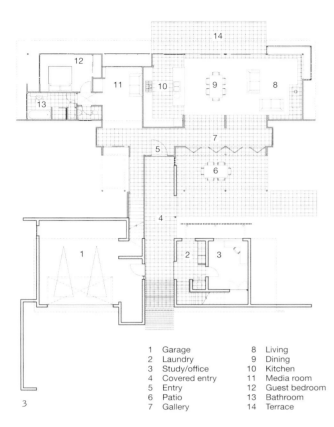

3

1	Garage	8	Living
2	Laundry	9	Dining
3	Study/office	10	Kitchen
4	Covered entry	11	Media room
5	Entry	12	Guest bedroom
6	Patio	13	Bathroom
7	Gallery	14	Terrace

4

1	Balcony		
2	Master bedroom		
3	Closet		
4	Ensuite		
5	Void		
6	Bathroom		
7	Guest bedroom/living		
8	Kitchenette		
9	Deck		

0   3m

1   A glass-roofed gallery delineates circulation from the main entry
2   The house blends into its rural setting among the grapevines
3   Lower floor plan
4   Upper floor plan
5   The one- and two-story wings are related by similar roof pitches and materials
6   The gallery links indoor living with outdoor living
7   Living spaces expand to a roofed courtyard for year-round outdoor living

Photography: Ian Jack

6

5

7

Steven Ehrlich Architects

WALDFOGEL RESIDENCE
Palo Alto, California, USA

This 8800-square-foot house on a flat, half-acre site a mile from Stanford University takes its cues from the urbanity of the community and the sophistication of its owners, who wanted a home suitable for displaying their collection of contemporary art. || The house opens on all sides through **a pinwheel plan that forms four distinct courtyards**. Two two-story volumes are connected by taut horizontal planes that extend beyond the building envelope and are clad in gray Rhinezinc. The entrance is flanked by an axial wall of poured-in-place concrete, which continues indoors to become the north–south circulation spine of the house; carved alcoves along its length house the couple's unique ceramics collection. || The entrance court doubles as a terrace for a double-height dining room paneled in mahogany. The first volume, which contains the living room and the husband's study to the north, shares another paved court extending out to the garden, and the kitchen and family room in the southern volume open onto a separate garden and pool. At the upper level, the master suite and study are linked across a glass bridge to the children's and guest bedrooms. A floor-to-ceiling window wall adjacent to the glass bridges and stairway brings light into the finished basement.

4

4   Internal space extends visually and physically into the landscape
    through the use of large sliding doors and glass corners
5   Glass bridges link the wings of the home
6   A second-floor guest bedroom
7   Second floor plan
8   First floor plan
9   Basement plan

Photography: Sharon Risedorph

5

6

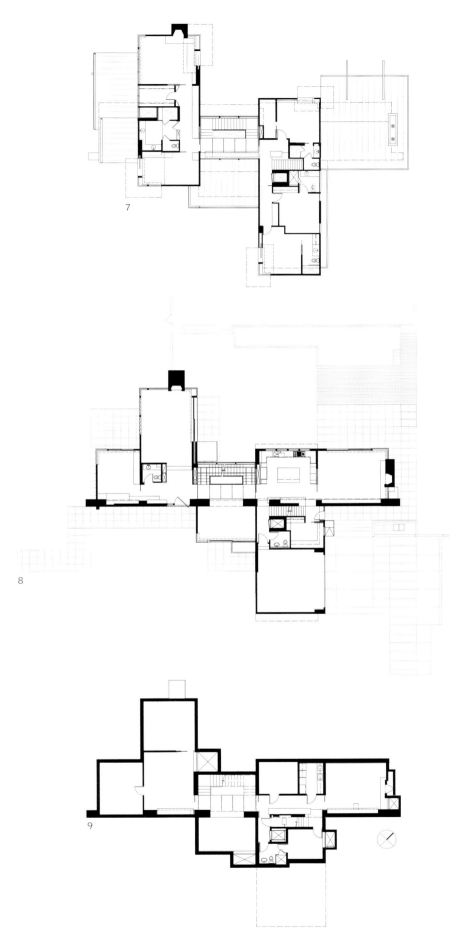

7

8

9

C2 Architects

WELLES HOUSE

County Down, Northern Ireland

This new house is located southeast of Belfast, not far from the coastal town of Bangor. The secluded site is surrounded by mature landscaping and has extensive views of the countryside, Belfast Lough, and beyond. || The original brief was to refurbish and extend the existing 1930s house by removing internal walls and introducing double-height spaces, thus giving a more contemporary feel by introducing greater light and movement. But as the brief developed, it became clear that the original house could not meet all the client's requirements. A new scheme was designed and was enthusiastically received by the client. || **The rural setting dictated natural materials** while the contemporary nature of the house demanded a reinterpretation of their use. || The view from the site influenced the design of the new scheme and was central to the orientation and positioning of the living environment. The glass-enclosed first floor gives a sense of freedom and space; the freestanding structures define specific areas. In contrast, the ground floor, which provides further accommodation, is characterized by solidity and enclosure. || The two floors blend together by way of the grand glazed entrance, and a large, curved cedar wall, which fuses the exterior with the interior. The transparent and the solid, one floating above the other, create a subtle play of elements in this superb country house.

1 Entrance
2 Back view with pool
3 Dining/living area
4 Studio and bridge
5 First floor plan
6 Ground floor plan

Photography: Khara Pringle Photographic

4

5

1 Roof terrace
2 Studio
3 Glass bridge
4 Kitchen
5 Dining area
6 Fireplace
7 Glass floor panel
8 Living area
9 Master bedroom
10 Dressing
11 Master bathroom
12 Stair from balcony
13 Bedroom 2
14 Ensuite
15 Bathroom
16 Bedroom 3
17 Fireplace
18 Family area
19 Bedroom 4
20 Sauna
21 Entrance hall
22 Entrance canopy
23 Utility
24 Storage
25 Lobby
26 Garage
27 Plant room
28 Bridge over pool

6

1

2

WESKetch Architecture

WINDSONG

Seaside Park, New Jersey, USA

So many restoration projects begin with a familiar phrase: 'this place has potential' or 'that old house must have been something in its day.' This home was a modest Victorian with character and presence, but years of the shore's salty winds and intense sun had taken their toll. A sensitive addition and carefully detailed renovation have successfully breathed new life to this bayside home, while fulfilling the promise of its potential and revitalizing its historic charm. || The house is entered through a double cascading staircase that perfectly accentuates its coastal feel. The residence, originally constructed at the turn of the 19th century, underwent a renovation and addition that not only kept the home's historic charm intact, but also added new components that seamlessly blend with the historical elements of the residence. More than a century on, however, these now-outdated renovations had been complicated by the decline and decaying nature of the house. Floorboards were sinking and the bathrooms were in complete

disrepair. Windows were drooping and previous modifications to the home had now become unsightly and unnecessary. || With the help of historic photographs, the architects set about restoring the pristine charm. Flying trusses at the end of the gabled roof, combined with blusters, spindles, and porch railings, lend an authentic Victorian feel to the outside of the home. Inside, the living spaces were smartly renovated to handle extended family visits. The old bathrooms were removed and three new bathrooms were stacked in a dominating tower feature. || The combination of renovations to the existing residence and new additions that respect the character and history of the original have been successfully merged into a home that can be enjoyed by multiple generations of family at once. With these sensitive updates, it will continue to provide **a seaside haven for generations to come.**

1   Double cascading staircase entry
2   Historically renovated façade
3   A sensitive addition to the back of the house

3

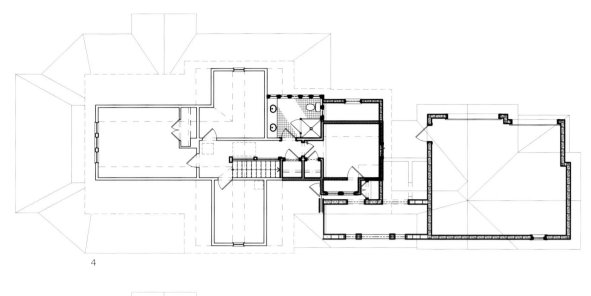

4

7

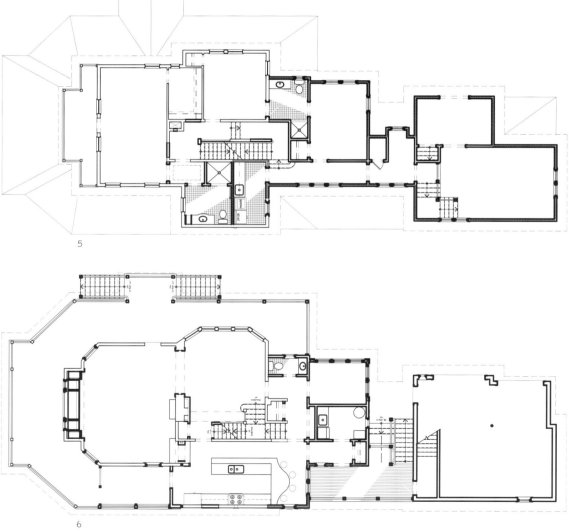

5

6

8

Photography: Bruce Nelson (1–3); Jay Rosenblatt (7–9)

9

1   Connection with the water
2   Iron bark timber was used to represent wharf piles
3   The building has a strong connection with its
    surroundings and environment
4   The portholes create interesting light quality
5   Living with the water
6   The strong form provides a sense of protection against
    the elements
Photography: Charles Martin

Novak & Middleton Architects Ltd

WORSER BAY 119

Wellington, New Zealand

This house is located in the seaside community of Worser Bay, Wellington. The neighborhood consists of an eclectic mix of seaside cottages and newer houses in various states of repair. The site is located adjacent to Worser Bay beach with views across to Wellington Harbour and Baring Head. || The house has been designed as a composition of solids and voids, maintaining privacy from neighboring properties and creating a focus toward the water and Wellington Heads. || The owners' brief called for a house that could function as **a beach house as well as a home**. The house had to respond to the dramatic and variable environment, providing a sense of shelter but also a connection with the surrounding land and sea. The weather can vary from still, clear days when the harbor is like a mirror, to gale-force winds and airborne salt spray that threaten anything that is not fixed down. || The house consists of a primary two-story form that accommodates the owners' day-to-day living. Large, open-plan areas, interconnected between the two levels, provide spaces where various functions can occur independently but remain connected. Solid-edge walls support a two-story glass façade to the northeast, maximizing sun and views across the beach and the water. Bedroom spaces are sheltered and restful areas, removed from the open-plan environment. || Solids and voids are present in the treatment of the exterior façade. The walls to the neighboring properties are intentionally solid, providing privacy and shelter. Beyond these façades, solidity gives way to dramatic use of space and light. Heavy iron bark wharf timbers, sourced from an old railway bridge, sail-cloth screens, and familiar porthole windows create a design that sits comfortably into its seaside environment. || The use of solid forms, together with expansive use of glass, heightens the experience of the site, giving the feeling of being close to the elements but protected from them at the same time. The house creates a sense of shelter in close connection with its environment.

3

5

4

6

1

2

blank studio

XEROS RESIDENCE

Phoenix, Arizona, USA

This house is sited within a 1950s-era neighborhood where the urban grid of Phoenix is overtaken by the organic landforms of the North Mountain preserve. Located at the end of two dead-end streets, the Xeros Residence is positioned on the upward slope of a 50- by 250-foot double site, facing the mountain preserve to the north and the city center to the south. || The building plan includes a two-story, lower-level design studio that descends into the earth. A single-story residence above the studio is accessed solely by an external stair. The path to the studio level requires guests to pass behind the mesh screen and descend a short flight of stairs into an exterior, mesh-enclosed forecourt. A stainless-steel water feature leads down the steps and terminates at a reflecting pool. A steel-framed glass door offers entry into the studio from the courtyard. || To access the residence, the visitor ascends an exterior steel staircase to an upper-level balcony before entering the common room (sitting, dining, and kitchen). A central gallery leads to the cantilevered master suite/media room. This space is completely glazed on the north façade to enjoy the mountain preserve views. To complete the cycle of movement, a cantilevered yellow-glass framed 'Romeo and Juliet' balcony allows views back to the city and across the long axis of the building. || Called 'Xeros' (from the Greek for 'dry') as a reminder that **all solutions should be in direct response to the environment**, the building has several environmentally responsible features. The form turns an opaque face toward the intense western afternoon sun and the more exposed faces to the south and east are shielded by an external layer of woven metal shade mesh. The long, narrow lot precipitated the very tall form with its petite footprint that allows the maximum amount of site to be retained for vegetation. Drought-tolerant species are positioned around the residence to add to the shading effect of the screen. The primary building material is exposed steel (used as structure, cladding, and shading) that is allowed to weather naturally and meld with the color of the surrounding hills.

1   Detailed exterior view of the residence entry stair and
    shade mesh
2   Cantilever at north façade of residence
3   Early dawn view of the southeast corner of the residence

3

4

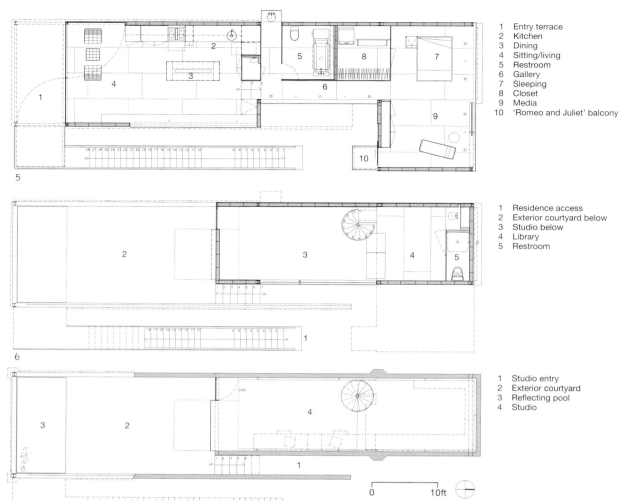

1	Entry terrace
2	Kitchen
3	Dining
4	Sitting/living
5	Restroom
6	Gallery
7	Sleeping
8	Closet
9	Media
10	'Romeo and Juliet' balcony

5

1	Residence access
2	Exterior courtyard below
3	Studio below
4	Library
5	Restroom

6

1	Studio entry
2	Exterior courtyard
3	Reflecting pool
4	Studio

0   10ft

7

8

Photography: Bill Timmerman

9

10

Dekleva Gregoric Arhitekti

XXS HOUSE
Ljubljana, Slovenia

The XXS House is located in the Krakovo district of Ljubljana. In the Middle Ages, the village of Krakovo supplied the nearby monastery with fresh food; today, it is a highly protected historical area that includes significant Roman ruins. || Strict building regulations determined that the basic dimensions of this new house were not to exceed those of the pre-existing house, which a hundred years ago was a service building to an adjacent traditional house. The task was to integrate all residential functions in a very small volume, and on a tiny site, to suit the needs of the clients who live in the country and for whom this was to be an 'urban holiday home.' Ultimately, **the total area of just 43 square meters led to the 'XXS' label for the house**. || Since the house faces north, it was a challenge to bring direct and indirect sunlight into the living spaces on the ground floor. The heritage protection regulations allow light shafts on the roofs, but light was masterfully brought in by turning the shafts toward the sky. This major alternation of the volume opened up completely new attic space suitable for use as a bedroom. A huge wall-sized sliding window opens up the space to the intimate atrium and allows for indirect lighting. || The selection of the façade materials and detailing reflected the desired, almost industrial, appearance of the house. The concept of raw materials stretches from the exterior to the interior: fiber-cement panels in their primer mode are used for the roof and yard façade, and 'béton brut' (unfinished or raw concrete), terrazzo, plywood, iron, and felt are used indoors.

1   Roof and façade shows use of non-traditional materials
2   Local context
3   The concept of raw materials stretches from exterior to interior

3

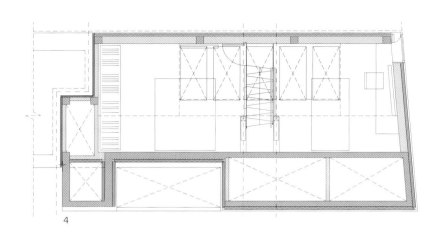

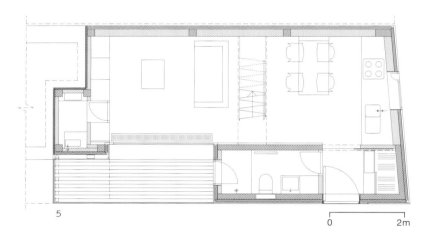

4

5

0   2m

4   Upper floor plan
5   Ground floor plan
6   The living area extends toward the mini atrium
7   Attic sleeping space with a series of roof windows
8   Steel stairs toward the ground floor living area
9   Bathroom
10 Attic bedroom
11 Connection to ground floor

Photography: Matevz Paternoster

6

7

8

9

10

11

INDEX OF ARCHITECTS

INDEX OF ARCHITECTS (continued)

Nebular Hypothesis

Lunar Halo

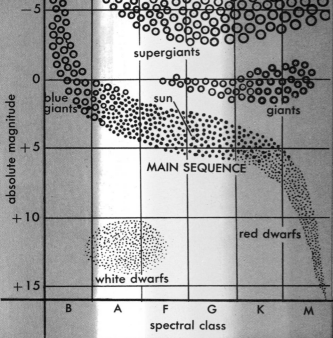
Main Sequence of Stars

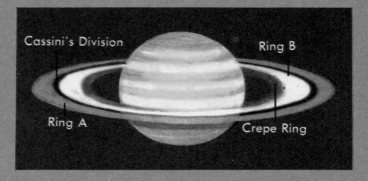
Rings of Saturn

New Moon

CELESTIAL LATITUDE

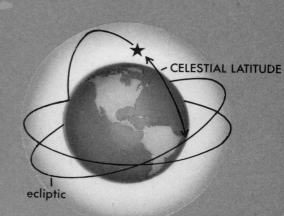
ecliptic

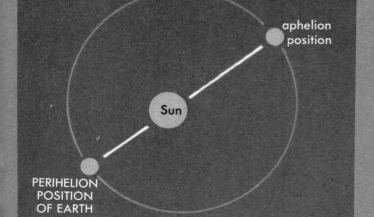
aphelion position

Sun

PERIHELION POSITION OF EARTH

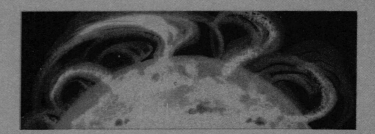
Solar Prominences

FOR JONATHAN AND JAMES

THE ABC's OF ASTRONOMY

AN ILLUSTRATED DICTIONARY

THE ABC's OF
ASTRONOMY

AN ILLUSTRATED DICTIONARY

Roy A. Gallant

Illustrated by John Polgreen

DOUBLEDAY & COMPANY, INC., GARDEN CITY, NEW YORK

OTHER BOOKS BY ROY A. GALLANT

Exploring the Moon	**Exploring Mars**
Exploring the Universe	**Exploring the Weather**
Exploring the Sun	**Exploring Chemistry**
Exploring the Planets	**Man's Reach into Space**

Exploring under the Earth

The Author's thanks to Colin A. Ronan, Fellow of the Royal Astronomical Society, for his helpful suggestions regarding the manuscript of this book, and to Lloyd Motz, Associate Professor of Astronomy, Columbia University, for his careful checking of text and illustrations.

Library of Congress Catalog Card Number 61–5048.
 Lithographed in the United States of America. 9 8 7 6 5

Contents

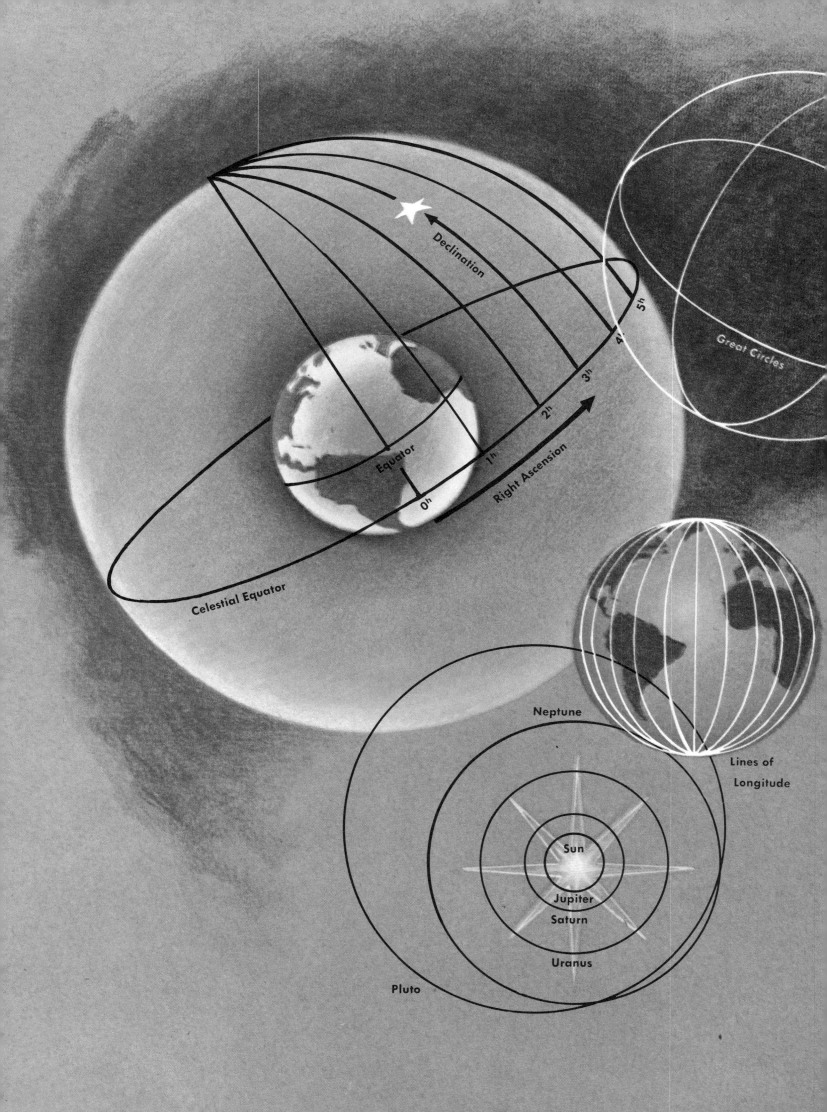

Declination

Right Ascension

Equator

0ʰ   1ʰ   2ʰ   3ʰ   4ʰ   5ʰ

Celestial Equator

Great Circles

Lines of
Longitude

Neptune

Sun

Jupiter

Saturn

Uranus

Pluto

Saturn

Vanguard

Moon

How to Use This Book

The *ABC's of Astronomy* has been planned for the amateur astronomer—for the beginner who is still at the stage of groping his way through the jungle of terminology and for the advanced amateur who is carefully observing and recording what he sees.

The book is organized in four sections: 1. The Dictionary of Terms defines more than 500 terms that any amateur astronomer must know if he expects to understand the various magazines and books he will be reading as his interest in astronomy grows. The Dictionary of Terms is carefully cross-referenced in such a way that the beginning amateur will find, under the entry *Stars*, for example, all he may want and need to know about the composition of stars for the time being; yet cross references at the end of the listing refer him and the advanced amateur to more advanced information: star classification by spectral analysis, the mass-luminosity curve, and so on. Throughout

the Dictionary of Terms are sketches and diagrams that show at a glance many of the concepts the amateur finds difficult to grasp in words alone.

2. Eighteen Reference Tables give kilometers-miles equivalents, centigrade-Fahrenheit temperature equivalents, the occurrence of meteor showers, comets, the nearest stars and the brightest stars with their magnitudes, a comprehensive table of the planets, and much more information which the amateur usually finds only by consulting several different books.

3. A detailed Map of the Constellations and the stars that form them also gives the astronomical and popular names of the stars.

4. The section on Telescopes shows with diagrams the principles underlying reflecting and refracting telescopes, the spectroscope, and radio telescopes. The reader will also find detailed maps of the Moon and Mars to aid him in his observations.

Dictionary of Terms

A

A-stars:
Stars can be classified by their spectra, which give a "measure" of their surface temperature. On the scale O, B, A, F, G, K, M, R, N, S, the O stars are hottest and the R, N, and S stars are coolest. The *A-stars,* such as Sirius, are white and have a surface temperature of 7500°C.–11,000°C. But you may also find A_1, A_2, A_3, through A_9 stars; the lower the number, the hotter the star. (See *Stars.*)

Aberration of Lenses:
Because a lens bends the many colors making up white light unequally, the image of an object seen through a lens will appear distorted with colored fringes. This is called *chromatic aberration.* Because a lens is usually made with its surfaces curved like part of a sphere, the light rays that pass through its center are bent less than the rays that pass through its edge, so an image seen through the lens will appear out of focus. This is called *spherical aberration.*

Aberration of Light:
An apparent change in position of the stars due to the motion of the Earth in its orbit around the Sun, and the fact that light travels at a definite speed. This change is too small to be seen by the unaided eye or even with a small telescope.

Absolute Magnitude:
The apparent magnitude any star would have if it were 32.6 light-years, or ten parsecs, away from the Earth, or 191,600,000,000,000 miles. (See *Magnitude.*)

Absolute Zero:
The temperature at which all molecular motion is thought to stop. On the Kelvin scale *absolute zero* is written as 0° K. and is equal to −273.1° C. on the centigrade scale.

Absorption of Light:
A "swallowing up" of light by an object. Generally speaking, black surfaces absorb light and white surfaces reflect light. When a surface absorbs light, its temperature rises. Dust and gas in space absorb light.

Acceleration:
When an object is constantly changing its velocity it is said to be undergoing *acceleration.* For example, when the speedometer needle of a car steadily climbs to 60, the car is *accelerating;* but when the car reaches 60 and continues to cruise at that speed, it is no longer *accelerating.*

Accidental Errors:
Errors in observational measurement which cannot be estimated beforehand. Their existence is one of the reasons scientists make more than one measurement of an observation.

Achromatic Lens:
A lens which shows an image that is free of colored fringes. (See *Aberration.*) An *achromatic lens* is made by assembling a pair of lenses, one of crown glass and the other of flint glass.

Airglow:
At night the sky appears to shine with a weak glow. Radiant energy from the Sun seems to cause this; in stronger doses it produces the auroras.

Albedo:
The amount of sunlight reflected by a planet, compared with the amount it receives, is known as the *albedo* of a planet.

Almanac:
A table of days, weeks, months, containing times of sunset, sunrise, phases of the Moon, and other astronomical information.

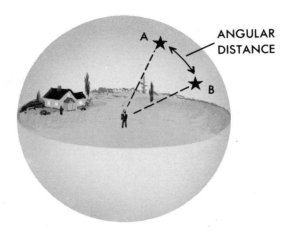

Almucantar:

That small circle on the celestial sphere passing through a star or planet and which is parallel to the horizon; it is, therefore, a circle of equal altitude.

Altazimuth:

An instrument used to determine the altitude and azimuth of a star or planet.

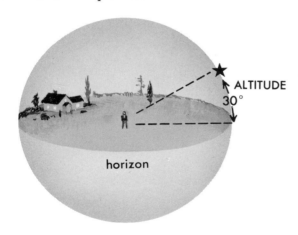

Altitude:

The angular height of a body above the horizon. For example, a star has an *altitude* of 30° when the angle between the star, observer, and horizon is 30°.

Ammonia:

A colorless gas made of one part nitrogen and three parts hydrogen (NH_3). Household *ammonia* is a weak solution of this gas in water.

Andromeda Nebula:

A galaxy or vast cloud of dust, gas, and stars in the constellation Andromeda. Known as Messier 31, the nebula is visible to the naked eye (magnitude 5.0) and has a diameter of about 120,000 light-years. It is about 1,500,000 light-years away.

Angular Distance:

The distance between two objects measured by an angle. The *angular distance* between two stars, for example, could be found if you project a line to star A and another line to star B. The angle formed at your position becomes the *angular distance.*

Angular Velocity:

The rate at which an object moves through an angle as the object travels along a curve. For example, the tip of a clock hand moves faster than a point midway down the hand, but both the tip and the midpoint have the same *angular velocity*— 6° per minute.

Annual Equation:

Because the Earth's distance from the Sun varies as the Earth travels in its orbit, the Sun's gravitational attraction on the Moon changes. This change affects the Moon's speed about the Earth. This inequality in the Moon's motion is known as its *annual equation.*

Annular Eclipse:

An eclipse of the Sun when the Moon coincides with but does not completely fill the Sun's disk; when a ring, or annulus, of sunlight is visible.

Anomalistic Month:

(See *Month.*)

Anomalistic Year:

(See *Year.*)

Anomaly of a Planet:

The angular distance of a planet from its perihelion position, measured in the direction of the planet's motion across the sky.

Aperture:

The opening that admits light to an optical instrument; in telescopes, the diameter of the object glass or mirror.

Apex, Solar:

That point on the celestial sphere toward which the solar system appears to be moving.

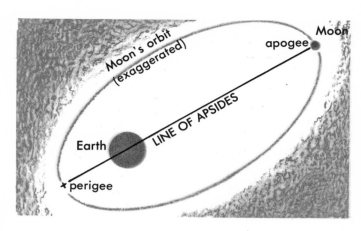

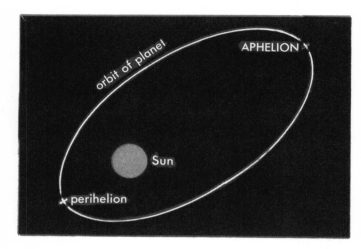

Aphelion:

The most distant point from the Sun a planet or comet may reach as it travels in its orbit.

Aplanatic:

When the chromatic and spherical aberrations have been corrected by the proper combination of lenses in a telescope, the telescope is said to be *aplanatic.*

Apogee:

The most distant point from the Earth that the Moon, planets, and satellites may reach as they travel in their orbits.

Apparent Motion:

(See *Motion.*)

Appulse:

The apparent close approach of two stars, when actually one star may be hundreds of millions of miles behind the other, but our depth perception is not good enough to reveal the real distance.

Apsis:

A term which means "perigee" and "apogee." The Earth, for example, is in *higher apsis* when it is farthest from the Sun; it is in *lower apsis* when it is nearest the Sun.

Apsides, Line of:

A line joining the farthest and nearest points of a planet (aphelion, perihelion) in its orbit around the Sun; a line joining the farthest and nearest points of the Moon as it circles the Earth.

Arc:

Any part of a curve.

Armillary Sphere:

In early astronomy, an instrument consisting of metal rings that represented the main circles of the celestial sphere.

Asteroids:

(See *Minor Planets.*)

Astrolabe:

In early astronomy, an instrument used to measure the altitude and positions of celestial bodies.

Astrology:

A so-called science in which people attempt to foretell future events in life by the position and "influence" of the stars and planets.

Astronomical Clock:

A clock that measures sidereal (star) time, not solar time.

Astronomical Unit:

A measure of distance equal to the average distance of the Earth from the Sun—which is about 92,907,000 miles. There are 63,300 *astronomical units* to one light-year.

Astronomy:

The science dealing with celestial bodies, their distances, magnitudes, sizes, motions, relative positions, and composition. The word comes from the Greek and means "the arrangement of the stars."

Astrophysics:

The science that deals mainly with the composition of stars and planets.

Atmosphere:

The envelope of gases that surround planets and other celestial bodies. The Earth's atmosphere is made of 78 per cent nitrogen, 21 per cent oxygen, and 1 per cent argon, helium, neon, ozone, carbon dioxide, and other gases. (See Table of Planets, Sun, and Moon, p. 90–91.)

Atom:

The smallest possible piece of an element that can take part in a chemical reaction. An atom retains all the properties of its element.

Aurora:

A glow of colored lights in the northern and southern skies, caused by charged particles streaming from the Sun and entering the Earth's atmosphere. *Auroras* are most prominent when there is strong sunspot activity (see *Sunspots*). In the Arctic: *aurora borealis,* called the "northern lights"; in the Antarctic: *aurora australis.*

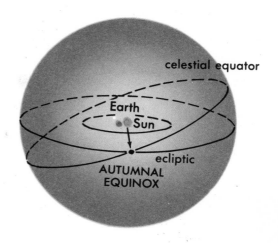

Autumnal Equinox:

About September 21, at which time the Sun crosses the celestial equator from north to south. On *autumnal equinox* the hours of sunlight and darkness are nearly the same everywhere on Earth, but afterward the days begin to get shorter in the Northern Hemisphere. *Autumnal equinox,* then, is one of the two points where the ecliptic crosses the celestial equator. (For the other point, see *Vernal Equinox.*)

Axis:

The Earth is said to rotate around an *axis,* which is simply an imaginary straight line running from the North Pole to the South Pole. An *axis,* then, is an imaginary or real line around which a body rotates.

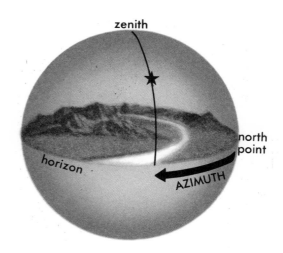

Azimuth:

The *azimuth* of a star is measured as shown in the diagram. It is measured in degrees clockwise along the horizon from north point to the foot of the star's vertical circle.

B

B-stars:

Highly luminous bluish stars with surface temperatures of 15,000°C.–35,000°C., such as Rigel and other stars in the constellation Orion. (See *A-stars* for additional information; also *Stars.*)

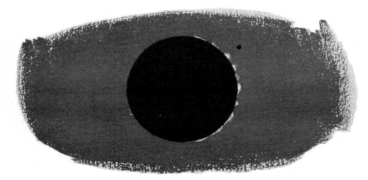

Baily's Beads:

As the Moon eclipses the Sun, the Sun's crescent becomes slimmer and slimmer until finally only a narrow line of light is left. Just before this narrow line disappears it breaks up into "beads," as described by the British astronomer Francis Baily. The Moon's mountains and valleys, which block out some of the Sun's light but allow some to shine through, cause the bead effect.

Barlow Lens:

A special lens used to increase the power of a telescope's eyepiece. It is a small achromatic lens (with negative focus) placed just behind the eyepiece so it is between the eyepiece and object glass.

Barred Spiral Galaxies:

Unlike normal spiral galaxies with dense round nuclei, the *barred spirals* have arms that wind outward from the ends of a central bar. Some of them have arms that sweep around so that they nearly touch both ends of the central bar. Because there

are no *barred spirals* close to us, we know little about them; however, they seem to have vast clouds of dust and gas.

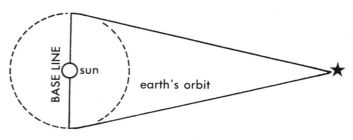

Base Line:

The "bottom" line of a triangle on which the triangle stands. In measuring the distance of the Earth from the Sun, the *base line* is approximately the Earth's radius. In measuring the distance of the Earth from a star, the *base line* is the diameter of the Earth's orbit.

Bayer Catalogue:

In 1603 Bayer classified the stars by their relative brightness in their constellations. He used the letters in the Greek alphabet as keys to brightness: for example, alpha designates the brightest star in a group; beta, the next brightest; gamma, the next, and so on through omega, which is the last letter in the alphabet. In the constellation Aries, the brightest star is Hamal but is designated Alpha Arietis. The next brightest is Sheratan and is designated Beta Arietis.

Belts of Jupiter:

The planet's atmosphere appears to have several bands lying parallel to its equator. They change color from time to time and rotate at different speeds. Sometimes the bands appear pink, tan, light yellow, or greenish blue.

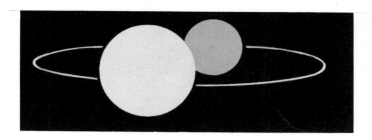

Binary Stars:

Two stars which appear to revolve about each other, but which actually revolve about a common center. Also called *double stars,* many binary systems have stars of different colors, so they are interesting to see through a telescope. Mizar, in Ursa Major, for example, has a companion called Alcor. There are millions of such *binary stars.*

Binocular:

Any optical instrument is called *binocular* if it enables both eyes to look through it at the same time: field glasses, for example.

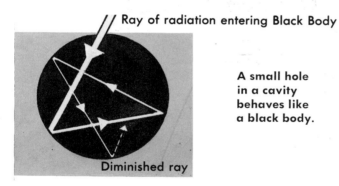

Ray of radiation entering Black Body

A small hole in a cavity behaves like a black body.

Diminished ray

Black Body:

A body that does not reflect any of the radiation striking it; so it absorbs all radiation. But no such ideal body exists. Even the blackest piece of paper we can make reflects some radiation.

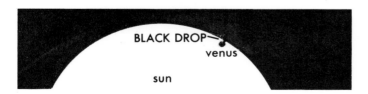

BLACK DROP

venus

sun

Black Drop:

As Venus begins to cross the Sun's disk, it appears to have a black area behind it. This is an optical effect caused by the dark disk of the planet against the bright disk of the Sun. The *black drop* effect is also seen as Venus begins to ease its way off the Sun's disk.

Blink Microscope:

Astronomers use this instrument to find out whether a particular star (or other celestial object) has changed its position relative to neighboring stars. This is done with two photographs of the star, taken at different times. The astronomer looks at both photographs through the *blink microscope;* he sees one photograph with his left eye and the other with his right as they are alternately hidden and covered quickly. If the star has changed position, it will appear to jump back and forth as the microscope is made to "blink."

Bode's Law:

In 1772 the German astronomer Johann Bode showed the distance of the planets from the Sun by using a mathematical law devised earlier by Titius of Wittenberg, Germany. To a series of numbers, each (except for the second) twice the value of the preceding one, (0, 3, 6, 12, 24, 48, 96, 192) he added 4, which gave 4, 7, 10, 16, 28, 52, 100, 196. These numbers, he said, represented the distance of the planets from the Sun, taking the Earth's distance as 10. See table which compares Bode's distance with actual distance. (Neptune and Pluto are not given because they had not been discovered during Bode's life. Pluto, however, does not fit in the scheme.)

Planet	Bode's Distance	Actual Distance
Mercury	4	3.9
Venus	7	7.2
Earth	10	10
Mars	16	15.2
Asteroids	28	27.7
Jupiter	52	52
Saturn	100	95.4
Uranus	196	191.8

Bolide:

(See *Fireball.*)

Bolometer:

An instrument used to measure very small quantities of radiant heat in the infrared section of the spectrum. With the *bolometer* astronomers can measure heat radiation from a variety of celestial bodies.

Bolometric Magnitude:

The magnitude of a star, taking into account all its radiation and not, as with visual magnitudes, the visible radiation only.

C

Calendar (Gregorian):

This is the calendar we use today. To make the calendar keep pace more exactly with the seasons, Pope Gregory XIII in 1582 revised it. At that time the old Julian Calendar lagged behind the seasons by eleven minutes a year. Over several hundred years this lag would amount to several days, so the calendar would have to be readjusted. To correct this defect, Pope Gregory brought the then existing calendar up to date by canceling ten days from it. When he made the change it affected the calendar in such a way that Thursday, October 4 was followed by Friday, October 15. To keep the calendar in pace with the seasons in the future, the Pope's advisers proposed that three leap years be omitted every 400 years. He did this by saying that leap years would come every four years *except* when the number of the year ends in 00 and is not divisible by 400. So 1900 and 2100 are not leap years, but 2000 and 2400 are.

Calendar (Julian):

Julius Caesar decided that the old Roman Moon calendar, which had only 355 days to a year, should be changed to keep pace with the solar year of 365¼ days a year. In revising the calendar in 47 B.C., he first adopted the solar year of 365 days, but then found that he had a quarter of a day (or six hours) left over at the end of each year. To solve this problem, he said that every four years there would be an extra day added to the calendar (leap year) to account for the four left-over periods of six hours, which added up to twenty-four hours, or one day.

Canals of Mars:

Numerous straight lines, as seen by some astronomers through the telescope, linking certain areas on Mars. The *canals* were first reported as channels, or *canali,* by the Italian astronomer Schiaparelli in 1877, then were popularized as "canals"

by the American astronomer Percival Lowell several years later. Lowell regarded them as vast man-made waterways built by an intelligent form of life. Hardly any astronomer believes this theory today; in fact some astronomers deny that the canal markings exist at all; they think that the lines are only optical illusions. Yet some astronomers claim to have seen them clearly.

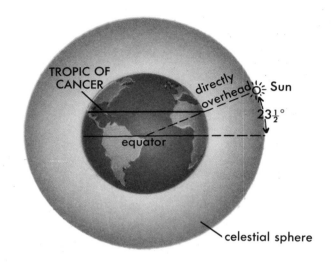

Cancer, Tropic of:

The northernmost latitude at which the Sun appears directly overhead—23½° North Latitude.

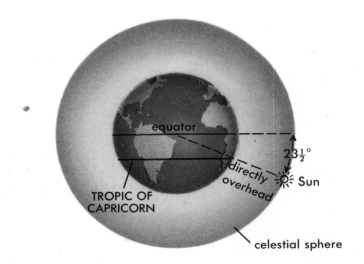

Capricorn, Tropic of:

The southernmost latitude at which the Sun appears directly overhead—23½° South Latitude.

Carbon Dioxide:

A colorless, odorless gas made up of one part carbon and two parts oxygen (CO_2). This is the gas that bubbles out of soda pop when you remove the bottle cap.

Cardinal Points:

The four major points on the compass—North, South, East, and West.

Cassegrainian Telescope:

(See special section on Telescopes, p. 107.)

Cassini's Division:

A 1700-mile gap between the two major rings of Saturn, discovered by J. D. Cassini in 1675.

Catalogue of Stars:

A list of stars giving details of apparent positions in space (right ascension and declination), their brightness (magnitude), and other information (for example, their spectral class, proper motion, and so on).

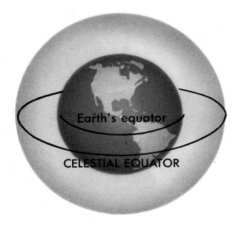

Celestial Equator:

The equator on the celestial sphere; more properly, the circle formed where the plane of the Earth's equator cuts the celestial sphere.

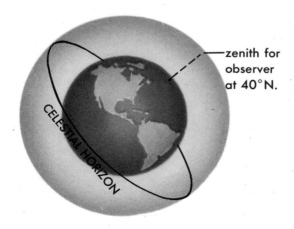

Celestial Horizon:

A great circle determined by a plane which is perpendicular to the Earth's radius at the observer's position and which cuts the celestial sphere.

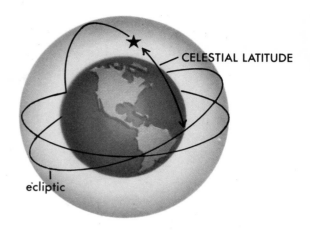

Celestial Latitude:

The angular distance of a star, measured from the ecliptic along a great circle which is at right angles to the ecliptic.

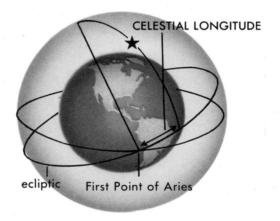

Celestial Longitude:

The angular distance of a heavenly body, measured along the ecliptic in an eastward direction, counted from the First Point of Aries.

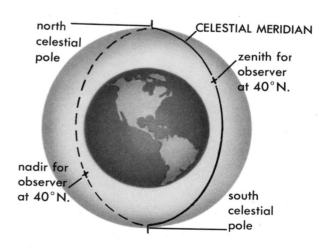

Celestial Meridian:

On the celestial sphere, the great circle passing through the nadir, zenith, and celestial poles.

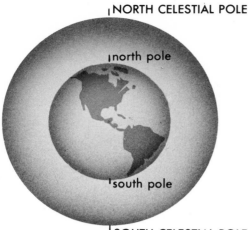

NORTH CELESTIAL POLE

north pole

south pole

SOUTH CELESTIAL POLE

Celestial Poles:

On the celestial sphere, those points which correspond to the Earth's North and South poles. Picture them as extensions of the Earth's axis.

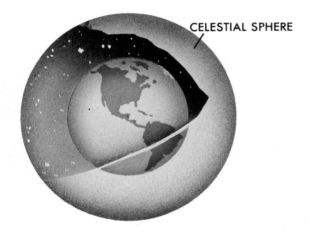

CELESTIAL SPHERE

Celestial Sphere:

The stars and planets appear to move along the inner surface of a great hollow globe, one hemisphere of which you see as you observe the stars. The Earth lies at the center of the *celestial sphere*.

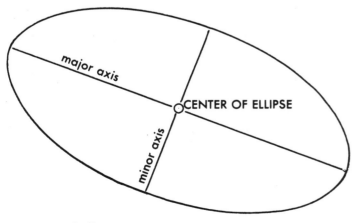

major axis

CENTER OF ELLIPSE

minor axis

Center of Ellipse:

The point of intersection of the major and minor axes of an ellipse.

Center of Gravity:

The point inside a body at which the mass of the body may be pictured as being concentrated for purposes of discussing its motion. This is more accurately described as the "center of mass." In a rod it's the rod's balancing point. In a sphere, equally dense throughout, it is at the center of the sphere. But the *center of gravity* will change position if the sphere is more dense in one section and less dense elsewhere.

Centigrade Temperature:

Temperature measured on a thermometer scale on which water freezes at 0° and boils at 100° at standard atmospheric pressure. (Also called Celsius temperature.) To convert from centigrade to Fahrenheit, see *Fahrenheit*. (See also the conversion table on p. 119.)

Centrifugal Force:

That force, due to a body's motion in a curved path, which makes the body tend to move at right angles to its curved path. In a weight swung round on a string, the *centrifugal force* shows up as a pull on the string. As the Earth circles the Sun it experiences a centrifugal force pulling against the restraining gravitational force that holds it in its orbit. As the Earth rotates on its axis, *centrifugal force* makes the planet bulge at its equator. *Centrifugal force* is equal to, but the opposite of, centripetal force.

Centripetal Force:

That force which prevents a revolving body from flying off on a tangent. It is equal to, but the opposite of, centrifugal force.

Cepheid Variables:

(See *Variable Stars.*)

Chromosphere:

That layer of the Sun's gases that appear as a glowing, dark-red rim during an eclipse. The *chromosphere* layer is about 9000 miles deep and is made up largely of hydrogen, helium, and calcium. At the top of the *chromosphere* the temperature may rise as high as 100,000°C., but is about 6000°C. in its lowest regions.

Chronograph:

An instrument used to mark the time of star transits. Essentially the instrument consists of a clock, a rotating paper-covered drum, and a pen. As the pen traces a continuous line on the drum, the clock gives the pen a slight jerk once every second. When the star which the astronomer is watching crosses the hairline of his instrument, he presses a button that gives the pen extra jerks. These mark on the records the exact time of the star transit.

Chronometer:

A very accurate clock used by ships at sea to determine longitude.

Circumpolar Stars:

Stars which never appear to set. They remain visible above the horizon throughout the night.

Civil Year:

(See *Year*.)

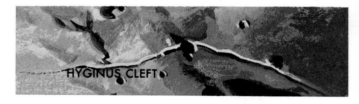

Clefts (on Moon):

Long narrow hollows in the Moon's surface, reaching depths of 1000 feet or more and extending for hundreds of miles in length.

Clepsydra:

Water clock used by the Babylonians, Egyptians, Greeks, and Romans. In principle it consisted of a container of water which emptied slowly through a hole in the bottom. The amount of water that leaked out measured the lapse of time.

Clock Stars:

Stars used by astronomers to check the accuracy of clocks.

Clouds of Magellan:

Two extremely large star systems seen in the southern skies. They are regarded as stellar satellites of the Milky Way. Visible from any place south of 15° North Latitude. (Also called Nubecula Major and Nubecula Minor.)

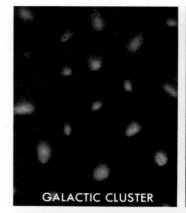

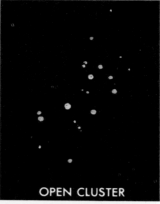

GALACTIC CLUSTER   OPEN CLUSTER

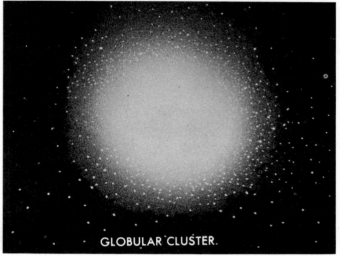

GLOBULAR CLUSTER.

Clusters:

1. *Galactic*—clusters of many galaxies in space. 2. *Globular*—clusters of a great number of stars comparatively packed together in space and spherical in shape. They surround our own galaxy and exist also in the galaxy of Andromeda. 3. *Open*— a star group with no particular shape but which moves through our galaxy; the Pleiades, for example.

Coal Sack:

A dark (nebula) patch seen in the constellation Southern Cross. It is a great cloud of dust and gas which blots out light from stars shining behind it.

Color Index:

Because the eye is most sensitive to the green-yellow part of the spectrum, and photographic plates used in astronomy are most sensitive to the blue end of the spectrum, the magnitude of a star will be differently assessed by the eye and a photographic plate. The photographic magnitude minus the visual magnitude is known as the *color index;* if positive, the star is red; negative, blue.

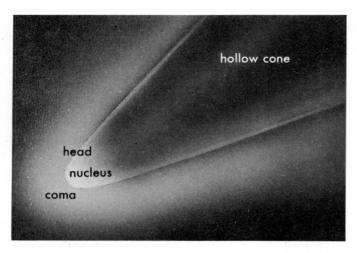

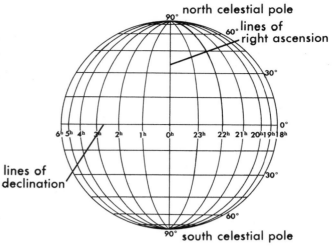

Comet:

A loose swarm of particles that travels around the Sun in a long elliptical orbit. The visible part of a comet is the gas envelope that surrounds its central condensation, or nucleus, and that trails off as a long tail. Small comets are usually without tails. Some comets make their appearance at regular periods; others appear only once, either being later broken up or leaving the solar system. (See Comets, p. 116.)

Complement of an Angle:

The *complement of an angle* of 30° is 60°—the difference between the angle and 90°

Compound:

In chemistry, the chemical union of two or more elements. Carbon dioxide (CO_2) is a *compound* of carbon and oxygen, which have been chemically joined.

Compression of a Planet:

The amount by which a planet's poles are flattened. The *compression of a planet* equals $\frac{e-p}{e}$ (*e* is the equatorial diameter, *p* is the polar diameter).

Conjunction:

Measured with reference to the Sun. Mercury and Venus (which lie nearer to the Sun than does the Earth) are said to be in *inferior conjunction* when between the Sun and the Earth, and in *superior conjunction* when beyond the Sun. The remaining planets are in *conjunction* when their celestial longitude (their right ascensions) are the same as that of the Sun. The Moon is in *conjunction* when its celestial longitude is the same as the Sun's.

Co-ordinates:

Latitude and longitude are *co-ordinates* which enable us to locate a given point on the Earth's surface. The position of celestial bodies can also be given by *co-ordinates*—right ascension and declination—which are the equivalent on the celestial sphere of terrestrial longitude and latitude.

Constellation:

The grouping of certain stars on the celestial sphere. The ancients recognized the groups as human and animal figures; for example, Orion "the Hunter" and so on. By international agreement, astronomers recognize eighty-eight *constellations*. (See section on Star Maps starting on p. 58.)

Copernican System:

In 1543 the Polish astronomer Nicholas Copernicus published a book which set forth the idea that the Earth and other planets revolved around the Sun. At the time most astronomers believed that the Sun, stars, and planets revolved about the Earth.

Corona:

1. *Solar corona*—the outermost layer of gases of the Sun. During an eclipse the *corona* can be seen as a diffuse cloud of pearly white gas. Made up mostly of hydrogen and helium, the *corona* stretches millions of miles out from the Sun, but shrinks and swells from time to time. Its temperature is thought to be between 800,000°C. and one million degrees C. 2. *Auroral corona*—the northern lights form streamers that extend beyond the overhead point, or zenith. When this happens they meet and form a patch called the *auroral corona*.

Coronagraph:

The instrument used for studying the corona in daylight and for taking motion pictures of the Sun's activity.

Cosmic Rays:

High-speed subatomic particles originating in space and also from the Sun. They can penetrate three feet of lead or three thousand feet of water. When *cosmic ray primaries* enter the Earth's atmosphere they break up into *secondary* particles, which reach us at ground level. The atmosphere, then, protects us from the harmful primaries.

Cosmogony:

The study of how the universe originated.

Cosmology:

The application of science in an attempt to understand the universe as an orderly system.

Continuous Creation Theory:

(See *Steady State Theory.*)

Counterglow:

(See *Gegenschein.*)

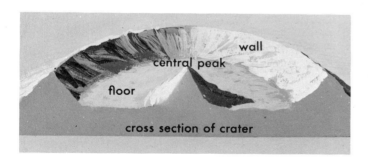

cross section of crater

Craters (on Moon):

Circular walled structures ranging over the Moon's visible surface. They have central peaks and mountainous walls that range in height from only a few feet to 20,000 feet. The craters range in size from only about half a mile across to about 200 miles across. Some astronomers think that a storm of meteorites made the craters, others that they were formed by volcanic activity. (For location and names of Moon's craters, see The Moon, p. 96.)

Crepe Ring:

The innermost ring of Saturn, measuring 10,000 miles wide; known also as *Ring C* and the *Dusky Ring*.

Culmination:

When a celestial body reaches its highest point in the sky and crosses the observer's celestial meridian.

Cusps:

The pointed ends of the Moon, Venus, and Mercury when these bodies are seen as crescents.

Cusp Caps:

Two bright patches that sometimes appear at the "horns" of Venus when the planet appears as a crescent. Two astronomers have suggested that the *cusp caps* may be the ice-covered poles of Venus, but most astronomers doubt this since Venus seems eternally hidden beneath a cloudy atmosphere.

Cycle:

The time during which a celestial event repeats itself over and over again. You can regard one trip of the Earth around the Sun as one cycle. *Cycle of eclipses:* the period of time when solar and lunar eclipses take place in the same order.

D

Dark Nebula:

A vast cloud of dust and gas that does not contain stars, which make some nebulae glow with a dull light. Hence *dark nebulae* appear as black patches when seen against a background of bright gas or other stars.

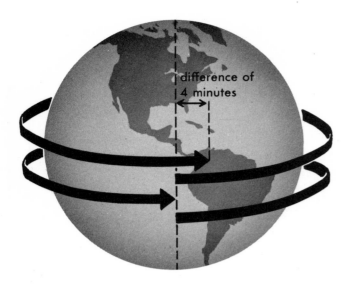

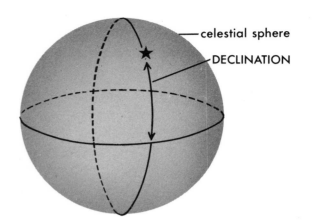

March or April; then set them back in September or October.

Day:

1. *Apparent Solar Day*—the length of time it takes the Earth to rotate once on its axis, using the departure and return of the Sun to a given meridian; measured from noon to noon or midnight to midnight. 2. *Mean Solar Day*—as it circles the Sun, the Earth moves at different speeds—faster when it is close to the Sun in December and slower when it is at the long end of its orbit in June. This variation in orbital speed makes the apparent solar day longer in winter than in summer. To give each day of the year exactly the same length of time, astronomers have invented the "mean" Sun, which does not vary its speed across the sky. Or looking at it another way, they have invented a "mean" Earth, which moves in its orbit at a constant speed. Apparent solar time, then, is sometimes ahead of mean solar time and sometimes behind it. The difference is known as the "equation of time." 3. *Sidereal Day*—the length of time it takes the Earth to rotate once on its axis, using the departure and return of a star to a given meridian; measured from noon to noon or midnight to midnight. Because the apparent position of the Sun is affected not only by the rotation of the Earth on its axis, but also by its orbital motion round the Sun, a sidereal year contains 366¼ sidereal days compared with the 365¼ solar days. Thus 24 sidereal hours equal about 23 hours and 56 minutes of solar time.

Daylight Saving Time:

To gain earlier morning daylight hours for work, we set our clocks ahead (usually one hour) in

Declination:

The angular distance of a star or planet north or south of the celestial equator, measured along a great circle passing through the star or planet and the celestial pole. A star north of the equator has a $(+)$ declination; south it has a $(-)$ declination.

Declination Circle:

A great circle passing through the celestial pole. The declination of heavenly bodies is measured on the *declination circle*. (See also *Hour Circle*.)

Degree:

The circle is divided into 360 equal units called *degrees*. An angle of 90°, then, is one fourth of a circle; an angle of 180° (or a straight line) is one half of a circle. Also a unit to measure temperature.

Density:

The amount of matter contained in a given volume, expressed as mass per unit volume. *Density* is expressed as the relationship between the weight of a given volume of matter and an equal volume of water. For example, a cubic foot of water weighs 62.5 pounds, and a cubic foot of mercury weighs about 845 pounds. Giving water a value of 1, the *density* of mercury is 13.5 grams per cubic centimeter. The *mean density* of the Earth is about 5.5 grams per c.c., meaning that it weighs about five and a half times as much as an equal volume of water. (See also *Specific Gravity*.)

Descending Node:

The point where a planet's orbit crosses the ecliptic as the planet is moving from north to south.

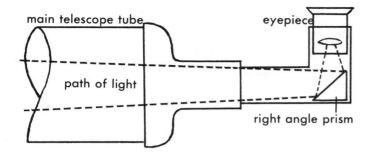

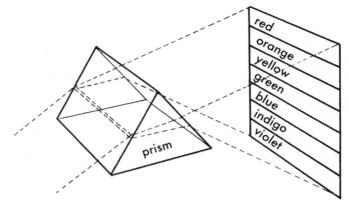

Diagonal Eyepiece:

A special telescopic eyepiece that reflects light at right angles to the tube; used in a refracting telescope for observing celestial objects near the zenith.

Dichotomy:

To cut in two. A description of the Moon, Venus, and Mercury when they are exactly half lighted.

Diffraction:

The spreading of light around very small objects. Thus if light comes from a very small source, fringes, alternately bright and dark, are visible at the edges of shadows.

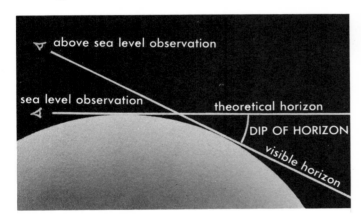

Dip of Horizon:

An observation is always made above sea level so the visible horizon will always appear farther away than it should. In other words, the visible horizon appears lower than the theoretical horizon. The amount of such a lowering is the *dip*.

Direct Motion:

(See *Motion*.)

Disk:

That part of the surface of the Sun and planets which you can see. Because the stars are so far away we see them as pin points of light, not as disks.

Dispersion of Light:

When white light is passed through a prism, it is broken up into its individual colors, or wave lengths.

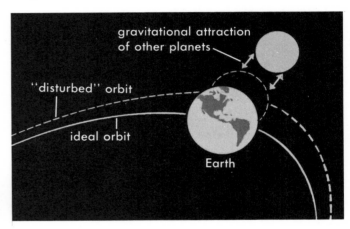

Disturbing Forces:

Any force which disturbs the exact elliptical motion of a celestial body. As it circles the Earth, the Moon is disturbed in its orbit by the gravitational attraction of the Sun, planets, and the equatorial bulge of the Earth. The Earth's motion is disturbed by the gravitational attraction of the other planets, and so on throughout the solar system.

Diurnal Motion:

(See *Motion*.)

Domes:

A term used to describe mounds shaped like giant potlids on the Moon's surface.

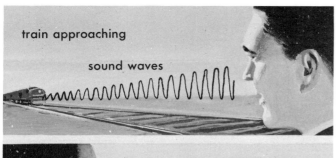

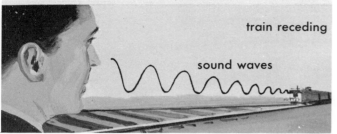

Doppler Effect:

As a train approaches you, its whistle has a high pitch; then as the train passes you, the pitch of the whistle becomes lower. This change in pitch is caused by a crowding up of the sound waves from the whistle as the train is approaching, then a spreading out of the waves as the train passes. During the train's approach the frequency of the sound waves is high, while the wave length is short. After the train passes, the frequency becomes low, while the wave length becomes long. A similar effect is produced in light. (See *Red Shift*.)

Double Star:

(See *Binary Stars*.)

Driving Clock:

A device fitted to an equatorial telescope to rotate the polar axis and so automatically cause the telescope to "track" a celestial object.

Dwarf Stars:

A class of small, faint stars which have used up all their hydrogen. Although small, they are extremely dense. For example, one dwarf known as Kuiper's Star is as massive as the Sun but is only about the size of Mars. A thimbleful of its material would weigh many tons. The *white dwarf* stars lie outside the main sequence and are quite hot, considering their faintness. Other *white dwarfs* include Sirius B, Procyon B, Omicron Eridani (all members of binary systems); but there must be many more which are too distant to be seen. (For additional information see *Main Sequence*.)

Durchmusterung:

A German word meaning a systematic cataloguing of stars. Thus the *Bonner Durchmusterung* is a catalogue of stars made at Bonn, Germany.

Dynamometer:

An instrument that measures the magnifying power of telescope eyepieces.

E

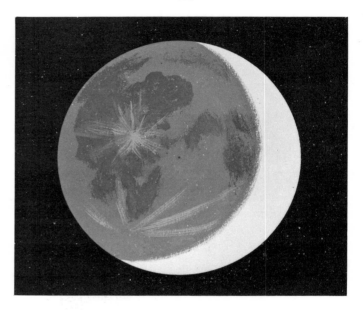

Earthshine:

Just before and just after new moon, the dark part of the Moon is dimly lighted by reflected light from the Earth. This reflected light is called *earthshine*.

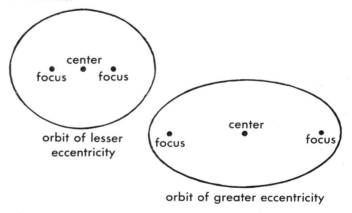

Eccentricity:

Pluto is said to have a highly *eccentric* orbit. In an ellipse the amount of *eccentricity* is found by measuring the distance of either focus from the center of the ellipse and dividing it by the length of the semi-major axis. *Eccentricity* of an orbit is usually expressed as a decimal fraction.

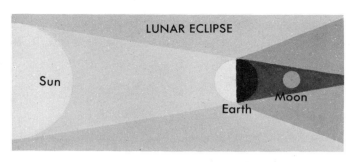

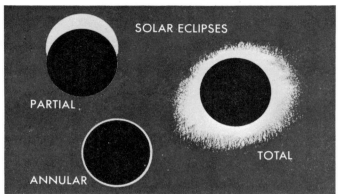

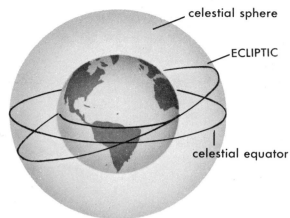

Eclipse:

The partial or total blocking from view of a celestial object by another one passing in front of it. A *lunar eclipse* occurs when the Moon passes through the Earth's shadow. *Solar eclipses:* 1. *Partial*—the Moon blocks only part of the Sun from view; 2. *Total*—the Moon completely covers the Sun's disk; 3. *Annular*—the Moon covers all the Sun's disk but, because at its greatest distance from the Earth, it does not appear quite so large as the Sun, it leaves a narrow rim of the photosphere visible.

Eclipsing Binaries:

Some binary star systems are so far away that even a telescope cannot show them as two separate stars. When the two stars are lined up as they circle each other, their combined light is roughly halved because one star is temporarily hidden behind the other. At times of such alignment the binary system appears dimmer than usual.

Ecliptic:

The path the Sun appears to travel across the sky in one year. It forms a great circle on the celestial sphere.

Egress:

The emergence of Venus, Mercury, and the moons of the planets from the disks of their parent objects as they cross them. For example, Venus' moving off the Sun's disk during transit.

Einstein Shift:

A small shift in the spectral lines of stars, due to their own gravitational fields. This effect was foreseen in working out the applications of the theory of relativity by Einstein.

Element:

A substance made up entirely of the same kind of atoms. Such a substance cannot be broken down into a simpler substance by chemical means. Examples: gold, oxygen, lead, chlorine.

Elevation:

The *elevation* of a star is its altitude — its angular height above the horizon.

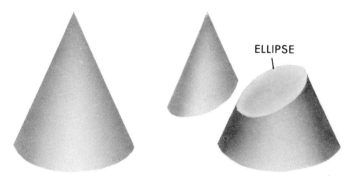

Ellipse:

The closed curve formed when you cut through both sides of a cone at an angle to the cone's axis.

Elliptic Motion:

The Earth is in *elliptic motion* around the Sun, meaning that the Sun is one focus of the ellipse the Earth traces as it moves in its orbit. Any celestial object that moves in an ellipse around a second object, which is a focus of the ellipse, is in *elliptic motion*.

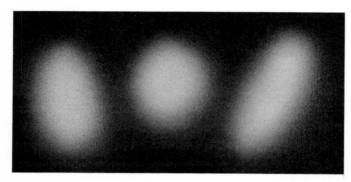

Elliptical Galaxies:

These are flattened sphere-shaped galaxies; some are very elongated, others nearly perfect globes. We cannot see any structure in these star systems, nor is there evidence that they contain gas and dust clouds.

Encke's Comet:

A short-period comet discovered by the German mathematician J. Encke in 1786. It has a period of 3.3 years and does not move beyond the orbit of Jupiter. Like many other comets, it is barely visible to the naked eye.

Encke's Division:

A narrow gap within Saturn's outermost ring, called Ring A.

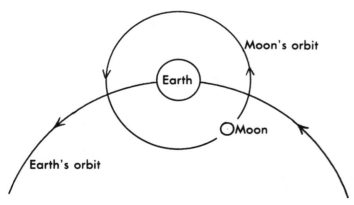

Epicycle:

A small circle whose center lies on the rim of a large circle. For example, the path traced by the Moon (as seen from the Sun) as the Moon circles the Earth is an *epicycle* because its center is the Earth, which itself traces a circular path about the Sun.

Equation of Time:

The difference between apparent solar time and mean time (see *Day*).

Equator:

That great circle of the Earth lying midway between the poles and from which north and south latitudes are measured. The plane formed by the *equator* is at right angles to the Earth's axis.

Equatorial Mounting:

(See p. 113–114.)

Equatorial Telescope:

A telescope mounted equatorially.

Equinoctial Points:

The two points at which the Sun's ecliptic crosses the celestial equator. One is called the First Point of Aries and the other is called the First Point of Libra.

Equinoxes:

The two days of the year when the hours of sunlight and darkness are very nearly the same all over the globe. This is about March 21 (*vernal equinox*) and about September 21 (*autumnal equinox*).

Errors of Observation:

No scientific measuring instrument is ever completely free from errors. Most errors can be found and allowed for. Even so, no scientific measurement will be exactly correct and the *errors of observation* take account both of undiscovered or unmeasurable errors of instruments and errors due to the "personal equation" of an observer. (See also *Personal Equation* and *Accidental Errors*.)

Escape Velocity:

That minimum velocity required of an object in order to break away from its parent body never to return. *Escape velocity* for the Earth is about seven miles a second. For the Moon it is about 1.4 miles a second. (See Table of the Planets, Sun, and Moon, p. 90–91.)

Ether:

A kind of substance once thought to occupy space.

Supposedly the *ether* was a necessary medium which carried light and radio waves across space. Today scientists regard the *ether* theory as an unnecessary assumption.

Evection of Moon:
An unevenness in the Moon's motion about the Earth.

Exterior Planets:
Those planets lying beyond the Earth: Mars, Jupiter, Saturn, Uranus, Neptune, and Pluto.

Extragalactic:
A term applied to any object lying outside our own galaxy.

Extraterrestrial:
A term applied to any object lying beyond the limits of the Earth.

Eyepiece:
The lens, or lenses, at the eye end of a telescope. The *eyepiece* magnifies the image formed by the object glass or main mirror of the telescope.

F

F-stars:
Stars with surface temperatures 6000°C.–7500°C., such as Canopus. *F-stars* usually appear yellowish. (See *A-stars* for additional information; also *Stars.*)

Faculae:
Bright clouds of gas in the Sun's atmosphere. They hang above sunspots or above a position where a group of sunspots is about to break out or has broken out and disappeared.

Falcated:
When Mercury, Venus, or the Moon are in the crescent phase they are said to be *falcated*.

Fahrenheit Temperature:
The thermometer scale on which water freezes at 32° and boils at 212°. Nine *Fahrenheit* degrees equal five centigrade degrees. To convert from Fahrenheit to centigrade subtract 32 from the Fahrenheit reading, multiply by five, then divide by nine. To convert from centigrade to Fahrenheit, multiply the centigrade reading by nine, divide by five, and add thirty-two. (See Centigrade and Fahrenheit scale, p. 119.)

Field Stars:
Those stars which appear in the field of view of a telescope. *Field stars* may be observed along with other objects also in the field of view and used as standards for comparison.

Field of View:
That part of the sky visible through a telescope. The *field of view* in a low-power telescope is larger than it is in a high-power telescope.

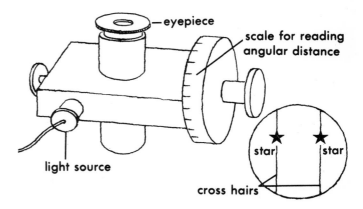

Filar Micrometer:
A device (fitted to a telescope) with two vertical movable cross wires. Used, for example, in measuring the separation of some binary stars.

Finder:
A small telescope with a large field of view attached to a larger telescope (with a smaller field of view). The purpose of a *finder* is simply to locate celestial objects quickly. It contains cross wires so that an object bisected by them lies in the field of view of the main telescope.

Fireballs:
Exceptionally large meteors which become brilliant when they enter the Earth's atmosphere. They become visible at a height of from 80 to 100 miles above the ground.

First Point of Aries:
Point where the Sun crosses the celestial equator in spring, traveling in a northward direction (also called *vernal equinox*).

First Quarter of Moon:
(See *Quarters*).

Flare Stars:

Among the red dwarf stars are some that flare up violently, first increasing in brilliance then fading back to normal within a few minutes.

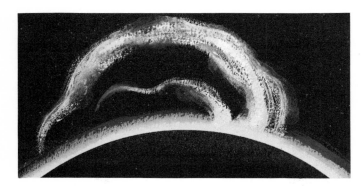

Flares, Solar:

Great loops of glowing gas that burst out of the Sun, often reaching 200,000 miles or higher into the Sun's sky. *Flares* have a life of only a minute or so and their brilliant flash lasts only a few seconds.

Flocculi:

Great clouds of hydrogen and calcium associated with sunspots. They appear above the photosphere.

Focal Length:

The distance in feet from the center of a lens to the point where the light rays bent by the lens meet.

Focal Ratio:

In a telescope, the focal length divided by the object-glass diameter, expressed as f/ratio.

Focus:

1. The point where light rays from infinite distance meet after being bent through a lens or reflected by a curved mirror. 2. Focus of an ellipse. (See *Ellipse.*)

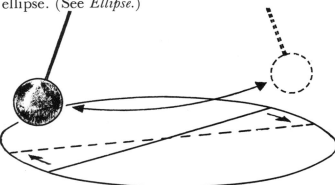

Foucault's Experiment:

To prove that the Earth rotates, Jean Foucault, in 1851, set a pendulum swinging in a north-south direction. During each swing the pendulum appeared to shift its plane gradually clockwise. Since we know that the plane in which a pendulum swings does not shift, Foucault correctly said that the floor beneath the pendulum was turning, or more properly, that the Earth was rotating.

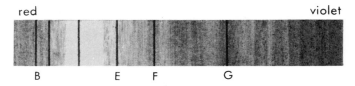

Fraunhofer Lines:

In 1814 Joseph Fraunhofer plotted the dark lines he noticed in the continuous color band of the spectrum of the Sun. The lines are caused by the absorption of certain wave lengths of white light before they can reach us—hence the dark lines. They are absorbed by elements in the Sun's chromosphere.

Full Moon:

When the whole disk of the Moon is visible; this occurs when the Moon is in opposition to the Sun.

G

G-stars:

Two typical *G-stars,* which are yellow in color, are Capella and the Sun. They have surface temperatures 5100°C.–6000°C. (See *A-stars* for additional information; also *Stars.*)

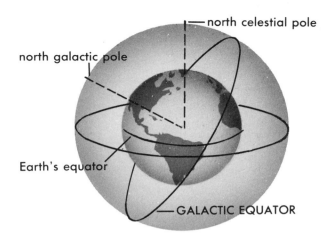

Galactic Equator:

The central plane of the Milky Way. It cuts the plane of the Earth's equator at an angle of 62° in two places—in the constellation Aquila and just east of Orion.

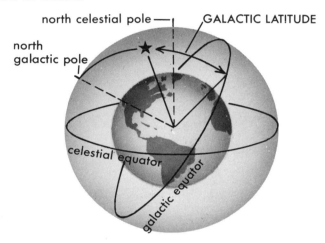

Galactic Latitude:

Angular distances measured north and south of the galactic equator are called *galactic latitudes*.

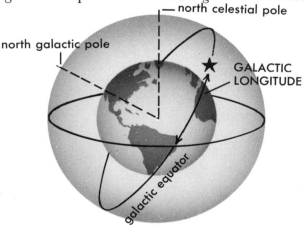

Galactic Longitude:

Measured in a northerly direction along the galactic equator, beginning where the Milky Way's and Earth's equatorial planes cross in Aquila.

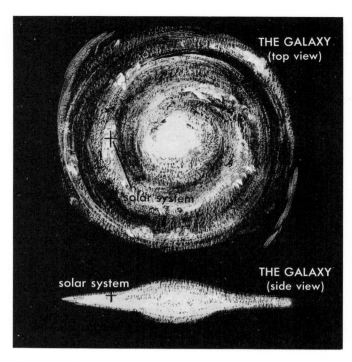

THE GALAXY (top view)

solar system

solar system

THE GALAXY (side view)

Galaxy, the:

The name given to the huge star system of which the Sun is a member (the middle parts of which we see as the Milky Way). *The galaxy* is shaped like a flattened disk with a central bulge. It may contain as many as 100,000 million stars and has a diameter of about 80,000 light-years. In addition to the stars themselves, *the galaxy* contains great clouds of dust and gas out of which new stars are constantly being formed. Like a giant pin wheel *the galaxy* rotates, but different parts of it have different speeds. The part containing the Sun takes about 200 million years to complete one rotation. The Sun lies close to *the galaxy's* central plane and about 25,000 light-years from the central bulge, which is about 10,000 light-years deep. Astronomers have classified the general groups of stars which make up *the galaxy: Population I* stars, which are found mostly in the spiral arms; and *Population II* stars, which are found mainly at *the galaxy's* center. We see the Milky Way as a luminous band stretching across the sky because of our position within *the galaxy*. Because we see it edge on, the stars appear to be tightly packed, but this is only an optical effect. We now know that there are at least 10,000 million galaxies within the range of today's telescopes; and quite likely there are many times this number that we cannot see. (See also *Barred Spiral Galaxies, Elliptical Galaxies, Irregular Galaxies, Spiral Galaxies*.)

Gegenschein:

An extremely faint glow in the sky opposite the Sun's position. Associated with zodiacal light and also called "Counterglow," the *Gegenschein* patch is best seen in September when its size appears to be about forty times the Moon's diameter. (See also *Zodiacal Light*.)

Geocentric System:

Referring to the solar system and meaning that the Earth is at the center with the Sun and planets revolving around it.

Geodesy:

The science that studies the shape, size, dimensions, and variations of the Earth's gravity.

Geoid:

An ideal figure of the Earth with the mean sea level extending over all the continents. The *Geoid* is spheroidal in shape.

Giant Planets:

Those planets of large diameter, including Jupiter, Saturn, Uranus, and Neptune.

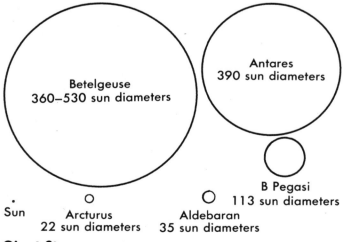

Giant Stars:

Tremendously bright stars with relatively low surface temperatures. Betelgeuse, for example, is a *giant star* with a diameter of about 200 million miles. When most stars are formed, they are red in color, then orange, and yellow as they become hotter. They then become giant stars, but the life history of stars is a complex matter which is still not completely understood. The *giant* and *supergiant* stars lie outside the main sequence. To be so luminous, yet at the same time be so cool, they have to be extremely large. (For additional information see *Main Sequence*.)

Gibbous Moon:

That phase of the Moon when its disk is more than half lighted; between first quarter and full moon and between full moon and last quarter, at which times both limbs are convex.

Globular Clusters:

(See *Clusters*.)

Gnomon:

A sundial formed by a stick placed vertically in the ground.

Granulation:

A term that describes the appearance of the Sun's photosphere. Great clouds of glowing gas well up to the "surface," where they cool and become less bright. The bright and darker gas areas, then, appear as millions of "rice grains."

Gravitation:

The force of attraction between any two or more particles in the universe, no matter how large or small. The attraction between any two bodies is proportional to the mass of each and inversely proportional to the square of the distance between them. For example, if you double the distance between two bodies, you reduce their mutual attraction to one quarter.

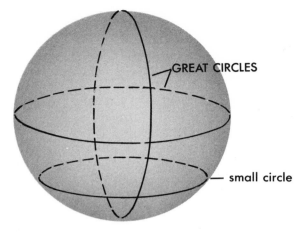

Great Circle:

Any circle whose plane cuts through the center of a sphere. All lines of longitude on the globe are *great circles,* but the only circle of latitude that is a *great circle* is the equator.

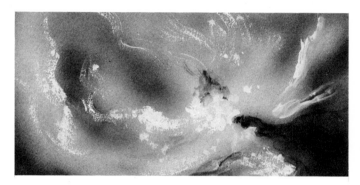

Great Nebula:

The brightest visible nebula, located in the sword of Orion. It is about 1000 light-years away from us and has a diameter of about sixteen light-years. It is composed of glowing gas and lies within our own galaxy.

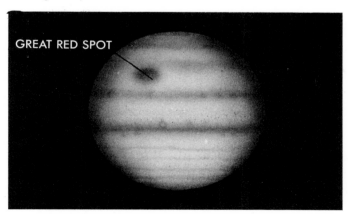

Great Red Spot:

A feature of Jupiter's outer atmosphere. It appears as a brick-red, pinkish, or gray football-shaped spot about 30,000 miles long and 7000 miles wide. It moves around the planet at irregular speeds.

Some astronomers think it is a gaseous feature; others have suggested that it may be a solid floating in Jupiter's atmospheric sea.

Green Flash:

As the Sun sets, the Earth's atmosphere bends its rays, the rays of different colors being bent by different amounts. The blue rays are bent the most and the red the least. Because the blue rays blend in with the color of the sky, the green rays are those which shine until the Sun has fully set. As the Sun sets, these green rays give the effect of a *green flash.*

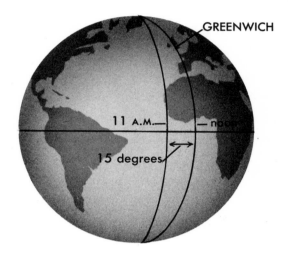

Greenwich Mean Time:

The standard time at Greenwich Observatory, England, measured by the mean sun. (See *Day.*) East of Greenwich clocks are kept ahead of GMT; west of Greenwich they are kept behind GMT. One hour difference is allowed for every 15° of longitude.

Gregorian Calendar:

(See description under *Calendar.*)

Gyroscope:

A heavy wheel which, when started spinning, will spin always in the same plane. It is mounted in such a way that the mounting can be turned this way and that, but the wheel will continue to keep its same plane of spinning relative to space.

H

Hale Telescope:

(See Telescopes and How They Work, p. 103.)

Halley's Comet:

The periodic comet named after Edmund Halley, who observed it in 1682. He worked out its orbit and predicted its return in 1759. It has a mean period of about seventy-seven years, but may vary by plus or minus two and a half years. Its next appearance is scheduled for 1987. The famous comet has a tail about 37 million miles long. (See *Comets*.)

Harvest Moon:

Throughout most of the year the Moon rises about fifty-two minutes later each night, but near autumnal equinox it rises at nearly the same time several nights running. This period is known as the *harvest moon* period.

Heliacal:

The *heliacal* rising of Sirius or any other celestial body means that the body rises or sets just after or just before the Sun.

Heliocentric System:

Referring to the solar system and meaning that the Sun is at the center with the planets revolving around it. (See *Copernican System*.)

Heliometer:

A special telescope whose object glass is cut down the middle so that by turning a screw one half can be moved up and the other moved down. The instrument can be used to find the diameter of the Sun and planets or the angular distance between the two stars making up a double star. This device is not widely used today.

Heliostat:

(See *Siderostat*.)

Helium:

An inert gaseous element with two protons and two neutrons in the nucleus and two electrons circling the nucleus. *Helium* is the second most abundant element in the universe. The energy in stars comes from the conversion of hydrogen into *helium*.

Hemisphere:

One half of a sphere; any plane cutting through the center of a sphere divides the sphere into two *hemispheres*.

Horsehead Nebula:

In the constellation Orion, a great dark cloud of dust and gas outlined by light from stars and gas shining behind it.

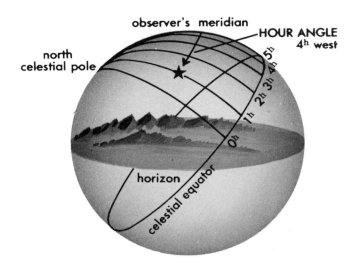

observer's meridian
HOUR ANGLE
4ʰ west
north
celestial pole
5ʰ
4ʰ
3ʰ
2ʰ
1ʰ
0ʰ
horizon
celestial equator

Hour Angle:

The angle measured westwardly along the equator from the foot of the observer's meridian to the foot of the hour circle passing through the celestial body. In other words, it is the angle between a celestial body and the meridian.

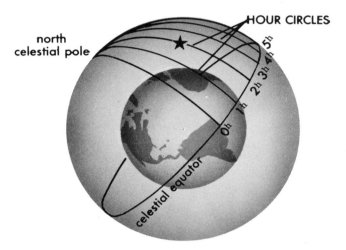

HOUR CIRCLES
north
celestial pole
5ʰ
4ʰ
3ʰ
2ʰ
1ʰ
0ʰ
celestial equator

Hour Circle:

A great circle passing through the celestial poles and a celestial body.

Hubble's Law:

The name given to the relationship of recession of galaxies and their distance from us—proposed by Edwin Hubble.

Hydrogen:

The element with the simplest possible atom, which consists of a single electron revolving about a single proton. *Hydrogen* is the "stuff" of the universe. It is thereby spread throughout space, and it makes up the bulk of stars. *Hydrogen* in stars changes into helium, and in the process generates great quantities of energy.

I

Immersion:

The disappearance of a planet behind the Moon, or of a satellite temporarily hidden from view as it passes behind its parent body.

Inclination of Orbit:

The angle between the plane of a planet's orbit and the plane of the ecliptic.

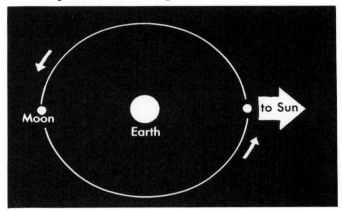

Moon
Earth
to Sun

Inequality, Moon's Parallactic:

At new moon, when the Moon is between us and the Sun, the Moon is pulled away from the Earth by gravitational attraction of the Sun. At full moon, when the Earth is between the Moon and the Sun, the Earth is pulled away from the Moon by gravitational attraction of the Sun. This elongation of the Moon's orbit toward the Sun is called *parallactic inequality*.

Inequality of Planets:

Lack of uniformity in the orbital motions of the planets. Some *inequalities* recur at regular intervals and others mount up with time.

Inferior Conjunction:

(See *Conjunction*.)

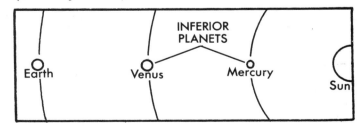

INFERIOR
PLANETS
Earth
Venus
Mercury
Sun

Inferior Planets:

Those planets which revolve around the Sun at a distance closer to the Sun than the Earth is; that is, Mercury and Venus.

Ingress:

When Venus or Mercury edges onto the Sun's disk during transit; also, when the moons of Jupiter and Saturn edge onto the disk of their primaries during transit.

Intercalation:

Adding one day to a year to make a leap year. The added days are called "intercalary," or leap days.

INTERNATIONAL DATE LINE
180°

International Date Line:

The 180° meridian, exactly halfway around the globe from the prime meridian, located at Greenwich, England. When you cross the *international date line* from east to west you advance the calendar by one whole day; from west to east you put the calendar back by one day.

Interferometer:

An instrument that causes light waves to interfere with each other and can be used to measure the wave length of light.

Interplanetary:

Among the planets; traveling from one planet to another.

Interstellar:

Among the stars.

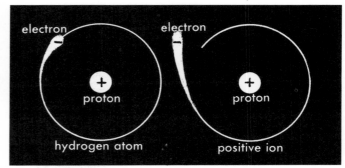

electron   electron

proton   proton

hydrogen atom   positive ion

Ionization:

Providing an electrically neutral atom with a charge. An atom that has lost an electron is left with a positive charge and is called a *positive ion*. An atom that gains an electron acquires a negative charge and is called a *negative ion*. In both instances the atom is said to be *ionized*.

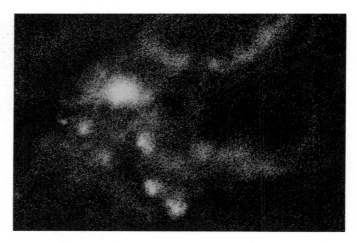

Irregular Galaxies:

Galaxies with an irregular shape. There are many in the neighborhood of the Milky Way. The two Clouds of Magellan are the nearest *irregular galaxies*.

Island Universe:

Any galaxy in the heavens.

J

Julian Calendar:

(See description under *Calendar*.)

Julian Date:

In some astronomical studies it is convenient to count the number of days that elapse between two observations. Mean noon on January 1, 4713 B.C., is taken as the starting point, so that the *Julian date* of January 1, 4712 B.C., is 365 (that is 365 days after the starting date).

K

K-stars:

Orange stars with surface temperatures 3600°C.– 5100°C. Arcturus is a *K-star*. (See *A-stars* for additional information; also *Stars*.)

Kelvin Temperature:

Another name for the absolute scale (see *Absolute Zero*). To convert from Kelvin to centigrade, subtract 273 from the Kelvin reading.

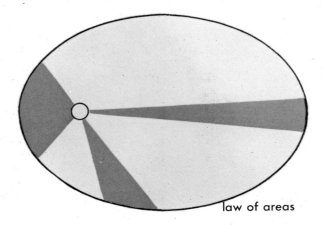

law of areas

Kepler's Laws of Planetary Motion:

In the early 1600s Johannes Kepler worked out his three laws of planetary motion, basing them on observations made by Tycho Brahe. They are: 1. The planets move in ellipses with the Sun at one focus; 2. The Law of Areas—the line joining the Sun and a planet sweeps out equal areas in equal times; 3. The Harmonic Law—the square of the time of revolution (in years) of any planet is equal to the cube of its mean distance from the Sun (in astronomical units). The three laws (with the third restated) also apply to the moons of planets and to artificial satellites.

L

Lagoon Nebula:

A nebula in the constellation Sagittarius.

Last Quarter of Moon:

(See *Quarter.*)

Latitude, Celestial:

(See *Celestial Latitude.*)

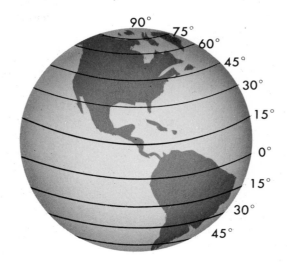

Latitude, Parallels of:

Imaginary circles north and south from the equator, the great circle along which longitude is measured. The *parallels of latitude* form circles whose planes are parallel to the plane of this great circle. Zero degrees latitude would be any place on the great circle. Ninety degrees North Latitude is the north pole of the great circle; ninety degrees South Latitude is the south pole.

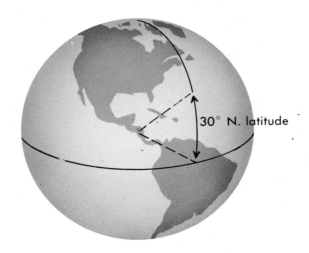

30° N. latitude

Latitude, Terrestrial:

The angular distance of any point on the Earth's surface north or south of the equator. For example, if a point is at 30° N. latitude a line running from the point to the center of the Earth and from the center to the equator, directly south of the point, will form an angle of 30°.

Leap Year:

A year with 366 days instead of 365. *Leap year* occurs once every four years, when the additional day is February 29. (See *Calendar*.)

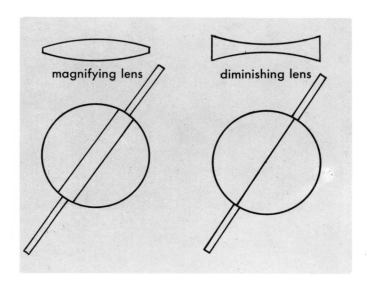

Lens:

A piece of glass whose surfaces are curved in order to bend light rays. Depending on how the light rays are bent, an object seen through the lens can be made to appear large or small.

Libration:

Because the Moon rotates only once during each revolution about the Earth we see only one hemisphere of its surface. Actually we see a bit more (four sevenths) because the Moon does not travel at a uniform speed in its elliptical orbit. Because its rate of rotation is uniform but its rate of revolution is not, we are able to see just around the edge of each limb from time to time. We call this effect *libration of longitude*.

Light-Year:

The distance light travels in one year, at a velocity of about 186,300 miles a second. One *light-year* equals about 6,000,000,000,000 miles.

Limb:

The rim of the disk of a stellar body such as the Sun, Moon, planets, stars.

Local Time:

The solar time at any place. Local noon is that moment when the Sun appears due south in northern latitudes.

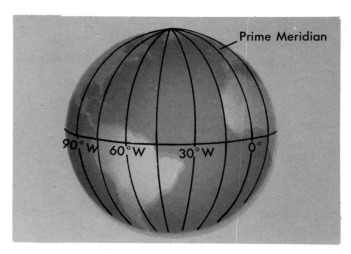

Longitude, Terrestrial:

The angular distance of any point on the Earth's surface measured east or west of the prime meridian, located at Greenwich. Longitude is measured 180° east and west from Greenwich. To say that Philadelphia is 75¼° W. longitude, means that a line drawn from Philadelphia to the center of the Earth, then from the center of the Earth to a point of the same latitude on the prime meridian forms an angle of 75¼°.

Lunar:

Relating to the Moon.

Lunar Halo:

A ring around the Moon caused by moonlight shining through ice crystals in the upper atmosphere. The halos are usually 22° wide.

Lunation:

The time from one new moon to the next—29 days, 12 hours, 44 minutes. Same as *synodical month*.

M

M-stars:

Orange-red giant and dwarf stars with surface temperatures from 3000°C. to 3500°C. Betelgeuse is an M-giant; Wolf 359 is an M-dwarf. (See *A-stars* for additional information; also *Stars*.)

Magellanic Clouds:

(See *Clouds of Magellan*.)

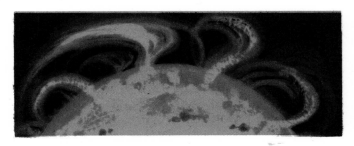

Magnetic Storm:

Whenever sunspots and certain solar prominences burst into activity, charged particles sweep into the Earth's atmosphere—most strongly in the polar and near-polar regions. During or a little after such times, compass needles quiver, we have auroral displays, and we may have radio blackouts.

Magnification:

In a telescope, the ratio of the focal length of the object glass to the focal length of the eyepiece. For instance, in a telescope with an eyepiece focal length of ½ inch and an object glass focal length of 36 inches, the magnification is 72 diameters, written "× 72."

Magnitude of Stars:

1. *Apparent Magnitude*—the apparent degree of brightness of a star. The higher the magnitude number of a star, the fainter it appears in the sky. Some of the nearly brightest stars we see have a magnitude of 1 and are called first-magnitude stars. A star of magnitude 2 is two-and-a-half times fainter than a second-magnitude star, and so on. The faintest stars you can see on a clear night are of 6th magnitude. Exceptionally bright stars have magnitudes of less than one and are given negative values. For example, the apparent brightness of the Sun is −27 (because it is so close to us). 2. *Absolute Magnitude*—This is defined as the *apparent magnitude,* assuming the star to be 10 parsecs from the Earth. (A parsec is equal to 19,160,000,000,000 miles; or 3.26 light-years.) The Sun has an *absolute magnitude* of 4.7. Other stars, although they appear not particularly bright have *absolute magnitudes* ranging up to −9.

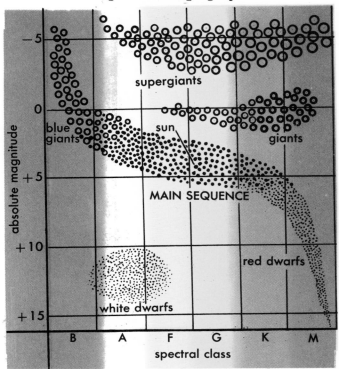

Main Sequence of Stars:

The Hertzsprung-Russell Diagram on this page shows how stars can be grouped when their absolute magnitudes are plotted against their spectral classes. When the stars were first plotted this way, astronomers discovered a close relationship between the spectral class and absolute magnitude. When grouped this way, most of the stars fall along a smooth band called the *main sequence,* beginning with the bright and massive hot B-stars and ending with the faint and lightweight, cool M-stars. Stars which do not fall along the *main sequence* are the supergiants, giants, and white dwarfs, The Sun lies near the middle of the *main sequence*. (See *Spectral Class of Stars;* also *Stars*.)

Major Axis of Orbit:

In an ellipse, the line passing through the two foci.

Mare (on Moon):

Large areas of rock, probably solidified lava, stretching 700 miles or more over the surface. (For location and names of the Moon's "seas," see The Moon, p. 96.)

Mass:

The amount of matter contained in a body.

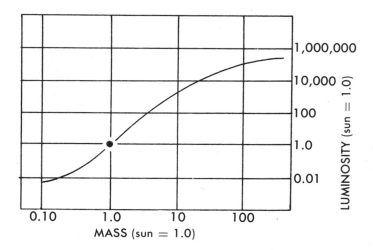

Mass-Luminosity Curve:

The mass and luminosity of stars are closely related. Generally, the greater the mass, the greater the luminosity. If the known masses of a representative group of stars are plotted against their luminosities, the stars lie along a single curve. The white dwarf stars are the only ones that fall outside this curve. (For additional information see *Main Sequence, Dwarf Stars, Giant Stars*.)

Mean Motion:

(See *Motion*.)

Mean Solar Time:

The hour angle of the mean sun. Expressed as time, 1 hour equals 15° of motion of the mean sun. (See *Day*.)

Mean Sun:

An imaginary sun that traces its path along the equator at a uniform rate of speed throughout the year (which the real Sun does not do because of the Earth's varying speed in its orbit). The *mean sun* is used to calculate mean time. (See *Day*.)

Mean Time:

The time kept by your watch, measured by the mean sun. (See *Day*.)

Megaparsec:

A million parsecs, or 3,260,000 light-years.

Meridian:

A line of longitude on the Earth's sphere or a similar line on the celestial sphere.

Messier Objects:

In the 1700s the French astronomer Jean Messier, while looking for comets, made a numbered list of bothersome "objects to avoid." Since Messier's time we have identified these "objects" as nebulae (although some of them are star clusters). **M 31** is the Messier number for the Andromeda Galaxy; **M 42** is the Orion Nebula. (See section on Star Maps starting on p. 58.)

Meteors:

Stone, stone-iron, and iron fragments that travel in swarms or as lone objects through space, circling the Sun. They are as small as grains of sand or so large that they weigh many tons. When a *meteor* enters the Earth's atmosphere, it usually vaporizes by frictional heat produced by its rapid passage through the air. The average speed of *meteors* through space is about 90,000 miles an hour. Known also as "shooting stars," these objects flare into prominence about seventy-five miles above the Earth, are visible for a second or so, then disappear at a height of about fifty miles above the ground. Their remains fall to earth as fine dust. About a ton of meteoric dust falls to Earth each day, which means that millions of *meteors* enter our atmosphere every twenty-four hours. Both the "sporadic" meteors (those that travel alone) and the "shower" meteors (those that travel in swarms) may be remains of "leftover" matter when the planetary system was formed some five billion years or so ago. Many *shower meteors* appear at regular intervals, returning year after year. The known showers are named after the constellations out of which the meteor swarms seem to flow, or "radiate" (see Meteor Showers, p. 117). The Leonid Shower, for example, is named after the constellation Leo; the Orionids after Orion, and so on.

Meteorites:

When a meteor survives its journey through the atmosphere without vaporizing and strikes the ground, it is called a *meteorite*. The largest one known, called Ahnighito, was found in Greenland and weighs 34 tons. *Meteorites* made mostly of iron are called *siderites;* those formed of iron and stone are called *siderolites;* those made mostly of stone are called *aerolites.*

Meter:

A measure of length equal to 39.37 inches.

Methane:

A poisonous, gaseous compound whose molecule is made up of one atom of carbon and four atoms of hydrogen (CH_4). Also known as "marsh gas," it is present in large amounts in the atmospheres of Jupiter, Saturn, Uranus, and Neptune.

Micrometeor:

Meteors about the size of grains of sand.

The Arctic sun seen at 20 minute intervals

Midnight Sun:

Within 23½° of the poles the Sun is visible twenty-four hours a day during parts of the summer, so the Sun can be seen at midnight.

Milky Way:

The luminous band of light seen on any clear night. The effect is caused by our looking into our galaxy edge on, and so we see millions of stars that appear to be crowded together, the effect being a haze. The term *Milky Way* is sometimes used to designate our galaxy.

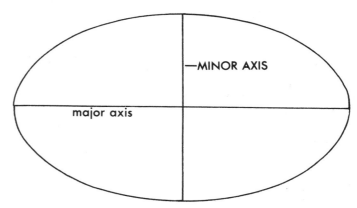

Minor Axis of Orbit:

In an ellipse, the line crossing the major axis at right angles midway along the major axis.

Minor Planets:

Between the orbits of Mars and Jupiter are thousands of objects that revolve about the Sun as the planets do. More than 2000 of these *minor planets,* or asteroids, have been observed to date. They are thought to be composed of stone and iron. Some are as large as houses, others are mountain-sized and much larger. Those that sweep in close to Earth are called Earthgrazers. The swarm of *minor planets* may well be one source of meteors. One theory suggests that the *minor planets* may be the fragmented remains of a planet that once occupied an orbit between Mars and Jupiter but was destroyed. (See Minor Planets, p. 89.)

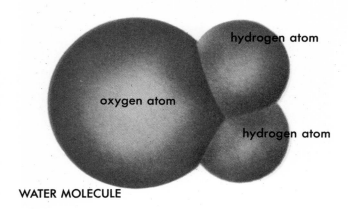

WATER MOLECULE

Molecule:

The smallest possible piece of a substance that still retains all the properties of the substance. For example, a molecule of water, written H_2O, consists of two atoms of hydrogen joined to one atom of oxygen. These atoms in combination form a single molecule of water.

Monochromatic Filter:

A filter allowing the light of only one particular color to pass through it.

Month:

1. *Anomalistic*—the length of time it takes the Moon to circle the Earth once, measuring its travel time from one perihelion to the next: 27 days, 13 hours, 18 minutes, 37.4 seconds. 2. *Nodical*—the length of time it takes the Moon to pass through one of its nodes and return to it: 27 days, 5 hours, 5 minutes, 35.8 seconds. 3. *Sidereal*—the length of time it takes the Moon to circle the Earth once, using the stars as a reference point: 27 days, 7 hours, 43 minutes, 11.5 seconds. 4. *Synodical*—the length of time it takes the Moon to circle the Earth once, using the Sun as the reference point (that is, the time lapse between two successive conjunctions with the Sun): 29 days, 12 hours, 44 minutes, 2.7 seconds.

Motion:

1. *Apparent*—the motion of any celestial object as seen from the Earth, which itself is moving. 2. *Real* —the motion of any celestial object as it would be seen from the Sun. 3. *Direct*—the apparent motion of the planets in a west-to-east direction among the stars. 4. *Diurnal*—As the Earth rotates on its axis from west to east, the stars, Sun, Moon, and planets appear to move across the sky from east to west. This *apparent motion* is called *diurnal motion*. 5. *Retrograde*—Because the Earth and the other planets are constantly revolving about the Sun, we sometimes see the planets moving from east to west among the stars. This particular *apparent motion* is called *retrograde*. Phoebe, one of Saturn's nine moons, unlike the other moons, has *retrograde motion*, meaning that it is seen to cross Saturn's disk from east to west. 6. *Proper*—Many of the "fixed" stars appear to us never to move; for example, those making up the constellations. In reality they do move, but only the finest instruments can detect their motion over a period of years. 7. *Mean*—the velocity of a moving body if the body traced a circular orbit (rather than elliptical) with a radius equal to the mean distance of the body from its primary.

Multiple Stars:

Many points of light in the sky appear as single stars, but a telescope reveals them as a group of stars. Castor, for example, is made up of six stars.

N

N-stars:

Orange-red stars with surface temperatures around 2600°C. (See *A-stars* for additional information; also *Stars*.)

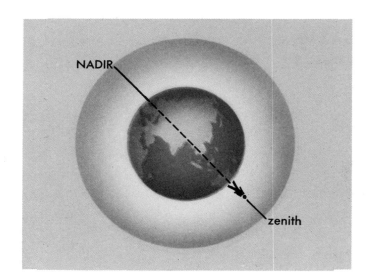

NADIR

zenith

Nadir:

On the celestial sphere the point opposite the zenith. A plumb line points toward the *nadir*.

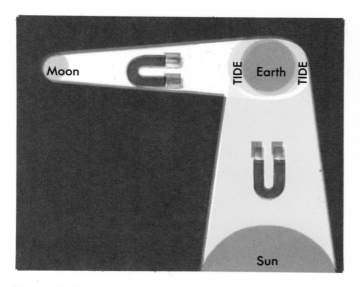

Neap Tides:

When the Sun and Moon are at right angles to one another we have *neap tides*. These are relatively weak tides because the Sun and Moon are attracting the Earth's ocean water from two different directions. We have *neap tides* whenever the Moon is in first quarter or in last quarter.

Nebular Hypothesis:

In 1796 Laplace published a theory explaining the origin of the solar system. He suggested that a great spinning disk of gas and dust threw out rings which condensed and so formed the planets. The central bulge of gas and dust contracted and formed the Sun. Around 1900 Laplace's theory fell out of favor. Astronomers criticized it by saying that such a rotating disk would not cast off rings and that, if it did, the rings would not condense into planets.

TRIFID NEBULA

Nebulae:

Great clouds of dust and gas within our galaxy. Some of these clouds glow with light provided by nearby stars, or a few stars within the cloud. Others are simply dark patches outlined by light from stars shining far behind them. A planetary nebula is a globe of dust and gas enclosing one or more stars. NGC 3587 in the Great Bear is an example. Another is the Ring Nebula in Lyra; and another is the Owl Nebula in Ursa Major. Two examples of bright nebulae which glow are the Trifid Nebula in Sagittarius and the Gaseous Nebula in Orion.

New Moon:

When the Moon is in direct line between the Sun and the Earth, or in conjunction with the Sun.

Newtonian Telescope:

(See Newtonian Reflector, p. 106.)

Nodes:

The orbits of the planets and comets cross the ecliptic at two points called the *nodes*. When a planet is crossing the ecliptic from south to north, it is at the *ascending node;* from north to south, the *descending node.*

Nodical Month:

(See *Month.*)

Nonagesimal Point:

The highest point along the ecliptic at any given time.

Noon:

1. *Apparent*—when the visible Sun crosses the observer's meridian. 2. *Mean*—when the mean sun crosses the observer's meridian. (See *Day, Apparent Solar;* and *Day, Mean Solar.*)

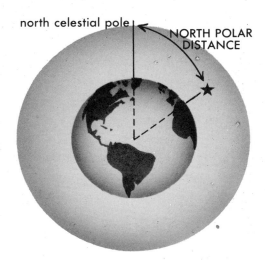

North Polar Distance:

On the celestial sphere, the angular distance of a star or other celestial object from the north pole.

North Polar Sequence:

A selected number of stars near the north celestial pole whose magnitudes have been accurately measured. These stars are used as reference stars in determining the brightness of others.

Northern Lights:

(See *Aurora.*)

Nova:

A star that for some reason not yet fully understood bursts into brilliance. Within a few days a typical *nova* may become 60,000 times brighter than usual, then it becomes somewhat less brilliant, and after a few months or longer returns to its pre-nova magnitude. Certain planetary nebulae may be the result of *novae.*

Nucleus, of Comets:

(See *Comets.*)

O

O-stars:

Among the hottest of the normal stars, greenish white and with surface temperatures of 35,000°C. and higher. (See *A-stars* for additional information; also *Stars.*)

Object Glass:

The lens, or system of lenses, at the far end of a telescope. (See Refracting Telescopes, p. 108.)

Objective Prism:

A large prism placed in front of the object glass of a telescope. Through this prism the spectra of many bright stars may be photographed at the same time.

Oblateness:

A bulging at the equator of a rotating sphere. The Earth is an *oblate* spheroid because it bulges slightly at the equator.

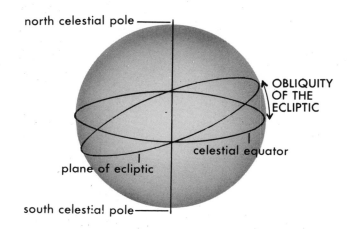

Obliquity of the Ecliptic:

The plane of the equator forms an angle of about 23½° with the plane of the ecliptic; this angular difference is known as *obliquity of the ecliptic.*

Occultation:

When one celestial object crosses your line of sight and so hides a second object behind it. The hidden body is said to be *occulted.*

Opaque:

A material is *opaque* if light cannot pass through it.

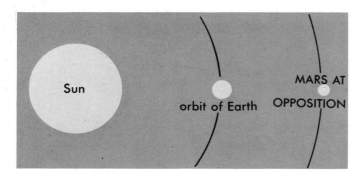

Opposition:

The position of a planet when the Earth lies directly between it and the Sun.

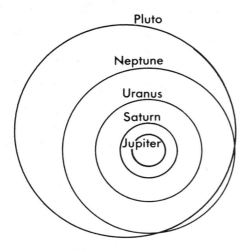

ORBITS OF OUTER PLANETS

Orbit:

The path one celestial object traces as it circles another. The Earth and other planets each have their own *orbits* around the Sun. The Moon travels in an *orbit* around the Earth.

P

Palomar Reflector:

The 200-inch telescope at Mount Palomar Observatory in California. (See pp. 103, 107.)

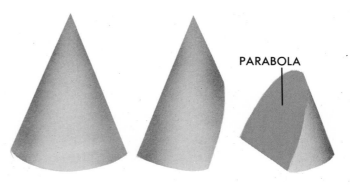

Parabola:

The open curve formed by slicing a cone along a line parallel to one side of the cone. Parabolic mirrors bring parallel light rays to a focus. They also reflect into parallel rays light coming from the focus. Reflecting telescopes and automobile headlights both employ the *parabolic* principle.

Parallax:

When you view an object from two different positions the object appears to change place. Look at a nearby tree first through one eye, then through the other by winking rapidly with one eye and then with the other and the tree will appear to jump back and forth. This apparent change in position of the object is called *parallax*. By viewing a nearby star from opposite points on the Earth's orbit, we measure its angle of shift, the parallax, and so determine its distance from the Earth.

Parsec:

A measure of distance equal to 19,160,000,000,000 miles.

Partial Eclipse:

(See *Eclipse*.)

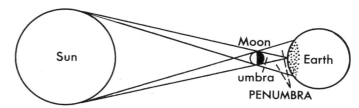

Penumbra:

During an eclipse the shadow cast on the Earth is made up of two parts (see diagram): the *penumbra* and *umbra*. If you see the eclipse from the (inner) *umbra* shadow, you see a total eclipse; if you see it from the (outer) *penumbra* shadow, you see a partial eclipse.

41

Periastron:

In the real orbit of a binary star system, that point at which the two stars come closest together.

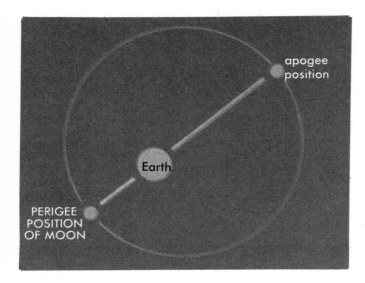

Perigee:

That point in the orbit of the Moon at which it reaches its closest possible distance to the Earth; also of artificial satellites' closest approaches to the Earth.

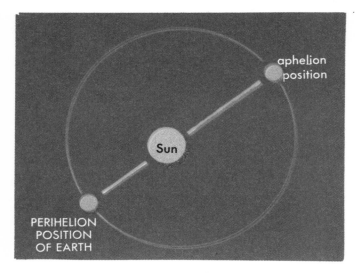

Perihelion:

That point in the orbit of a planet or other member of the solar system at which it reaches the closest possible approach to the Sun.

Period:

The length of time it takes any member of the solar system to complete one trip around the Sun; the length of time between two successive maxima or minima of variable stars; the time it takes two stars in a binary system to complete one revolution about their common center of mass.

Period-Luminosity Law:

Astronomers have found that certain variable stars with equal *periods* of variation have the same absolute magnitude. Delta Cephei, for example, has a period of five and a third days and is about 660 times more luminous than the Sun. So according to the *Period-Luminosity Law,* any other variable star that has a period of five and a third days should also be 660 times more luminous than the Sun. If, then, we see such a star at some great distance, we can compute that distance by measuring the star's apparent magnitude.

Personal Equation:

The errors an individual observer himself makes as he observes and records celestial events.

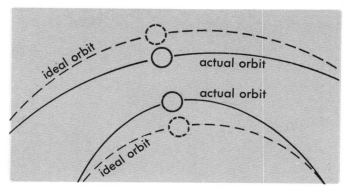

Perturbation:

The planets and their satellites do not move in exactly elliptical orbits because they all exert gravitational attractions on each other. This results in slight departures from elliptical orbits which are called *perturbations.* The existence of Neptune was predicted on the basis of the *perturbation* of Uranus. If an astronomer knows the amount of *perturbation* of a celestial body, he can work out the mass of the body exerting the disturbing force.

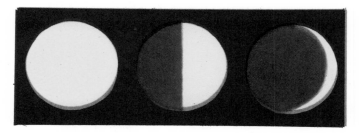

Phases:

The changing apparent "shape" of the Moon (also Venus and Mercury) as it appears full, half, and crescent-shaped.

Photometer:

An instrument that measures the intensity of light from the stars and planets.

Photosphere:

The so-called "surface" of the Sun. It has a granular appearance caused by great cells of gas welling up to the surface, cooling, and turning dark in contrast to the lighter, surrounding background. Each cell is about 700 miles across, about 200 miles deep, and lasts about four minutes. The temperature of the *photosphere* is about 6000°C.

Plane, Invariable:

The plane perpendicular to the combined rotational motion of the bodies in the Solar System.

Planetary Nebula:

(See *Nebulae.*)

Planetoids:

(See *Minor Planets.*)

Planet:

Celestial objects that shine by reflected light from a star about which they revolve. There are nine known *primary planets* that make up the solar system: Mercury, Venus, Earth, Mars, Jupiter, Saturn, Uranus, Neptune, Pluto. *Secondary planets* are the moons that circle Earth, Mars, Jupiter, and other *primary planets.* (For additional information see Table of the Planets, Sun, and Moon, p. 90–91.)

Plumb Line:

A line determined by a weight suspended from a string. It always points to Earth's center and is exactly perpendicular to a surface of water.

Pointers, the:

Two stars in the Big Dipper—Dubhe and Merak—which are in line with and "point" to the Pole Star.

Pole Star:

Polaris, the star now nearest the north celestial pole. (See also *Precession.*)

Poles, Celestial:

(See *Celestial Poles.*)

Poles, Terrestrial:

The end points of the Earth's axis—0° North Latitude and 0° South Latitude.

Population I Stars:

These are stars, like the Sun, which are associated with interstellar dust and gas in the spiral arms of our galaxy. *Population I* stars are relatively young and are believed still to be forming within our galaxy.

Population II Stars:

These are the stars that make up the dense nucleus of our galaxy and that form globular clusters. They are not associated with interstellar dust and gas, so *Population II* stars are not believed to be forming now. There are about ten times as many *Population II* stars in the galaxy as there are *Population I* stars.

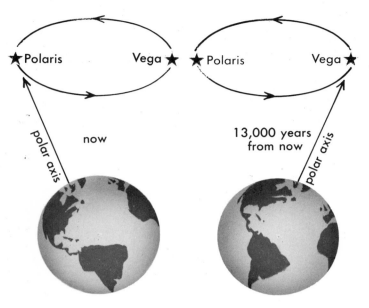

Precession:

A gradual change in the direction of tilt of the Earth's axis due to gravitational attraction of the Sun and Moon, which tend to pull the Earth's equatorial bulge into line. This double attraction causes the Earth to wobble slightly, like a spinning top. The axis completes one rotation in about 26,000 years, which means that Polaris has not always been the pole star, nor will it continue to be.

Prime Meridian:

Known also as the "Greenwich Meridian," it is zero degrees longitude—east and west of which longitude is measured. It is located at Greenwich, England.

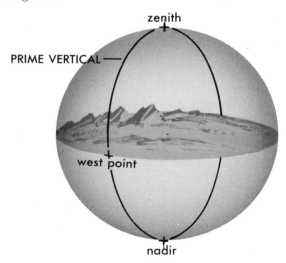

Prime Vertical:

The great circle passing through the zenith and nadir of the celestial sphere and through the west point on the horizon.

Prism:

A solid block of glass with surfaces inclined to one another. As light passes through the *prism,* different colors are bent (refracted) by different amounts and so form a spectrum.

Prominences:

Glowing masses of gas that loop and surge from the Sun's photosphere for distances of hundreds of thousands of miles. They can best be seen during an eclipse of the Sun or by special instruments such as the coronograph and the spectrohelioscope.

Proper Motion:

(See *Motion.*)

Ptolemaic System:

Claudius Ptolemaeus around A.D. 140 maintained that the Earth was the center of the universe; that the other planets, the Sun, and the stars all revolved about the Earth in uniform circular motion.

Q

Quadrant:

A quarter of a circle. Also a kind of sextant.

Quadrature:

When two celestial bodies are 90° of longitude apart, they are said to be at *quadrature.*

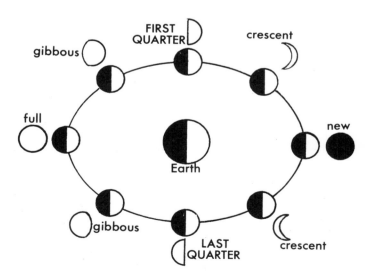

Quarter:

When the Moon is in first and last *quarter* of its journey round the Earth, one half of its disk, as seen from the Earth, is lighted by the Sun. At such time we say the Moon is half full.

R

R-stars:
Orange-red stars, not too common, with surface temperatures around 2300°C. (See *A-stars* for additional information; also *Stars*.)

Radar Detection of Meteors:
When meteors enter the Earth's atmosphere they ionize the air they pass through. Because this ionized air reflects radio waves, the paths and speeds of meteors can be measured by radar. The advantages of radar detection are many—for instance, neither daylight nor clouds interfere as they do in visual observation. Also, radar gives a written record of a meteor's flight path and speed.

Radial Motion:
That part of a star's motion which carries it away from or toward the observer. This motion is detected by a spectroscope.

Radiant:
During a shower of meteors, the meteor swarms appear to flow out of a particular constellation. This point from which they appear to flow is called the *radiant*. (See Meteor Showers, p. 117.)

Radiation:
Rays, wave motion, or subatomic particles emitted from any source.

Radiation Pressure:
Light, or other electromagnetic radiation, exerts a pressure in the direction of its motion. As comets circle the Sun, their tails always point away from the Sun rather than trail behind the comet. *Radiation pressure* causes this. It has been suggested that space ships fitted with sails might be driven across space by *radiation pressure*.

Radio Astronomy:
The study of radio waves emitted by certain stars, planets, galaxies, and nebulae.

Radio Interferometer:
The use of two or more radio telescope aerials to receive signals from the same radio sources in space. By a switching system, the signals from the various aerials interfere with each other in such a way that the multiple aerial system can detect signals from a smaller section of the sky than a single aerial can.

Crab Nebula

Radio Stars:
Stars and other bodies in space that emit radio waves. One of the strongest known radio sources in the sky is the Crab Nebula, which is thought to be the remains of a supernova star that was observed to explode about 900 years ago.

Radio Telescope:

(See p. 115.)

Rate of a Clock:

The amount of time an astronomical clock loses or gains over a twenty-four-hour period. If it gains time, the rate is negative; if it loses, the rate is positive.

The crater Copernicus surrounded by rays

Rays on Moon:

Long "arms" of light color extending like spokes of a wheel from certain craters on the Moon—the craters named Tycho and Copernicus in particular. The origin of the Moon's *rays* is unknown, but they may have been formed by the impact of meteorites striking the Moon's surface.

Real Motion:

(See *Motion.*)

Red Giants:

(See *Giant Stars.*)

Red Shift:

When the light from distant galaxies is examined through a spectroscope, the lines of the spectrum are shifted toward the red end of the spectrum. This shift toward the red indicates that the galaxies are moving away from us. (See *Doppler Effect.*)

Red Spot on Jupiter:

(See *Great Red Spot.*)

Reflecting Telescope:

(See pp. 106, 107.)

light refracted by lens

Refraction:

The bending of a ray of light as it passes from one transparent medium into another. When light passes through the atmosphere, its line of refraction is a curve; but when it passes through a lens, it is refracted at a sharp angle.

Refracting Telescope:

(See p. 108.)

Relativity:

Einstein's theory that it is impossible to measure absolute motion of objects in space, or the absolute instant at which an event occurs; that the velocity of light is the same for all observers; and that space and time must be regarded as an indivisible whole.

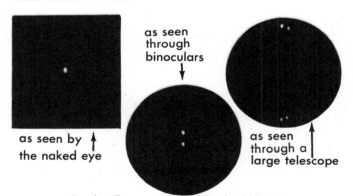

as seen through binoculars

as seen by the naked eye

as seen through a large telescope

Epsilon Lyrae, a "double double" star

Resolving Power:

A telescope's ability to separate two or more closely associated light sources. For example, to be able to distinguish that a binary star system (which will appear to the eye as a single star) is actually made up of two stars.

Retrograde Motion:

(See *Motion.*)

Revolution:

The motion of one body around another. The Moon revolves about the Earth; the planets revolve about the Sun.

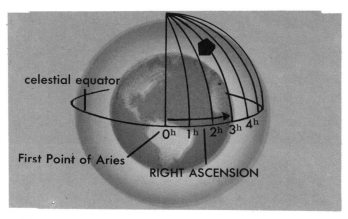

Right Ascension:

On the celestial sphere, the equivalent of terrestrial longitude. *Right ascension* is measured eastward along the celestial equator, beginning at the First Point of Aries.

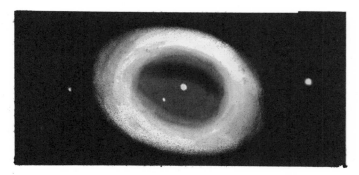

Ring Nebula:

A cloud of dust and gas which appears as a ring, surrounding one or more stars. The *Ring Nebula* in Lyra is actually a thin globe of dust and gas surrounding a star. It appears as a ring because we can easily see through the thin shell of gas between us and the star, but as we look through the edge of the globe the gas and dust appear thicker; this is an optical effect.

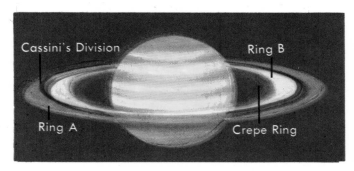

Rings of Saturn:

Billions of tiny globes of matter forming a thin disk around the planet Saturn. From outer edge to the opposite outer edge the rings measure about 171,000 miles and are between 10 and 40 miles thick. The outer ring, called *Ring A,* is 10,000 miles wide. Then there is a gap called *Cassini's Division,* which is 1700 miles wide. Next is *Ring B,* 16,000 miles wide, then *Ring C* (the Dusky or Crepe Ring) 10,000 miles wide; then another gap 9000 miles wide. The rings may have been formed long ago, when one of Saturn's moons ventured too close to the planet and was destroyed by Saturn's gravitational field; or the rings may have been formed from "leftover" material after Saturn itself was formed. The rings may be composed of tiny globes of rock encased in ice or frost.

Roche Limit:

If two bodies the size of planets come close enough to each other, the less dense planet will be broken apart by the gravitational field of the denser planet. The closest any two such bodies may approach one another without one being destroyed by the other is called the *Roche limit.*

Rotation:

The motion of a body around its axis. The Sun and all of the planets rotate, the Earth completing one *rotation* about every twenty-four hours. (See Table of the Planets, Sun, and Moon, p. 90–91.)

S

S-stars:

Orange-red stars, not too common, with surface temperatures around 2600°C. Most of these stars are variable, and practically none is visible without a telescope. (See *A-stars* for additional information; also *Stars.*)

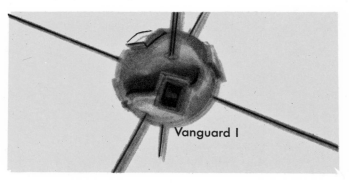

Satellite, Artificial:

Any man-made device that is placed into orbit around the Earth, Sun, or planets.

Satellites, Natural:

The natural moons of the planets. Or the planets themselves can be considered satellites of the Sun.

Scattering of Light:

When light passes through any medium, it is scattered by tiny particles making up the medium. 1. *Reflection*—When particles making up the medium are large compared with the wave length of light, the particles act as mirrors and so reflect the light in every direction. 2. *Scattering*—When particles making up the medium are small compared with the wave length of light, the particles scatter light in every direction, the amount of scattering depending on the wave length of the light. Molecules of the air scatter blue light more than red light, hence the blue color of the sky.

Schmidt Telescope:

(See p. 109.)

(See p. 109.)

Scintillation:

The apparent twinkling of the stars.

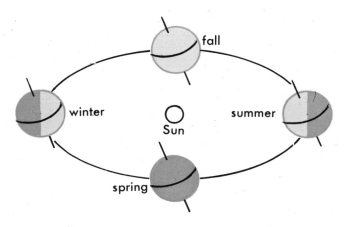

Seasons:

Because the Earth's axis is tilted with respect to the plane of its orbit, parts of the planet at certain times receive the Sun's rays more directly than other parts. When the north pole of the axis is tilted away from the Sun, the Northern Hemisphere receives the Sun's rays at an angle; we call this period winter. When the north pole is tilted toward the Sun, the Northern Hemisphere receives the Sun's rays in a direct line; we call this period summer. Many people think that summer and winter are determined by the distance of the Earth from the Sun, but this is not so. Actually, in winter in the Northern Hemisphere the Earth is closer to the Sun than it is in summer.

Selenography:

Study of the Moon's surface.

Sexagesimal:

Based on the division of a circle into 360 degrees, each degree subdivided into 60 minutes, and each minute further subdivided into 60 seconds.

Sextant:

An instrument used at sea to measure the altitude of celestial bodies.

Shell Stars:

Stars enclosed by a thin shell of gas which, in some cases, has been thrown off by the stars' rapid rotation.

Shooting Stars:

Another name for meteors.

Sidereal Month:

(See *Month*.)

Sidereal Period:

The length of time it takes a planet or any of the satellites to make one trip around their primaries with reference to the stars.

Sidereal Time:

The passage of time measured by the apparent motion of stars across the celestial sphere. *Sidereal time* is faster than solar time, a sidereal day consisting of only 23 hours, 56 minutes, 4 seconds, compared with a solar day of 24 hours. (See *Day*.)

Sidereal Year:

(See *Year*.)

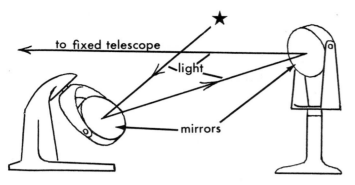

Siderostat:

An arrangement of flat mirrors that track a star as it moves across the sky. The mirrors reflect the star's image into a stationary telescope. *Siderostats* are used during field trips when it is inconvenient to set up an elaborate telescope mounting system with a clock drive.

Aries   Taurus   Gemini   Cancer

Leo   Virgo   Libra   Scorpius

Sagittarius   Capricornus   Aquarius   Pisces

Signs of the Zodiac:

The twelve constellations which lie along the Sun's path across the heavens: 1. *Aries* (the Ram); 2. *Taurus* (the Bull); 3. *Gemini* (the Twins); 4. *Cancer* (the Crab); 5. *Leo* (the Lion); 6. *Virgo* (the Virgin); 7. *Libra* (the Balance); 8. *Scorpio* (the Scorpion); 9. *Sagittarius* (the Archer); 10. *Capricorn* (the Goat); 11. *Aquarius* (the Water Bearer); 12. *Pisces* (the Fish).

Small Circle:

On a sphere, any circle whose plane does not pass through the center of the sphere. With the exception of the equator, all the circles forming the planes of latitude are *small circles*.

Solar:

Relating to the Sun.

Solar Cycle:

The days of the week do not fall on the same calendar-numbered days in successive years. Once every twenty-eight Julian years, however, the days of the week do have the same calendar numbers.

Solar Day:

The length of time between two successive Sun crossings of the observer's meridian, measured from noon to noon or midnight to midnight. (See *Day.*)

Solar System:

The *solar system* is made up of one star (the Sun) with nine planets having a total of thirty-one known moons, plus many other bodies—comets, meteors, and the asteroids.

Solar Time:

The passage of time measured by the apparent motion of the Sun across a given meridian.

Solar Tower Telescope:

(See p. 110.)

Solar Year:

(See *Tropical Year.*)

Solstice:

The highest and lowest points from the celestial equator reached by the Sun as it travels along the ecliptic. The northernmost point is called *summer solstice* (June 22); the southernmost point is called *winter solstice* (December 22). The *summer solstice* point lies in Gemini and the *winter solstice* point lies in Sagittarius. At these points the Sun appears to stand still momentarily—hence "solstice."

South Tropical Disturbance:

A feature (not understood) seen in Jupiter's atmosphere. It lies between the planet's equator and the Great Red Spot, is about 45,000 miles long, and moves faster than the Red Spot, passing it once every two years or so.

Specific Gravity:

The weight relationship between any substance and an equal volume of water. When we say that the *specific gravity* of the Earth is 5.5, we mean that the Earth weighs five and a half times more than a globe of water the same size as the Earth. *Specific gravity* is expressed as a pure number, while density is expressed in grams per cubic centimeter.

Spectral Class of Stars:

By examining the spectrum of a star, astronomers can classify the star. Stellar spectra consist of bright continuous backgrounds crossed by many dark fine lines called absorption lines. Those stars whose spectral lines are similar are placed in the same class. The classes are designated by the letters O, B, A, F, G, K, M. In this lettered sequence the stars grow cooler from O to M. To classify a star, all the astronomer does is examine the star with a spectroscope; then he matches the dark lines in the star's spectrum with the dark lines typical of the B, F, K, or whatever group has those representative lines. There are in addition R, N, and S stars, but these are considered subtypes since they so closely resemble K and M stars. (See *Main Sequence, Mass-Luminosity Curve, Spectrum,* and *Wolf-Rayet Stars.*)

Spectroheliogram:

A photograph of the Sun made in monochromatic light. Such photographs show the Sun's faculae and prominences.

Spectroheliograph:

An instrument used for making spectroheliograms.

Spectrohelioscope:

An instrument like the spectroheliograph, but which is used for visual rather than photographic observations.

Spectrogram:

A photograph of a star's spectrum.

Spectrograph:

An instrument used to photograph the spectrum of a star.

Spectroscope:

1. *Prism*—an instrument fitted with a prism that separates the star's light into its individual colors, or spectrum. 2. *Diffraction Grating*—a spectroscope fitted not with a prism but with a grooved, polished glass surface with as many as 30,000 grooves to the inch. When a star's light falls on this grating, the different colors making up the light are diffracted at different angles and so form a spectrum. A *diffraction grating* spectrum of a star is sharper than a *prism* spectrum. (See pp. 110, 111.)

Spectrum:

1. *Dark Line* or *Absorption Spectrum*—a spectrum or bar of colored light of a celestial body crossed by dark lines. These dark lines are due to the presence of the atoms of various elements at a lower temperature than the main source emitting the light. For example, the solar spectrum is an absorption spectrum. The Sun's photosphere gives a bright, continuous bar of colors, but slightly cooler gases lying above the photosphere absorb energy at certain wave lengths and thus give rise to dark lines; 2. *Absorption Band Spectrum*—a spectrum crossed by dark bands. Such a spectrum is formed in a similar way to a *line spectrum* but the cooler gas is, in this case, made of molecules that give rise to bands instead of lines, as do separate atoms. 3. *Bright-Line Spectra*—In some stars the atmospheres are so hot that their atoms emit bright lines. The spectrum produced then consists of a continuous bright background crossed by still brighter lines.

Spectrum Analysis:

Determining what chemical elements are present in a star by examining the spectrum of the star.

Speed of Light:

About 186,300 miles a second.

Sphere:

A globe having every point on its surface at an equal distance from the center of the globe.

Spheroid:

A globe formed by rotating an ellipse around one of its axes. If it is rotated around its major axis, the globe formed will be a *prolate spheroid;* if around its minor axis, it will be an *oblate spheroid.*

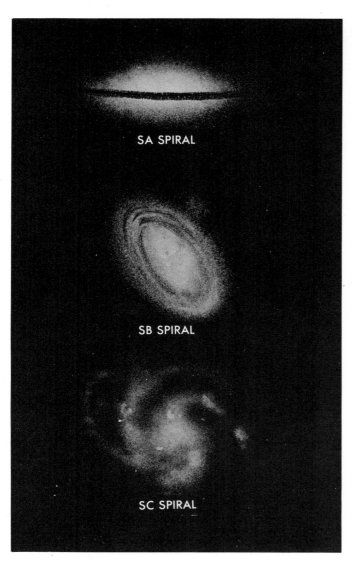

SA SPIRAL

SB SPIRAL

SC SPIRAL

Spiral Galaxies:

These make up the brightest groups of visible stars. They have a dense nucleus with less dense spiral arms winding outward. The Milky Way and the galaxy in Andromeda are both *spirals.* Hubble has classified the *spirals* as follows: those with a bright nucleus and dim arms are called *Sa spirals;* those with an equally bright nucleus and arms are termed *Sb;* those with bright arms and a dim nucleus are called *Sc.* The *spirals* are tipped at every angle in space so that we see some edge on, others flat, and still others tilted between these two positions.

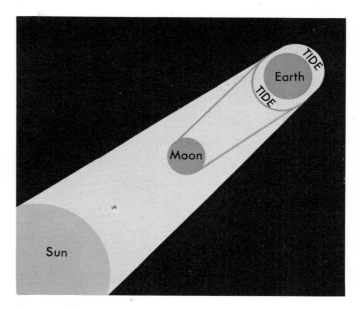

Spring Tides:

When the gravitational attraction of the Sun and Moon are in line (at new moon and full moon) we have *spring tides.* (See *Neap Tides.*)

Standard Time:

The time shown on your watch, depending on which time zone you live in. The time zones are set up east and west of the prime meridian at Greenwich, England. Traveling in a westward direction from Greenwich, you add one hour for every 15° of longitude you cross. From Greenwich to New York you cross five such time zones, so there is a five-hour difference in the standard times of the two places. *Eastern Standard Time* is called the (+5) zone because you add five hours; *Central Standard* (+6); *Rocky Mountain Standard* (+7); *Pacific Standard* (+8).

Stars:

Hot, glowing globes of gas, which shine by their own light. The Sun is a typical, and the closest, star. Most stars are tremendously large, compared with the planets; they contain enough matter to make a million or more Earths. Stars generate their energy not by chemical means, but by nuclear reactions not unlike those in a hydrogen bomb. Spectral analysis of the main sequence of stars has given us the following data: *O-stars*—prominent lines of ionized helium; *B-stars*—strong hydrogen lines, neutral helium; *A-stars*—strong hydrogen lines in the hotter A-stars, but lines associated with the metals begin to appear with the cooler A-stars, also ionized calcium; *F-stars*—weaker hydrogen lines, strong lines of ionized calcium; *G-stars*—still weaker hydrogen lines, stronger metals, strong ionized calcium traces of molecules; *K-stars*—weaker ionized calcium line. (See *O-stars, B-stars, A-stars, F-stars, G-stars, K-stars, M-stars.* See also *Magnitude of Stars, Main Sequence, Mass-Luminosity Curve, Spectral Class of Stars.*)

Star Clusters:
(See *Clusters.*)

Stationary Point:
The orbital position of a planet when it appears not to be moving among the stars; this is an effect due to the relative motions of the Earth and the planet.

Steady State Theory:
The astronomers Hermann Bondi, Thomas Gold, and Fred Hoyle have advanced the idea that the population of galaxies in space remains fairly constant throughout time. As old galaxies die, new ones are born ". . . at such a rate that their average density in space remains unaltered with time."

Stellar:
Relating to the stars.

Stereograms:
Photographs of the Moon taken at different times of libration. When seen through a stereoscope, they give the appearance of a spherical globe.

Summer Solstice:
(See *Solstice.*)

Sun:
The name of the star closest to the Earth, and the primary body around which all of the planets revolve. (See Table of the Planets, Sun, and Moon, p. 90–91.)

Sundial:
An instrument which records the passage of time by means of a plate mounted on a graduated plat-form. As the Sun moves across the sky, the shadow cast by the plate shortens and lengthens. The constantly changing position of the shadow over the graduated surface indicates the passage of time.

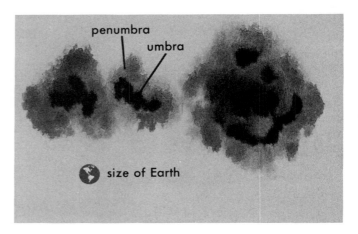

penumbra
umbra
size of Earth

Sunspots:
Great dark spots (up to 60,000 miles across) that break out periodically in varying numbers on the Sun's surface. Maximum activity occurs in periods of 11.1 years. Most of the spots appear about a third of the way between the Sun's equator and poles and have a life from only a few hours up to several days. They are thought to be great outbursts of gases that break out from deep inside the Sun. As the outrushing clouds of gas rise high above the Sun's surface, they cool and so appear dark against the lighter surface of hotter gases. Whenever a storm of *sunspots* occurs it is followed by magnetic disturbances within the Earth's atmosphere.

Supergiant Stars:
Enormous stars with a high luminosity. (See *Giant Stars.*)

Superior Conjunction:
(See *Conjunction.*)

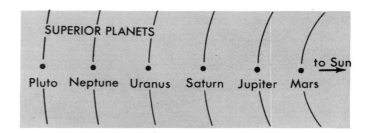

SUPERIOR PLANETS
Pluto   Neptune   Uranus   Saturn   Jupiter   Mars   to Sun

Superior Planets:
Those planets from Mars outward that lie at a greater distance from the Sun than the Earth.

Crab Nebula

Supernova:

A star whose brightness is tremendously increased by a catastrophic explosion. *Supernova* stars are about 10,000 times brighter than ordinary novae. Their absolute magnitude is around −16 or −17. In a single second a *supernova* releases as much energy as the Sun does over a period of sixty years. The *supernova* of the year 1572 could be seen clearly in daylight. In 1054 a star was observed to become a *supernova;* its remains today are what we call the Crab Nebula—a white dwarf star surrounded by a great bright cloud of gas and dust. No one fully knows what causes *supernovae.*

Synodical Month:

(See *Lunation.*)

Synodic Period:

The time between two successive conjunctions or oppositions of a planet.

Synodic Year:

(See *Year.*)

System:

One or more celestial objects which revolve about another. A double star forms a *binary system.*

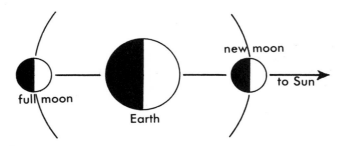

Syzygy:

Whenever the Moon is full or new; that is, when it is in conjunction with or in opposition to the Sun.

T

Telescope (astronomical):

An optical instrument used to view celestial objects. In principle it has two parts: 1. an objective lens or mirror which gathers light from a star (or other source) and brings the light to a focus as a tiny image; and 2. an eyepiece which enlarges the image. Because an astronomer wants to use as few lenses as possible in his instrument, an astronomical telescope always shows an inverted image.

Telescope Drive:

A device which moves a telescope slowly to keep pace with the apparent motion of the stars. With a *telescope drive* the observer does not have to move his telescope continuously to keep a given star in the field of view.

Temperature:

A measure of how hot or cold a body is. "Hotness" and "coldness" are determined by the atomic or molecular motion within a substance. The faster the molecules move, the hotter the substance is.

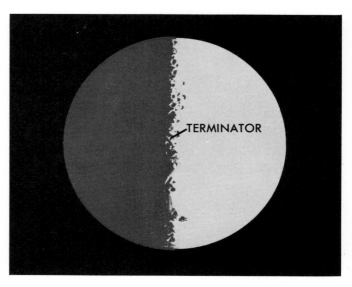

TERMINATOR

Terminator:

The line which divides the light and dark portions of a planet or satellite. At half moon the *terminator* is the line dividing the Moon's disk down the middle.

Terrestrial:

Relating to the Earth.

Theodolite:

A small telescope accurately mounted so that it can measure, with great precision, the altitude and azimuth of an object.

Thermocouple:

An instrument that measures heat from the stars. It consists of two wires each made of a different metal. Small amounts of heat from distant stars or planets can be detected by the wires. Where the wires are in contact, a voltage is set up when a star's heat strikes them. The greater the heat, the higher the voltage. A sensitive galvanometer is used to measure the voltage.

Certain regions of the world have daily tides of twenty feet or more.

Tides:

The rise and fall each day of the Earth's oceans, caused by gravitational attraction of the Moon and Sun. If the Moon were poised permanently above the Pacific Ocean, a great bulge of water would pile up there. But because the Moon moves across the sky, it pulls the bulge of water behind it. When the bulge approaches the shore, we say that we have a *high tide;* and when the bulge is pulled away from the shore we say that we have a *low tide*. Because of its greater distance from us, the Sun's ability to raise tides is only one third that of the Moon's. (See *Neap Tides* and *Spring Tides*.)

Tidal Friction:

The tendency of the tides to slow down the Earth's rotation, but the effect is very small.

Total Eclipse:

(See *Eclipse*.)

Transit:

Whenever Venus and Mercury cross the Sun's disk they are said to be in *transit;* also of satellites when they cross the disk of their primaries. *Transits* of stars occur when a star crosses the observer's meridian.

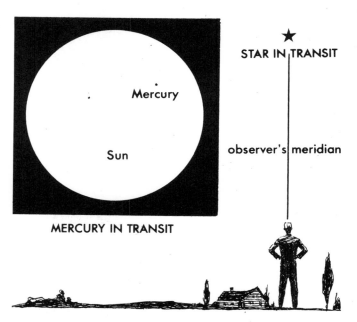

Transit Instrument:

A telescope (mounted so that it points due north and south) having hairlines in the eyepiece so that the observer can measure the exact instant a star crosses his meridian.

Tropical Year:

(See *Year*.)

True Horizon:

(See *Dip of Horizon*.)

True Sun:

The Sun we see in the sky; the term is used to distinguish it from the mean sun.

Twilight:

The hours between sunset and dark and between sunrise and the appearance of the Sun over the horizon. *Astronomical twilight* is that period when the Sun is less than 18° below the horizon.

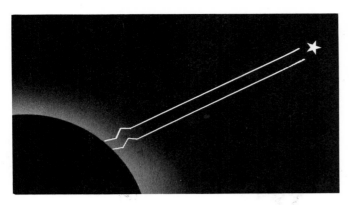

Twinkling:
The stars appear to change color and twinkle. This effect is caused by our seeing them through the Earth's atmosphere, which is in constant motion.

U

Umbra:
(See *Penumbra.*)

Universal Time:
The time used by astronomers when they record data. It is the same as *Greenwich Mean Time*.

Universe:
All that is contained in the vast expanse of space around us.

V

Variable Stars:
A star that is not uniform in its brightness; one that becomes bright (reaching "maximum") then grows dim (reaching "minimum"), repeating the cycle over a period of hours or years. *Variable stars* without proper names are given one or two letters with their constellation name following: for example, W Virginis and RV Tauri. Others are given the letter V followed by numbers and their constellation name: for example, V335 Sagitarii. 1. *Pulsating Variables*—These include many groups: a. *Beta Canis Majoris Stars* have short periods of only an hour or two. They are B-stars and are not too common; b. *Cluster Variables* have periods from one and a half to twenty-four hours and are white giants; c. *Classical Cepheids* are yellow supergiants with periods from one to forty-five days and are among the brightest of stars, with absolute magni-

tudes smaller than −2. *Type II Cepheids* generally have periods of sixteen to seventeen days; d. *RV Tauri Stars* have periods usually less than 100 days and are less regular than the Cepheids; e. *Long-Period Variables* are the red giants or supergiants having periods between 100 days and 1000 days. One cycle of these stars may differ considerably from the next cycle. 2. *Explosive Variables*— See *Nova* and *Supernova.* 3. *Irregular Variables*— These include two groups of stars: a. *Flare Stars* are found among many red, main-sequence stars. Within five minutes these stars throw off great flares in a violent display, increasing their brightness by one magnitude. Their outbursts are not predictable; b. *T Tauri Stars* grow bright and dim without warning. They all are associated with clouds of dust and gas which they seem to be drawing into themselves. When an excessive amount of the material is drawn to the star, the star brightens. All the *irregular variables* are red giant stars.

Variation:
A changing velocity in the Moon's motion caused by gravitational attraction of the Sun. The Moon moves fastest during full moon and new moon; slowest when it is in its first and last quarters.

Velocity:
The speed of a body in a given direction.

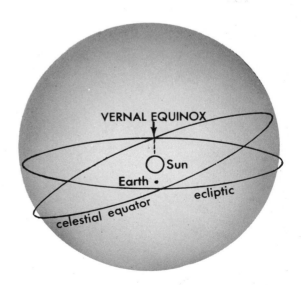

Vernal Equinox:
March 21, when the hours of sunlight and darkness are very nearly the same.

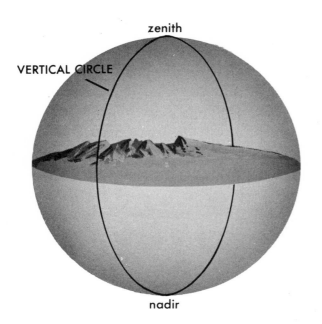

zenith

VERTICAL CIRCLE

nadir

Vertical Circle:

On the celestial sphere, a circle that passes through the zenith and nadir.

Violet Shift:

When the light from a star is examined through a spectroscope and the dark lines in its spectrum crowd up toward the violet, or short-wave end, it means that the star is moving toward us. (See *Red Shift* and *Doppler Effect*.)

W

W-stars:

(See *Wolf-Rayet Stars*.)

bright portion faces east

Waning Moon:

When the Moon's visible lighted portion grows smaller; that period between full moon and new moon.

Wave Length:

The distance between two successive "crests" or "valleys" of a wave of any sort. *Wave length* is found by dividing the velocity of a wave by its frequency.

bright portion faces west

Waxing Moon:

When the Moon's visible lighted portion is increasing; that period between new moon and full moon.

White Dwarfs:

(See *Dwarf Stars*.)

Winter Solstice:

(See *Solstice*.)

Wolf-Rayet Stars:

Stars associated with the early main sequence. Blue white, they are very hot stars with surface temperatures around 50,000°C. or more and belong to spectral class W.

Y

Year:

1. *Anomalistic Year*—the time between two successive passages of the Sun through the perigee of the Earth's orbit. An *Anomalistic Year* has 365 days, 6 hours, 13 minutes, 53 seconds. 2. *Civil Year*—the year shown on our calendars as having 365 days; but since there are 365¼ days we add a day once every four years and call that year Leap Year (see *Leap Year*). 3. *Sidereal Year*—the length of time it takes the Earth to make one trip around the Sun and return to the same position among the fixed

stars as seen from the Sun. A *Sidereal Year* has 365 days, 6 hours, 9 minutes, 9 seconds. 4. *Lunar Year*—12 lunar months having 354 days, 8 hours, 48 minutes, 34 seconds. 5. *Tropical Year*—the time between two successive passages of the Sun through the vernal equinox or First Point of Aries. A *Tropical Year* has 365 days, 5 hours, 48 minutes, 46 seconds (mean solar days); or 366 days, 5 hours, 48 minutes, 46 seconds (sidereal days).

Z

Zenith:

The point on the celestial sphere directly above the observer's head.

Zenith Distance:

The angular distance of a celestial object from the zenith of the observer.

Zenith Telescope:

A specially mounted telescope for accurately determining the zenith passage of a star.

Zodiac:

The zone stretching around the sky along the ecliptic. The Moon, Sun, and most of the planets revolve about the Sun in this zone.

Zodiacal Light:

A faint band of light stretching all along the ecliptic, the brightest part being near the Sun. The light may be sunlight reflected by a disk of space matter (possibly small meteors) stretching out around the Sun. It is best seen in clear air late in the evening in March and September. (See also *Gegenschein*.)

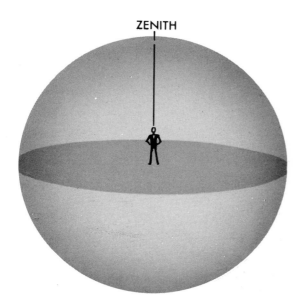

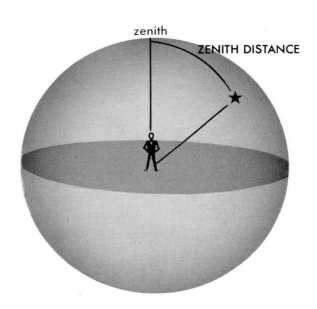

How to Use the Star Maps

On the following pages you will find six maps of the sky. They will familiarize you with the stars and constellations and show you how to locate sky objects quickly.

Most of the stars are identified by Greek letters (see page 121). You will also see two names for each constellation—its proper name and its Latin genitive. The Greek letters and Latin genitives are given because astronomers usually write about the stars by their "formal" names; for instance, the star Betelgeuse in Orion is known as Alpha Orionis.

All of the maps have been worked out for 9 P.M., but can easily be adjusted for earlier or later hours. Remember that during Daylight Saving Time your clock is moved ahead by one hour, so 9 P.M. Standard Time would be 10 P.M. Daylight Saving Time.

The maps show hour lines, which can be subdivided into 60 minutes; and minute lines, which can be subdivided into 60 seconds. These are called lines of *right ascension* (see dictionary terms) and correspond to lines of *longitude* on a map of the earth. The degree lines are also marked on the maps. Each degree can be subdivided into 60 minutes of arc ('). These are called lines of *declination* and correspond to the lines of *latitude* on a map of the Earth.

When you know the R.A. and Dec. (called *co-ordinates*) of any object in the sky, you can find it on a map. For example, on page 75 there is a photograph of **M 31,** the Andromeda Galaxy, with its co-ordinates listed. On your autumn star map first find 0ʰ40ᵐ then look down the map to 41°0' and you will find the position of **M 31.**

The seasonal maps show the line of the *ecliptic* —the apparent path the Sun follows across the sky. It is convenient to know which constellations fall on the ecliptic. Also, the planets very closely follow the ecliptic as they move across the sky.

The first map on these pages shows the stars that circle the *north celestial pole*. The twelve months of the year and the numbers from 0ʰ to 23ʰ appear around the edge of the map. These numbers represent 24 hours. For our purposes, one hour's time on the map is the same as an hour on our clock. But don't confuse the actual number of the hour with the time on your clock.

Let's say that it is 9 P.M. on an April evening. Face north and hold the map overhead with April at the very top. A weak flashlight, or one covered with red cellophane, will help you to read it more easily. You will see the stars in the sky arranged just as they are on the map. At 10 P.M. the map should be turned counterclockwise by one hour; at 11 P.M., by two hours, and so on. As the hours go by, you will see that the stars appear to be turning around the north celestial pole as you turn the chart in your hands.

The next four maps join the north circumpolar map at 50°N. Just as 9 P.M. was chosen as a convenient time, these maps are arranged by seasons for convenience. But, as the stars are steadily moving across the sky from east to west, you will no doubt use more than one map in an evening's observing. For instance, in the course of a long winter night you could see about two thirds of the constellations which are visible from your latitude and which appear on the maps.

To match a map to the stars in the sky, face south and hold the map overhead with the proper month of the year at the bottom of the page. If it is 9 P.M., the stars overhead will match the map. If it is 7 P.M., the stars directly overhead will be two hours to the right on the map. If it is 11 P.M., the stars overhead will be shown on the map two hours to the left.

The last map shows the stars that go around the *south celestial pole*. This map is used in the same way as the north circumpolar one with one exception. As the observer faces the south celestial pole (which, of course, can't be seen from the Northern Hemisphere), the stars will appear to be turning clockwise around the pole instead of counterclockwise as in the north.

Following each map are photographs of a few

spectacular objects found in the region of the sky shown by the map. Their co-ordinates are given under the photograph, and as you look back at the maps you can see exactly where each object is located, even though you cannot observe most of them without binoculars or a telescope.

The letter M stands for Messier (see glossary); NGC (New General Catalog); and IC (Index Catalog). The latter two are more recent systems of numbering celestial objects.

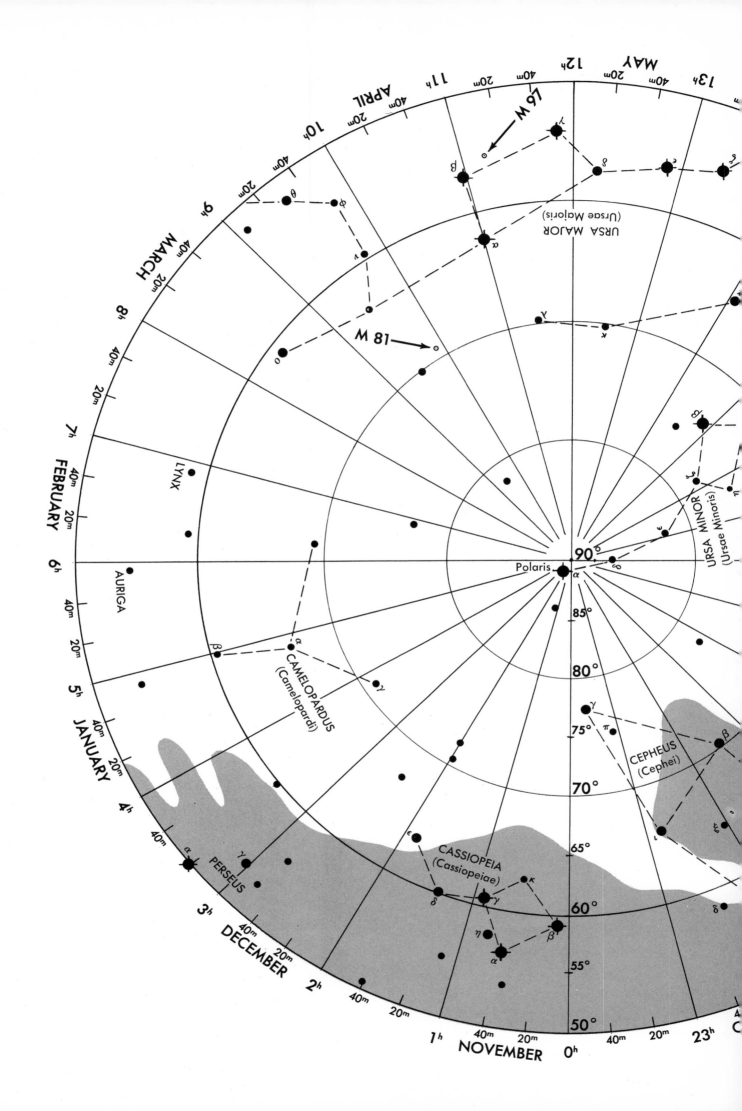

North Circumpolar Stars

For people who live in the northern latitudes, the north circumpolar constellations have no seasons. You can see them all at any time of the year, even though they are constantly changing position as they circle the celestial pole.

The north celestial pole is well marked by Polaris, a second-magnitude star in the Little Dipper. You can get your bearings outdoors instantly by locating the Pole Star. The Big Dipper, which is always easy to find, has two stars at the end of the bowl (Beta and Alpha) which point toward Polaris. The second star in the handle of the Dipper is an interesting naked-eye double star. Mizar, the bright star, is accompanied by Alcor, which can be seen faintly.

Although these two constellations are commonly referred to as "Dippers," they are Ursa Major and Ursa Minor, the Great Bear and the Little Bear.

Draco, the Dragon, winds in an S-curve through a large part of the sky, its tail tracing a line between the Dippers. It has no brilliant stars, but its shape can be seen quite distinctly.

Cepheus, the King, though not especially prominent, offers some interesting double stars and variables to watch.

One of the easiest constellations to find is Cassiopeia, the Queen, whose five major stars take the shape of a wide W or M. There are some fine clusters to be seen in this area with binoculars. It was in this constellation that a brilliant nova created much excitement in 1572. This new star appeared suddenly and became so bright that it could be seen even in the daytime, but by 1574 it had faded from sight.

```
KEY TO MAP
◉   1-1½ MAGNITUDE
✦   2-2½ MAGNITUDE
●   3-3½ MAGNITUDE
•   4-4½ MAGNITUDE
○   OTHER INTERESTING OBJECTS
SHADED AREAS REPRESENT MILKY WAY
```

M 81, NGC 3031, a bright spiral galaxy in Ursa Major with a brilliant nucleus and rather faint arms; taken with the 200-inch telescope.

R.A. 9ʰ 51ᵐ Dec. 69° 18′

M 81 taken with the 48-inch Schmidt. Below it can be seen **NGC 2976** and **3077.** Above it is **NGC 3034** or **M 82.** These two **M**-objects are impressive when viewed with low power because they can be seen in the same field.

R.A. 14ʰ 01ᵐ Dec. 54° 35′

M 101, NGC 5457, is a large and faint spiral galaxy in Ursa Major; taken with the 200-inch telescope.

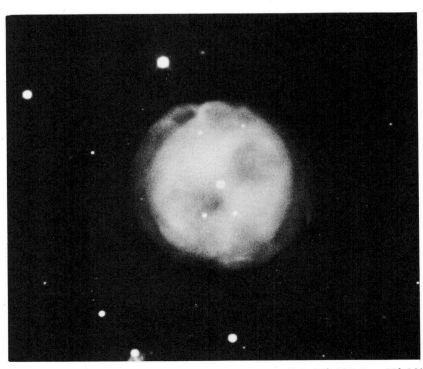

M 97, NGC 3587, the Owl Nebula in Ursa Major, photographed with a 60-inch telescope.

R.A. 11ʰ 12ᵐ Dec. 55° 18′

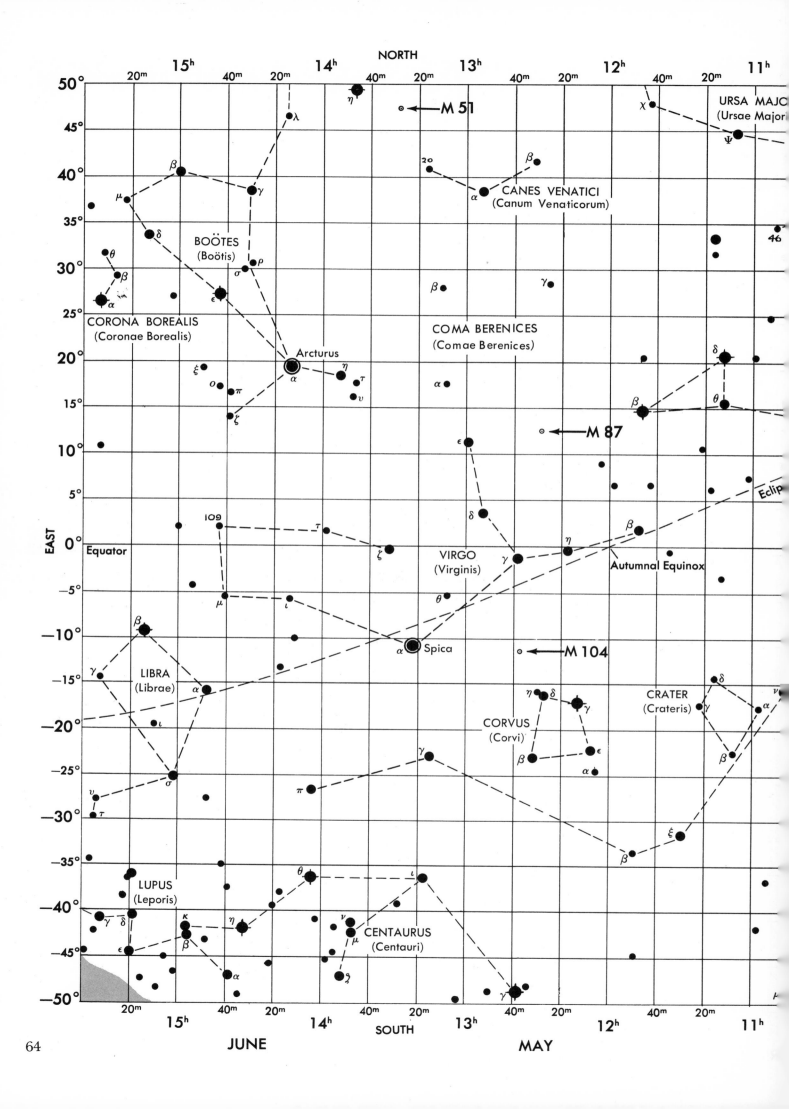

(star chart — left side)

10ʰ 20ᵐ 40ᵐ 20ᵐ 9ʰ 40ᵐ

λ
μ
31
21
O MINOR
(onis Minoris)
α
LYNX
(Lyncis)
κ ι

ι
CANCER
(Cancri)
μ
ε
ζ
γ
η
γ
δ
α

LEO
(eonis)
Regulus
α

ζ ε δ
θ η σ
ι
HYDRA
(Hydrae)
α
υ²
υ¹
μ

γ
PYXIS
(Pyxidis)
α
ANTLIA
(Antliae)
ε
β

Ψ
VELA
(Velorum)
λ

20ᵐ 40ᵐ 20ᵐ 40ᵐ
10ʰ 9ʰ

RIL

Stars of Spring

The appearance of Leo, the Lion, in the eastern sky is a welcome sign of spring. As the constellation swings higher in the sky, it dominates the southern heavens with its distinctive triangle and sickle. At the base of the sickle is Regulus, a first-magnitude blue-white star; and the eastmost star in the triangle is Denebola, (Beta Leonis) a second-magnitude star.

To the southeast of Leo lies Virgo, a constellation most notable for its brilliant blue star, Spica. South of Virgo and Leo, Hydra, the Sea Serpent, winds across the southern sky. It is the longest constellation in the sky, stretching 120°, or one third of the way around the heavens.

Two small, but interesting, constellations lie almost within the curve of Hydra. Corvus, the Crow, looks like an uneven square. When this constellation reaches its high point in the sky, about mid-May, the beautiful Southern Cross appears near the horizon. But to view it you must be far south in the United States. Directly west of Corvus is Crater, the Cup, a faint constellation of fourth-magnitude stars.

A bit northeast of Denebola in Leo is a lovely open star cluster with the delightful name of Coma Berenices, or Berenice's Hair. On a clear, dark night it can be seen as a dim patch of stars. Through binoculars it is an impressive sight and fills the whole field with separate stars.

KEY TO MAP

 1-1½ MAGNITUDE
 2-2½ MAGNITUDE
 3-3½ MAGNITUDE
 4-4½ MAGNITUDE
○ OTHER INTERESTING OBJECTS
SHADED AREAS REPRESENT MILKY WAY

M 87, NGC 4486, a globular galaxy in Virgo, taken with the 200-inch telescope. This field is rich with distant galaxies which can be identified only with a telescope.

Photographs: Mount Wilson and Palomar Observatories

M 104, NGC 4594, the Sombrero, is a spiral galaxy in Virgo, seen edge-on with the 200-inch telescope. The dark band is caused by dust and gas.

R.A. 12ʰ 28ᵐ Dec. 12° 40′

R.A. 12ʰ 37ᵐ Dec. −11° 20′

M 51, NGC 5194, the Whirlpool nebula in Canes Venatici, taken with the 200-inch telescope. In this unusual spiral system the satellite nebula appears to be whirling away from the main spiral.

R.A. 13ʰ 27ᵐ Dec. 47° 27′

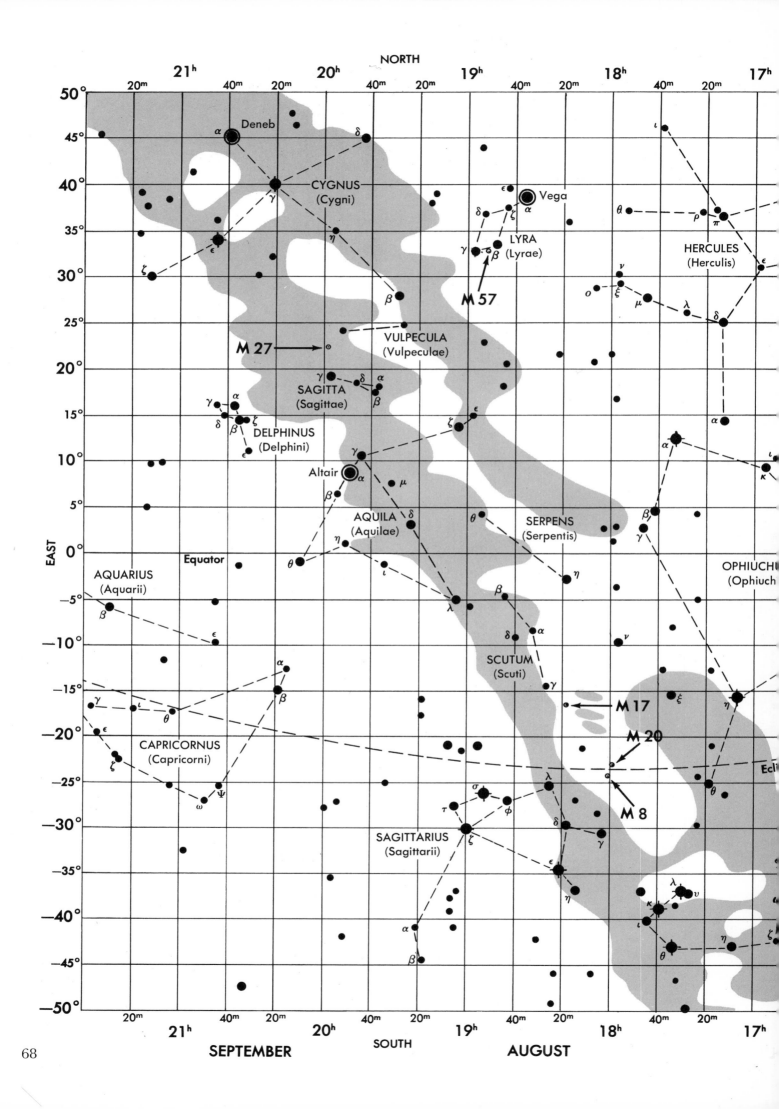

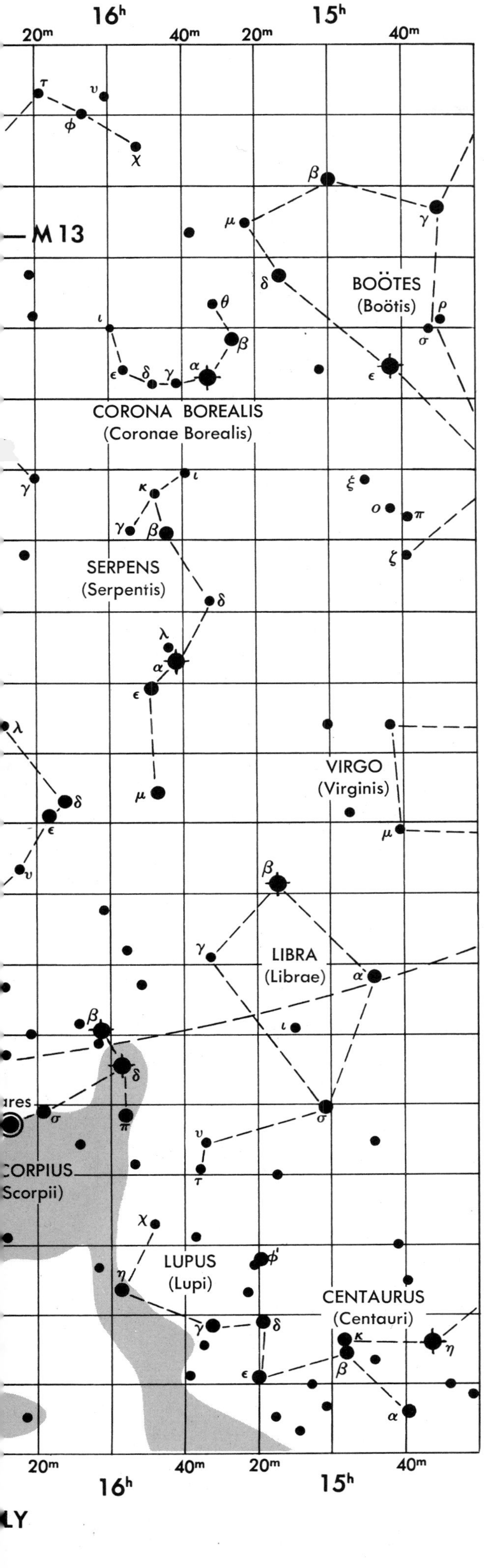

<!-- Star chart (left side) -->

16ʰ 20ᵐ 40ᵐ 20ᵐ 15ʰ 40ᵐ

τ υ
φ
χ

β
γ

— M 13
μ δ
θ **BOÖTES**
(Boötis)
ι ρ
β σ
ε δ γ α ε
CORONA BOREALIS
(Coronae Borealis)

ι
γ κ
ξ
ο π
γ β ζ
SERPENS
(Serpentis)
δ

λ
α
ε

λ
VIRGO
(Virginis)
δ
ε μ
μ

ν
β
LIBRA
(Librae)
γ α
ι
β
δ
res
σ π σ
SCORPIUS
(Scorpii)
ν
τ

χ
φ'
η **LUPUS**
(Lupi)
γ δ κ
CENTAURUS
(Centauri)
ε β η

α

20ᵐ 40ᵐ 20ᵐ 40ᵐ
16ʰ 15ʰ
LY

Stars of Summer

Throughout the summer months the Milky Way stretches across the sky like a powdery, sparkling cloud. During this season you will find many interesting constellations and many first-magnitude stars.

Boötes, the Herdsman, is a prominent constellation because of its one bright star, Arcturus (see Stars of Spring map). Arcturus is a giant among stars—30 times our sun's diameter and 80 times brighter. East of Boötes is a pretty half circle of stars, Corona Borealis, the Northern Crown. You will also find Hercules, a sprawling constellation, its center being an uneven square formed by four stars. When you become familiar with this square, you can learn to locate **M 13** on it. It looks like a dim, hazy star, but is actually a great globular star cluster.

Perhaps the most beautiful star in the sky is the brilliant blue-white Vega in the constellation Lyra. Also in Lyra is the well known *double-double* star (Epsilon Lyrae), a double star which can be split into four stars with a telescope. Following Lyra across the sky is Cygnus, the Swan, sometimes called the Northern Cross. It is probably the most prominent figure in the summer sky, headed by its bright star Deneb. South of Cygnus is Aquila, the Eagle, notable for its bright star, Altair. North of Aquila are two fascinating little constellations called Sagitta, the Arrow, and Delphinus, the Dolphin.

Scorpius, the Scorpion, is easy to identify among the constellations in the southern sky. Its main feature is the giant red star, Antares. With binoculars, many beautiful star clusters and nebulae can be seen as faint gray patches in the area around Scorpius and Sagittarius.

KEY TO MAP

◉ 1-1½ MAGNITUDE
✦ 2-2½ MAGNITUDE
● 3-3½ MAGNITUDE
• 4-4½ MAGNITUDE
○ OTHER INTERESTING OBJECTS
SHADED AREAS REPRESENT MILKY WAY

R.A. 16^h 40^m Dec. 36° 33'

M 13, NGC 6205, in Hercules, is the finest globular cluster in the northern sky, probably comprised of more than 100,000 stars. It can barely be seen with the unaided eye but is a fine sight in a telescope.

M 20, NGC 6514, the Trifid Nebula in Sagittarius, is a diffuse galactic nebula strange in appearance because of the dark lanes dividing it into irregular sections.

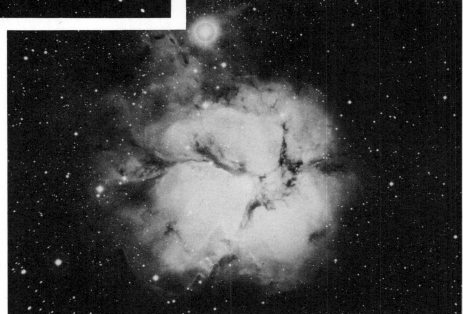

R.A. 17^h 59^m Dec. —23° 02'

M 8, NGC 6523, the great Lagoon Nebula in Sagittarius, is visible to the naked eye. This was taken with the 200-inch telescope.

Photographs: Mount Wilson and Palomar Observatories

R.A. 18^h 01^m Dec. —24° 23'

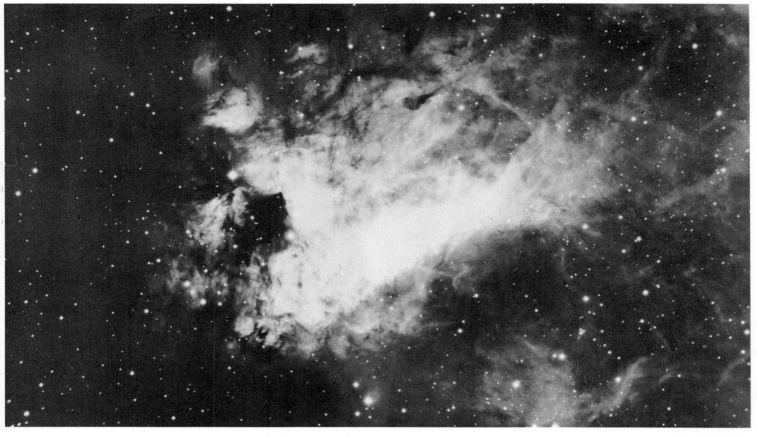

R.A. 18ʰ 18ᵐ Dec. —16° 12′

M 17, NGC 6618, the Horseshoe Nebula in Saggittarius, an area where the hunting is exceptionally good. There are many lovely clusters to be seen with binoculars or a small telescope.

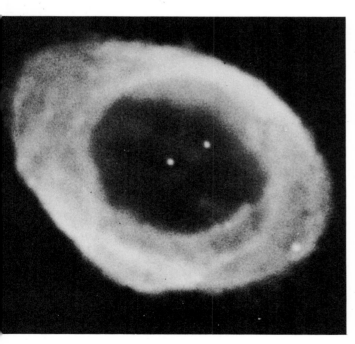

R.A. 18ʰ 52ᵐ Dec. 32° 58′

M 57, NGC 6720, the famous planetary Ring Nebula in Lyra. Although it looks like a smoke ring, it is really a gaseous shell caused by the explosion of the star in its center.

R.A. 19ʰ 58ᵐ Dec. 22° 35′

M 27, NGC 6835, the planetary Dumbbell Nebula in Vulpecula; taken with the 100-inch telescope. With low power it can be seen as two hazy patches of light.

71

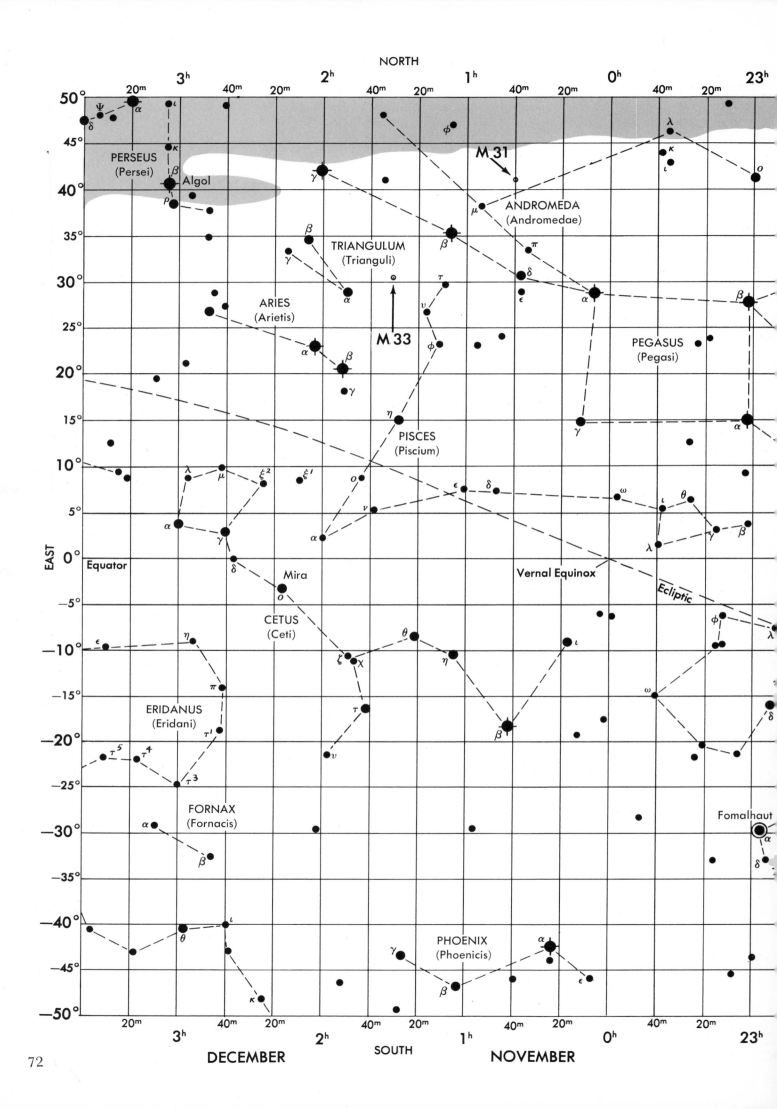

Stars of Autumn

Deneb α

CYGNUS
(Cygni) γ

π

ζ

ε

κ
ι

γ α
δ β ζ
ε

ε

DELPHINUS
(Delphini)

θ

π
ζ α
γ

QUARIUS
Aquarii)

β

ε

δ γ
ι
θ
ε

CAPRICORNUS
(Capricorni)

ζ

Ψ
ω

SCIS AUSTRINUS
(Piscis Austrini)

θ
β μ

GRUS α

The autumn constellations may not seem as spectacular as those of summer, but many of the summer figures, such as Cygnus, are really part of the autumn sky too.

Pegasus, the Winged Horse, is a prominent constellation, its main feature being the Great Square. In fact, the square takes up such a large part of the sky that you may have trouble locating it the first time. However, its four corners are clearly marked by bright stars. At first glance you might think that there are no stars inside the square, but you'll be surprised at how many you can count if you look closely.

Extending from the upper left corner of the square is the constellation Andromeda. It is here that you will find the Andromeda Galaxy—the great **M 31**. Although it appears only as a foggy patch, it is really a tremendous *spiral galaxy*, larger than the Milky Way.

To the south, Cetus, the Whale, has one especially notable feature. It has a "disappearing" star called Mira (a red *variable* star). In less than a year, Mira varies in brightness from a brilliant second-magnitude star to a tenth-magnitude star which can't be seen without a good telescope.

Low in the dim southern sky is one bright star. It is Fomalhaut, in the constellation Piscis Austrinus, the Southern Fish.

KEY TO MAP

- 1-1½ MAGNITUDE
- 2-2½ MAGNITUDE
- 3-3½ MAGNITUDE
- 4-4½ MAGNITUDE
- ○ OTHER INTERESTING OBJECTS
- SHADED AREAS REPRESENT MILKY WAY

R.A. 0^h 40^m Dec. 41° 0′

74

The central region of **M 31** taken with the 100-inch telescope in which the spiral structure can be seen in better detail.

M 33, NGC 598, a spiral galaxy in Triangulum offering a beautiful photographic subject for large instruments. This was taken with a 60-inch telescope.

◄

M 31, NGC 224, the Great Galaxy in Andromeda taken with the 48-inch Schmidt. It is visible to the naked eye and a most interesting object for telescopic study because of its similarity to our own galaxy. Both galaxies are spirals and nearly equal in size. The two small nebulae are satellites of **M 31.**

R.A. 1^h 31^m Dec. 30° 24'

75

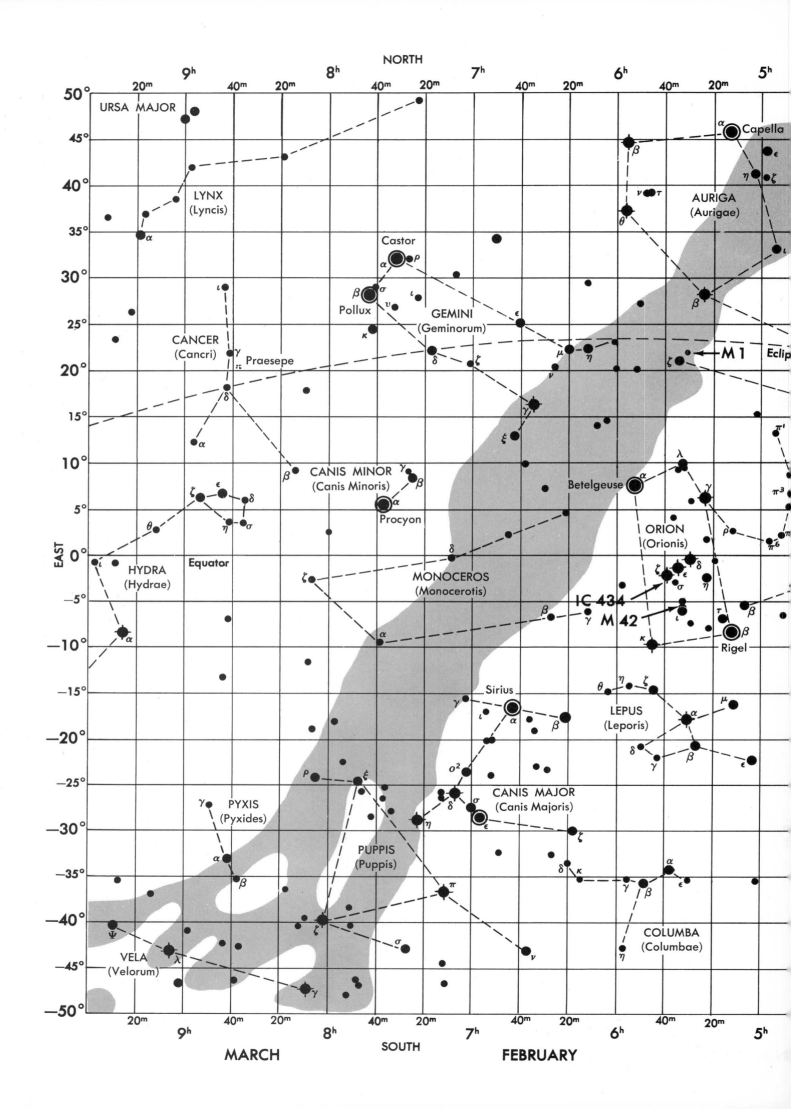

Star map showing constellations with coordinate grid.

Map labels (left page):

4ʰ 20ᵐ 40ᵐ 20ᵐ 3ʰ 40ᵐ

PERSEUS
(Persei)

δ
Ψ
α
ι
κ
β
Algol
ρ

ν
ε
ξ
ζ

M 45
Pleiades

ARIES
(Arietis)

Hyades
ε δ
TAURUS
θ (Tauri)
γ
ebaran

λ

ξ o

μ
λ CETUS
(Ceti)
α
γ
δ
ξ²

o¹
o²
δ ε η
γ
π
ERIDANUS
(Eridani)
τ¹

τ⁵ τ⁴
τ⁹ τ⁸ τ⁶
τ³
FORNAX
(Fornacis)
α
β

ι
θ
κ

NUARY

As the nights grow long, the winter sky offers a wealth of remarkable sights. Orion, the Hunter, has more bright stars than any other constellation. The two *supergiant* stars, Betelgeuse and Rigel, red and blue-white respectively, are diagonally opposite each other in the rectangle that forms the main figure. Across the center are the three bright stars of Orion's "belt," and hanging from the belt are the stars marking his "sword." What appears to be the middle star in the sword is the famed Great Nebula, **M 42**.

Northwest of Orion lies Taurus, the Bull, noted for its two lovely open star clusters. One, the Hyades, contains the first-magnitude star, Aldebaron. The Pleiades looks like a group of six small stars, but binoculars reveal many more. Taurus shares one star, (Beta Tauri) with the constellation Auriga, the Charioteer. Auriga is a five-sided figure featuring the brilliant yellow star, Capella, and many clusters that can be seen with binoculars.

Perseus, in the northwest though not one of the brightest constellations, has an interesting variable star, Algol, the "Demon Star." About every three days it dims, then returns to its original brightness.

Gemini, the Twins, lies east of Auriga and can easily be identified by its two bright stars, Castor and Pollux. East of Gemini is the faint constellation of Cancer, the Crab, with its lovely open cluster, **M 44,** or Praesepe.

Canis Major and Canis Minor, the Big Dog and the Little Dog, each has one bright star. The Little Dog star is called Procyon. The Big Dog star is Sirius, a blue star and the brightest in the whole sky.

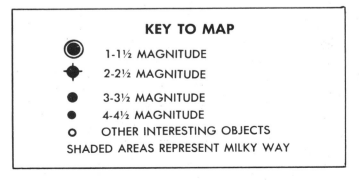

KEY TO MAP

◉	1-1½ MAGNITUDE
✦	2-2½ MAGNITUDE
●	3-3½ MAGNITUDE
•	4-4½ MAGNITUDE
○	OTHER INTERESTING OBJECTS

SHADED AREAS REPRESENT MILKY WAY

R.A. 03ʰ 44ᵐ Dec. 23° 57′

M 45, the Pleiades in Taurus, taken with the 18-inch Schmidt.

R.A. 05ʰ 32ᵐ Dec. 21° 59′

M 1, NGC 1952, the Crab Nebula in Taurus, taken with the 18-inch Schmidt.

R.A. 05ʰ 33ᵐ Dec. —05° 25′

M 42, NGC 1976, the Great Nebula in Orion, taken with the 100-inch telescope. This is one of the few nebulae that can be seen with the naked eye. With-out optical aid, it looks like a star. In the photo on the opposite page the nebulosity is faintly visible.

R.A. 05ʰ 39ᵐ Dec. —02° 10′

IC 434, the Horsehead Nebula in Orion, taken with the 200-inch telescope.

The same Horsehead Nebula surrounding Zeta Orionis, photographed with the Schmidt 18-inch camera. Note the triangle of bright stars.

Photographs on facing page and above: Mount Wilson and Palomar Observatories. Left: Photograph by John Polgreen.

A time exposure of Orion taken with an ordinary camera equipped with a clock drive. Notice the four main stars of the rectangle and the belt and sword. The outlined section represents the same area as photo above, right. Though there is no indication of the "Horsehead," you can see its exact location by comparing the pictures. The arrow points to M 42, the Great Nebula (see photo on opposite page).

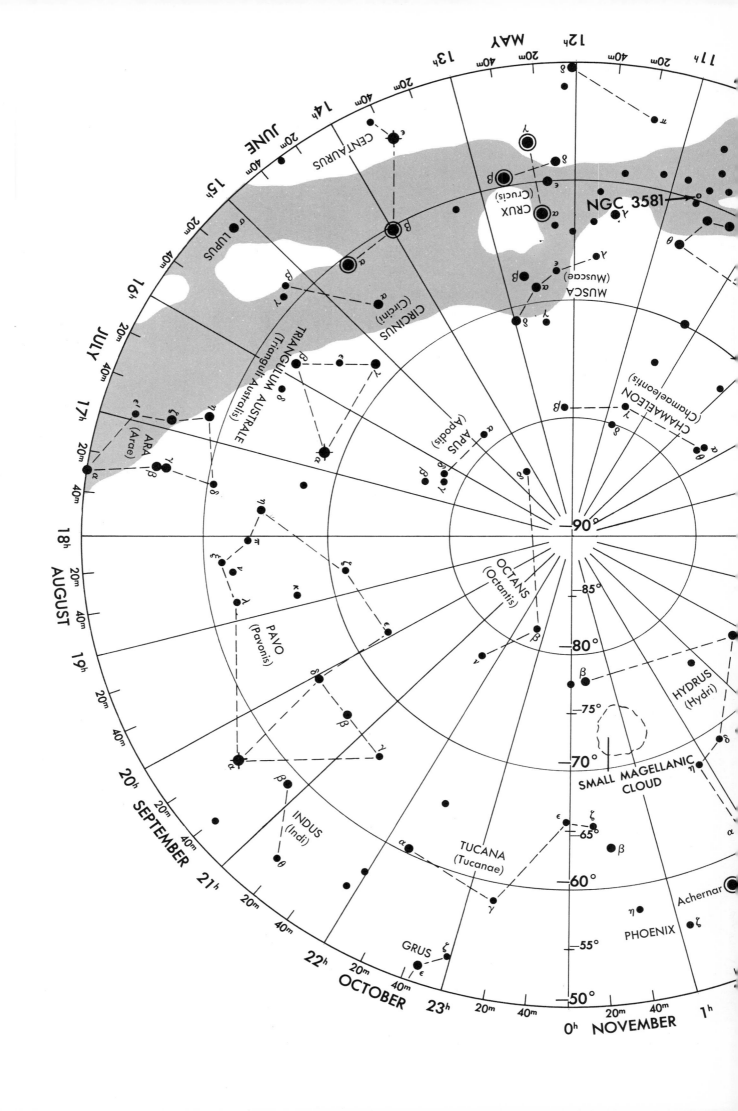

South Circumpolar Stars

The southern sky has neither a pole star nor any close bright star to mark the celestial pole. However, except for that particular area, the south circumpolar region offers a rich field for the observer in the southern latitudes.

The dominant part of the sky is in the region of Crux, the Southern Cross. Crux is a compact little constellation, its main figure formed by four brilliant stars, two of which more or less point to the pole. Near the brightest star, Alpha Cruxis is the "hole in the sky" known as the Coal Sack. This is a gaseous dark cloud that blots out the stars of the Milky Way behind it.

Not far from Crux is Centaurus, the Centaur, which is especially notable for two reasons: 1) for its two first-magnitude stars of yellow and blue; 2) for Proxima Centauri, the closest star to our solar system, at a distance of four and a half light-years away. It is located near Alpha Centauri. Despite its relative closeness, it is only an eleventh-magnitude star, so does not appear on the chart.

Probably the most unique feature of the southern sky is the Magellanic Clouds—two glowing star clouds resembling two "pieces" of the Milky Way. The Large Cloud appears to be about fourteen times the diameter of the full moon. Both have all types of celestial objects—clusters, nebulae, variables, and so on.

There are two more first-magnitude stars in the southern sky—Achernar at the very end of Eridanus, the River, and Canopus in the long figure of Carina, the Keel.

	KEY TO MAP	
	1-1½ MAGNITUDE	
	2-2½ MAGNITUDE	
	3-3½ MAGNITUDE	
•	4-4½ MAGNITUDE	

SHADED AREAS REPRESENT MILKY WAY

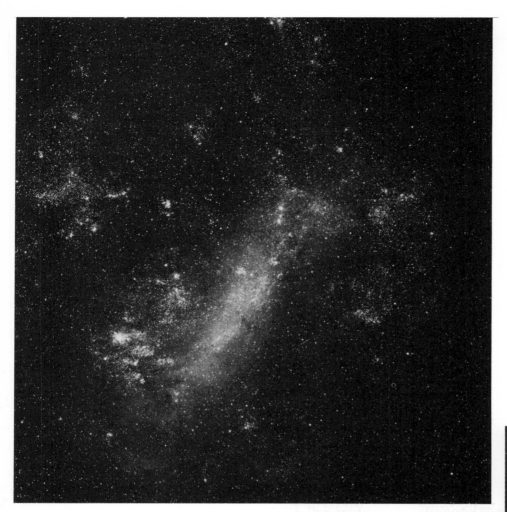

The larger of the two Magellanic Clouds, companions of the Milky Way, named for Ferdinand Magellan who saw them when he made his historic voyage around the world.

Photographs courtesy of Harvard College Observatory.

The smaller of the two Magellanic Clouds, this one in the constellation Hydrus. The first-magnitude star Achernar is at lower right.

The Great Nebula in Carina, taken with the 33—36-inch telescope, is one of the most beautiful nebulae in the southern sky.

A long time exposure of the Large Magellanic Cloud and the Small Magellanic Cloud taken with a 3-inch telescope. Although these "clouds" look as bright as the Milky Way, they are both star-packed galaxies at a distance of about 150,000 light-years from Earth.

The Nearest Stars

Name	Distance in Light-years	Apparent Magnitude	Spectral Type
Proxima Centauri	4.2	10.5	M?
Alpha Centauri	4.3	0.06	G0, K5
Munich 15040	6.2	9.7	M
Lalande 21185	8.1	7.6	M2
Wolf 359	8.3	13.5	M4
Sirius A	8.7	—1.6	A0
Innes' Star	9.6	11.7	—
B.D.—12° 4523	9.9	9.5	M5
Corboda Vh. 243	10.2	9.2	M0
Ross 248	10.2	13.8	M6
Tau Ceti	10.2	3.6	K0
Procyon	10.4	0.5	F5
Epsilon Eridani	10.5	3.8	K0
61 Cygni	10.7	5.6	K5
Lacaille 9352	11.2	7.4	M0
Sigma 2398	11.3	8.8	M4
Groombridge 34	11.6	8.1	M2
Epsilon Indi	11.6	4.7	K5
Krüger 60	12.5	9.3	K5
Van Maanen's	12.8	12.3	F0
Lalande 8760	12.9	6.7	M0
O.A. (N) 17415	13.2	9.3	K
B.D. 51° 658	13.6	9.2	—

The Brightest Stars

Name	Apparent Magnitude	Distance in Light-years	Spectral Type
Sirius	−1.58	9	A0
Canopus	−0.86	650?	F0
Alpha Centauri	0.06	4	G0, K5
Vega	0.14	26	A0
Capella	0.21	47	G0
Arcturus	0.24	41	K0
Rigel	0.34	540?	B8
Procyon	0.48	10	F5
Achernar	0.60	66	B5
Beta Centauri	0.86	300	B1
Altair	0.89	16	A5
Betelgeuse	0.92v.	190	M0
Alpha Crucis	1.05	230	B1
Aldebaran	1.06	57	K5
Pollux	1.21	32	K0
Spica	1.21	230	B2
Antares	1.22	360	M0
Fomalhaut	1.29	24	A3
Deneb	1.33	650?	A2
Regulus	1.34	56	B8
Beta Crucis	1.50	200	B1
Castor	1.58	43	A0

The Planets

The planets are among the most interesting objects in the sky. But to view them properly you need a telescope. For serious work you should have a 6- to 12-inch reflector, or a 3- to 6-inch refractor.

With a good telescope you will be able to see the belts of Jupiter, its moons, the spectacular system of rings circling Saturn, and surface features of Mars. Also you will see the planets in their multitude of colors.

Nearly every beginning amateur is disappointed when he has his first telescopic view of the planets. Usually he expects to see the planet as a large disk with sharp detail, as the illustrations in many astronomy books show. Not so. The disks of even Jupiter and Saturn are disappointingly small, and surface detail is often very hard to make out at first. But after several viewing sessions the eye begins to see more and more, as it learns what to look for, and the rewards gradually begin to mount.

For example, don't expect to see "canals" on Mars the first time you view the planet. After thirty years of observing, some professionals have yet to see them. On the other hand, you may see these curious markings on your second or third try. You can expect to see the subtle light and dark regions ("desert" and "vegetation" areas) change with the Martian seasons, as well as the polar frost cap which also changes with the seasons.

The other planets are less rewarding in what they have to offer. Mercury has very little, and is difficult to see because it is so small and so close to the Sun. Venus presents only a veil of clouds to her suitors, but a powerful pair of binoculars or a telescope will reveal her Moonlike phases as she circles the Sun. You should not have any trouble locating the planets once you have learned to use the Planet Finder on p. 92–93.

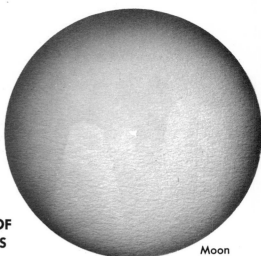

Phobos

Deimos

**RELATIVE SIZES OF
A FEW SATELLITES**

Moon

Ganymede

Europa

Hestia

Dione

Table of Satellites

Planet	Satellite	Mean Distance from Primary Thousands of mi.	Period in Days	Diameter in Mi.
Earth	Moon	238	27.32	2,162
Mars	Phobos	5.8	.32	10
	Deimos	14.6	1.26	5
Jupiter	Amalthea (V)	113	.50	100?
	Io (I)	262	1.77	2,320
	Europa (II)	417	3.55	1,950
	Ganymede (III)	666	7.15	3,200
	Callisto (IV)	1,170	16.69	3,220
	Hestia (VI)	7,120	250.66	100?
	Hera (VII)	7,290	259.66	30?
	Demeter (X)	7,300	260.5	10?
	Adrastea (XII)	13,000	625*	15?
	Pan (XI)	14,000	700*	20?
	Poseidon (VIII)	14,600	739*	30?
	Hades (IX)	14,700	758*	15?
Saturn	Mimas	113	.94	300?
	Enceladus	149	1.37	400?
	Tethys	183	1.89	800?
	Dione	235	2.74	1,000?
	Rhea	328	4.52	1,000?
	Titan	760	15.95	3,000?
	Hyperion	920	21.28	200?
	Iapetus	2,200	79.33	1,000?
	Phoebe	8,050	550*	200?
Uranus	Miranda	76	1.41*	150?
	Ariel	119	2.52*	500?
	Umbriel	166	4.14*	300?
	Titania	272	8.71*	800?
	Oberon	364	13.46*	800?
Neptune	Triton	220	5.87*	2,800
	Nereid	3,500	359.4	150?

*Means retrograde motion.

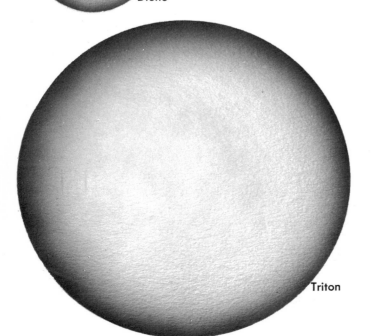

Triton

The Minor Planets

The minor planets, or asteroids, are not very promising as viewing objects for the amateur. Although the orbits of about 1600 of them have been plotted, you must know exactly where to look if you expect to see one. Except for Vesta, few of them appear as disks, even in large telescopes.

The first four discovered have diameters between 100 and 500 miles, but the diameters of the others are much smaller and all seem to be of irregular shape. A few of them, about a mile in diameter, sweep in surprisingly close to Earth. Hermes has come within 485,000 miles of us! At close approach these asteroids appear as faint stars rushing quickly across the sky.

(first 10 only)

Number	Name	Sidereal Revolution in Years	Diameter in Miles
1	Ceres	4.60	485
2	Pallas	4.61	304
3	Juno	4.36	118
4	Vesta	3.63	243
5	Astraea	4.14	?
6	Hebe	3.78	?
7	Iris	3.68	?
8	Flora	3.27	?
9	Metis	3.69	?
10	Hygeia	5.59	?

A TYPICAL ASTEROID COMPARED TO A CITY SKYLINE

NEPTUNE

PLUTO

URANUS

SATURN

RELATIVE SIZES OF MEMBERS
OF THE SOLAR SYSTEM

Table of the Planets, Sun, and Moon

	Mercury	Venus	Earth	Mars	Asteroids
Mean Distance from Sun in Miles	35,960,000	67,200,000	92,900,000	141,600,000	260,000,000
Mean Diameter in Miles	3100	7700	7918	4215	(See *Table of Minor Planets.*)
Mean Orbital Velocity (mph.)	107,900	79,000	67,000	54,200	——
Sidereal Period of Revolution	87.97 days	224.70 days	365.24 days	686.98 days	4.69 years
Period of Rotation	87.97 days	30 days ?	23 hrs. 56 mins.	24 hrs. 37 mins.	——
Density	3.8	4.86	5.52	3.96	?
Mass (Earth—1)	0.056	0.817	1.000	0.108	0.0002
Number of Satellites	None	None	1	2	——
Inclination of Equator to Orbit	?	?	23.5°	25.2°	——
Escape Velocity (mi. per sec.)	2.2	6.2	7	3.1	——
Atmosphere	Small traces of a few heavy gases such as carbon dioxide.	Carbon dioxide present in upper and lower cloud region; presence of oxygen and water vapor uncertain.	78% nitrogen; 21% oxygen; 1% argon, helium carbon dioxide, krypton, hydrogen xenon, ozone.	Mostly nitrogen, some carbon dioxide, traces of argon, small traces of oxygen and water vapor.	None.
Brightest Apparent Magnitude	—1.9	—4.4	—3.8 (as seen from Sun)	—2.8	+6 (and less)
Maximum Surface Temperature, F°.	770	140	140	86	?
Surface Gravity (Earth—1)	0.27	0.86	1.00	0.38	——

SUN

JUPITER · ASTEROIDS · MOON · MERCURY · VENUS · MARS · EARTH

Jupiter	Saturn	Uranus	Neptune	Pluto	Sun	Moon
483,400,000	886,200,000	1,782,000,000	2,794,000,000	3,671,000,000	——	From Earth—238,857
86,800	71,500	31,700	31,000	3600?	865,370	2162
29,400	21,700	15,310	12,240	10,800	——	2287
11.86 years	29.46 years	84.01 years	164.79 years	248.43 years	——	27 days 7 hrs. 43 mins.
9 hrs. 55 mins.	10 hrs. 38 mins.	10 hrs. 40 mins.	15 hrs. 48 mins.	6½ days?	Equatorial: 25 days Polar: 34 days	27 days 7 hrs. 43 mins.
1.33	0.71	1.26	1.6	?	1.41	3.34
318.356	95.223	14.580	17.264	0.926?	332,000	0.012
12	9	5	2	?	9+	None
3.1°	26.7°	98°	29°	?	7.2°	6.7°
37	22	13	14	?	384	1.4
Large amounts of hydrogen, methane, icy clouds of ammonia.	Large amounts of hydrogen, methane, ammonia crystals.	Large amounts of methane, ammonia crystals, some hydrogen and helium.	Large amounts of methane, with ammonia crystals, some hydrogen.	?	Mostly hydrogen and helium with traces of at least 27 other elements.	None.
—2.5	—0.4	+5.7	+7.6	+15	—27	—12.5
—216	—243	—300?	—330?	—350?	10,000	212+
2.64	1.17	0.92	1.12	1?	28	0.17

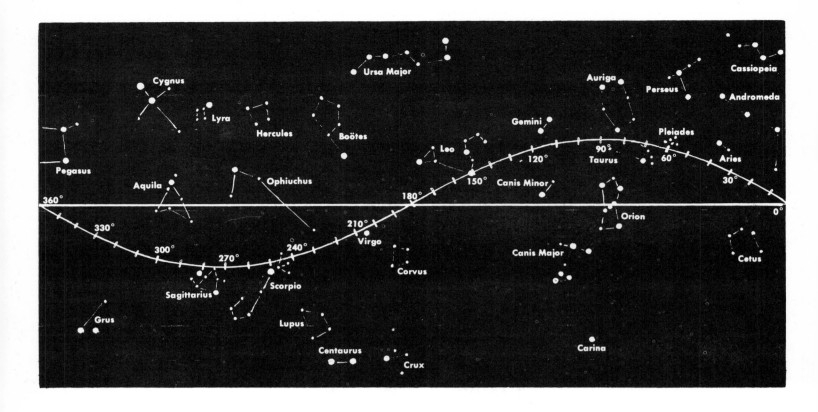

How to Find the Planets

The constellation chart (above) and the tables (opposite) will enable you to find Mercury, Venus, Mars, Jupiter, and Saturn through the year 1970, during the months these planets are visible.

To find the constellations shown in the chart, face south and hold the chart over your head. (This chart is for use only in the Northern Hemisphere.) Once you are able to find the constellations with ease, then you will be ready to spot the planets.

Suppose that the date is May 13, 1968, and that you want to observe Jupiter. First find the 1968 table and look in the Jupiter column opposite May. You will see the number 147. (All numbers in bold face indicate that the planets are visible only in the evening sky. The other numbers indicate that the planets are visible in the morning sky.) The 147 is Jupiter's longitude for this date. To find Jupiter, look along the white, wavy line which represents the approximate path of the planets as they move among the stars. Jupiter will be just to the right of 150, which is at the base of the constellation Leo. Six months later Jupiter would appear at longitude 180 in the morning sky between Virgo and Leo.

Notice that in all the tables the planets' positions are shown only for the 13th of the month. To find them around the beginning or end of the month, look to the right or left of the 13th date figure on the constellation chart.

The blank spaces in the tables mean that the planet is too close to the Sun to be seen. Mercury (the most difficult to observe) and Venus are visible only for a brief time after sunset and before dawn. Mercury will always appear within 6° of the ecliptic (wave line); Venus within 7°; Mars within 7°; Jupiter within 2° and Saturn within 3°.

With practice you will discover the best times to observe the planets as they circle the Sun.

PLANET:	MERC.	VEN.	MARS	JUP.	SAT.
DATE:	13	13	13	13	13
1962					
JAN.	—	—	286	—	—
FEB.	—	—	310	321	305
MAR.	328	—	331	328	308
APR.	—	—	356	334	310
MAY	74	79	18	339	311
JUNE	—	116	42	342	311
JULY	—	151	64	342	309
AUG.	—	186	85	340	307
SEPT.	197	216	104	336	305
OCT.	—	236	121	333	304
NOV.	—	—	136	333	306
DEC.	—	225	144	336	308

PLANET:	MERC.	VEN.	MARS	JUP.	SAT.
DATE:	13	13	13	13	13
1963					
JAN.	—	247	142	342	—
FEB.	299	279	131	348	315
MAR.	—	311	125	—	318
APR.	—	348	130	2	321
MAY	—	24	140	9	323
JUNE	59	62	155	15	323
JULY	—	—	172	18	322
AUG.	166	—	191	19	320
SEPT.	—	—	211	17	317
OCT.	—	—	232	14	316
NOV.	—	—	254	10	317
DEC.	281	288	277	10	319

PLANET:	MERC.	VEN.	MARS	JUP.	SAT.
DATE:	13	13	13	13	13
1964					
JAN.	—	326	300	12	322
FEB.	305	4	—	17	—
MAR.	—	37	348	23	328
APR.	—	70	12	—	332
MAY	32	93	35	38	334
JUNE	—	—	58	45	335
JULY	—	81	78	50	334
AUG.	167	97	100	55	332
SEPT.	164	126	119	56	330
OCT.	—	160	137	55	328
NOV.	—	197	154	51	327
DEC.	—	234	168	47	329

PLANET:	MERC.	VEN.	MARS	JUP.	SAT.
DATE:	13	13	13	13	13
1965					
JAN.	272	272	177	46	332
FEB.	—	—	176	48	—
MAR.	—	—	167	52	339
APR.	—	—	159	58	343
MAY	28	—	162	—	345
JUNE	—	—	173	72	347
JULY	138	136	188	79	347
AUG.	—	173	206	85	345
SEPT.	—	210	226	90	343
OCT.	—	245	247	91	341
NOV.	254	279	270	90	340
DEC.	243	306	293	87	341

PLANET:	MERC.	VEN.	MARS	JUP.	SAT.
DATE:	13	13	13	13	13
1966					
JAN.	—	—	317	83	343
FEB.	—	299	342	81	—
MAR.	—	310	4	82	350
APR.	357	337	—	86	354
MAY	—	10	49	92	357
JUNE	—	45	71	—	359
JULY	132	81	91	105	359
AUG.	123	118	113	112	358
SEPT.	—	—	132	118	356
OCT.	221	—	151	122	353
NOV.	—	—	169	124	353
DEC.	—	—	185	124	353

PLANET:	MERC.	VEN.	MARS	JUP.	SAT.
DATE:	13	13	13	13	13
1967					
JAN.	—	—	200	120	355
FEB.	342	348	210	116	358
MAR.	—	22	213	115	—
APR.	9	60	205	116	5
MAY	—	94	196	119	8
JUNE	106	128	197	124	11
JULY	—	154	208	—	12
AUG.	—	163	223	137	12
SEPT.	—	—	242	144	10
OCT.	225	157	263	149	8
NOV.	212	184	286	154	6
DEC.	—	218	309	156	5

PLANET:	MERC.	VEN.	MARS	JUP.	SAT.
DATE:	13	13	13	13	13
1968					
JAN.	—	255	334	155	6
FEB.	—	292	358	152	9
MAR.	326	328	20	148	—
APR.	—	—	42	146	16
MAY	—	—	64	147	20
JUNE	—	—	—	150	23
JULY	91	—	105	155	25
AUG.	—	—	125	—	25
SEPT.	197	194	145	168	24
OCT.	—	231	164	174	22
NOV.	—	269	183	180	20
DEC.	—	305	201	184	18

PLANET:	MERC.	VEN.	MARS	JUP.	SAT.
DATE:	13	13	13	13	13
1969					
JAN.	313	340	218	186	19
FEB.	301	11	235	185	21
MAR.	342	27	247	182	24
APR.	—	—	256	178	—
MAY	—	14	255	176	31
JUNE	—	37	245	177	35
JULY	—	68	242	180	37
AUG.	162	103	250	185	39
SEPT.	195	139	266	—	38
OCT.	182	176	285	197	36
NOV.	—	—	307	204	34
DEC.	—	—	329	210	32

PLANET:	MERC.	VEN.	MARS	JUP.	SAT.
DATE:	13	13	13	13	13
1970					
JAN.	—	—	352	214	32
FEB.	301	—	15	216	33
MAR.	—	—	35	215	36
APR.	43	43	56	212	—
MAY	—	80	77	209	43
JUNE	61	117	98	207	47
JULY	—	152	—	207	50
AUG.	168	186	137	210	52
SEPT.	—	216	157	215	52
OCT.	—	234	176	—	51
NOV.	—	—	196	228	48
DEC.	282	223	215	234	46

Map of Mars

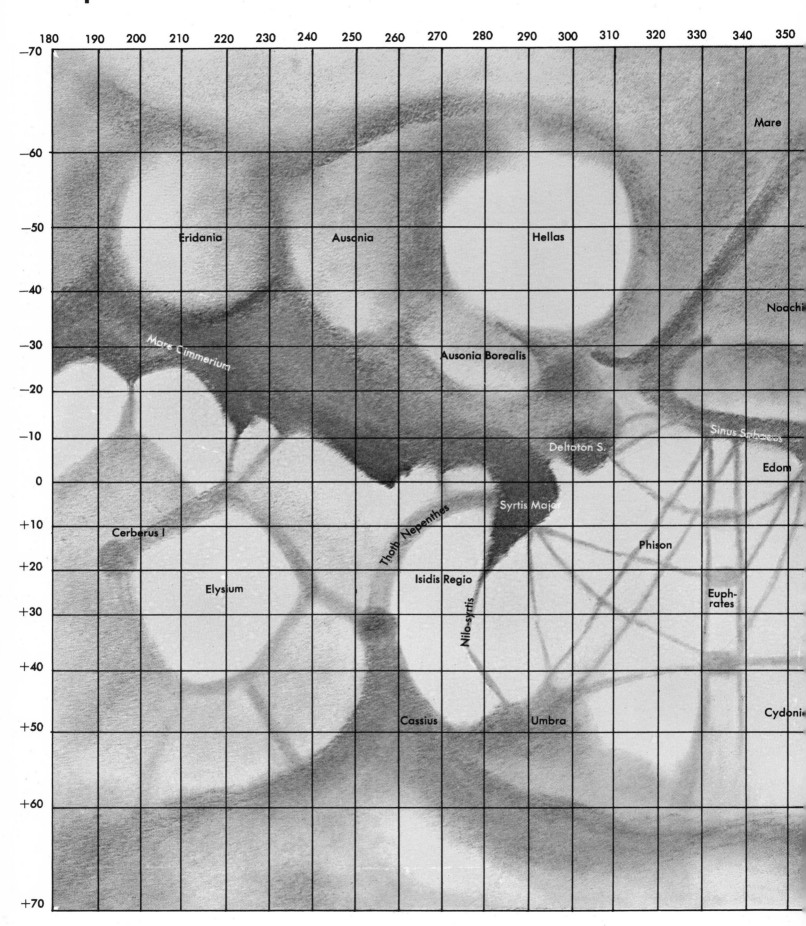

180	190	200	210	220	230	240	250	260	270	280	290	300	310	320	330	340	350

Mare

Eridania   Ausonia   Hellas

Noachi

Mare Cimmerium   Ausonia Borealis

Sinus Sabaeus

Deltoton S.

Edom

Syrtis Major

Cerberus I   Thoth Nepenthes   Phison

Elysium   Isidis Regio   Euph-rates

Nilo-syrtis

Cassius   Umbra   Cydoni

Stretched flat as a sheet of paper, this is what Mars' surface would look like. The canals, deserts, and other areas have Latin and Greek names. Map is based on observations by Antoniadi and other astronomers.

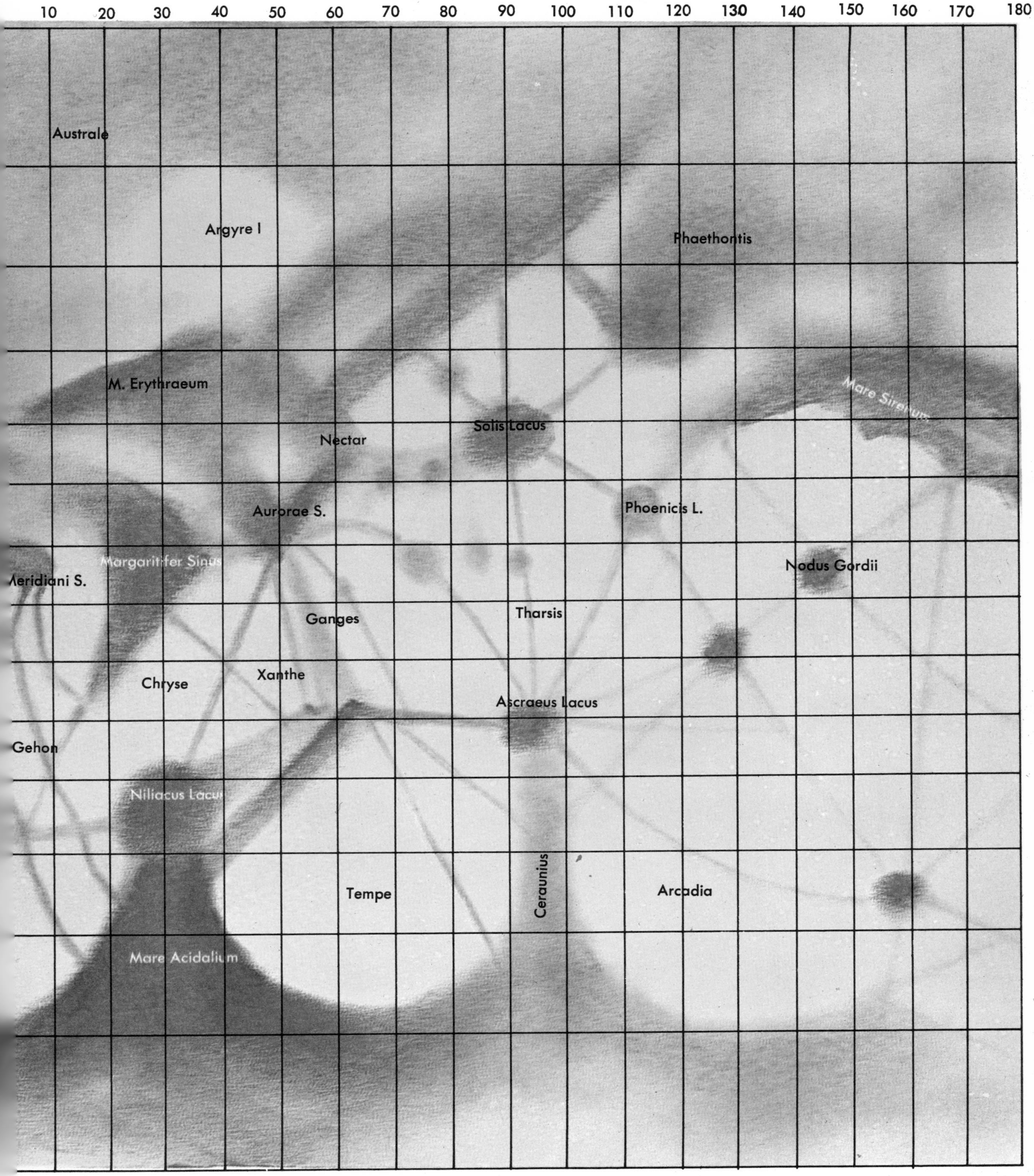

| 10 | 20 | 30 | 40 | 50 | 60 | 70 | 80 | 90 | 100 | 110 | 120 | 130 | 140 | 150 | 160 | 170 | 180 |

Australe

Argyre I

Phaethontis

M. Erythraeum

Mare Sirenum

Nectar

Solis Lacus

Aurorae S.

Phoenicis L.

Margaritifer Sinus

Meridiani S.

Nodus Gordii

Ganges

Tharsis

Chryse

Xanthe

Ascraeus Lacus

Gehon

Niliacus Lacus

Tempe

Ceraunius

Arcadia

Mare Acidalium

The Moon

On the following six pages you will find detailed maps of the Moon keyed with photographs which show a wealth of craters and lunar "seas." Because astronomical telescopes invert the image, the Moon's true north is shown at the bottom— but east and west are the observer's east and west.

For best viewing, search along the terminator (the sunrise-sunset line). It is here that the craters, mountains, and clefts will appear most sharply. Some of the large craters, such as Tycho and

Lick Observatory Photograph

THE WAXING CRESCENT MOON

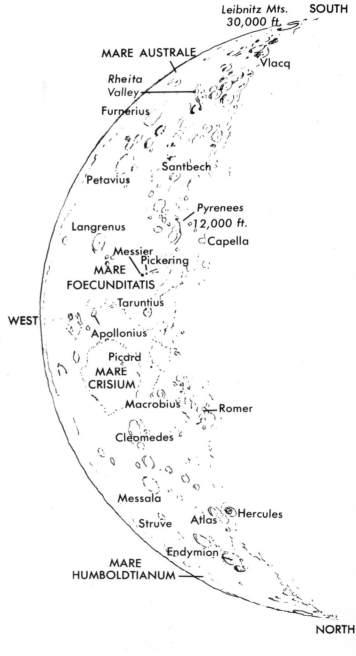

KEY
LUNAR "SEAS"
Lunar Craters and Walled Plains
Lunar Mountains and Other Features

Copernicus (page 100), measure 50 to 150 miles from rim to rim.

Some of the magnificent mountain ranges, such as the Leibnitz Mountains (page 96), rise to more than 20,000 feet. But most are about the same height as those on Earth. The Apennines, Caucasus, Doerfel Mountains, and Pyrenees all offer splendid viewing.

The lunar "seas," which seem to be vast areas of dried lava, are the most easily seen features of the Moon. Mare Serenitatis and Mare Tranquillitatis (page 98) are among the largest.

At a mean distance of 238,000 miles, the Moon is our closest companion. With practically no atmosphere, its day temperature reaches about 212°F.; its night temperature, −250°F.

Lick Observatory Photograph

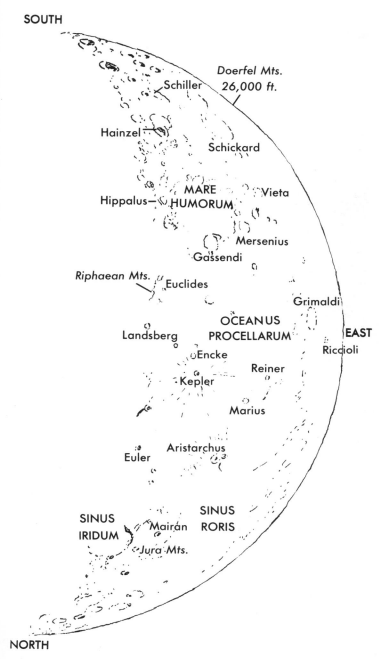

THE WANING CRESCENT MOON

KEY
LUNAR "SEAS"
Lunar Craters and Walled Plains
Lunar Mountains and Other Features

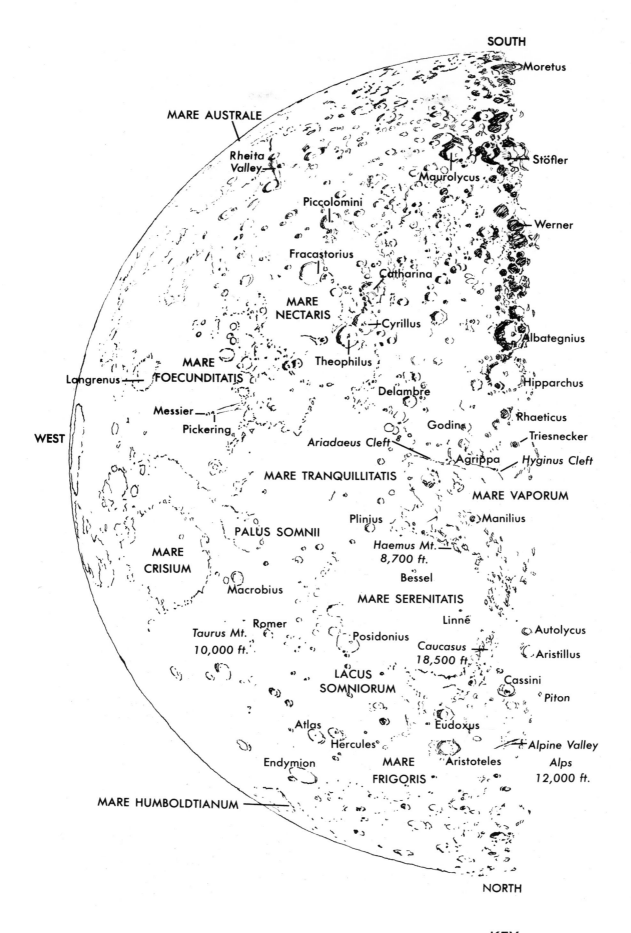

SOUTH

Moretus

MARE AUSTRALE

Rheita
Valley

Stöfler

Maurolycus

Piccolomini

Werner

Fracastorius

Catharina

MARE
NECTARIS

Cyrillus

Albategnius

Theophilus

MARE
FOECUNDITATIS

Hipparchus

Langrenus

Delambre

Messier

Godin

Rhaeticus

Pickering

Triesnecker

Ariadaeus Cleft

Agrippa

Hyginus Cleft

WEST

MARE TRANQUILLITATIS

MARE VAPORUM

Plinius

Manilius

PALUS SOMNII

Haemus Mt.
8,700 ft.

MARE
CRISIUM

Bessel

Macrobius

MARE SERENITATIS

Linné

Romer

Autolycus

Posidonius

Taurus Mt.
10,000 ft.

Caucasus
18,500 ft.

Aristillus

LACUS
SOMNIORUM

Cassini

Piton

Atlas

Eudoxus

Hercules

Alpine Valley

Endymion

MARE
FRIGORIS

Aristoteles

Alps
12,000 ft.

MARE HUMBOLDTIANUM

NORTH

THE WESTERN HEMISPHERE OF THE MOON

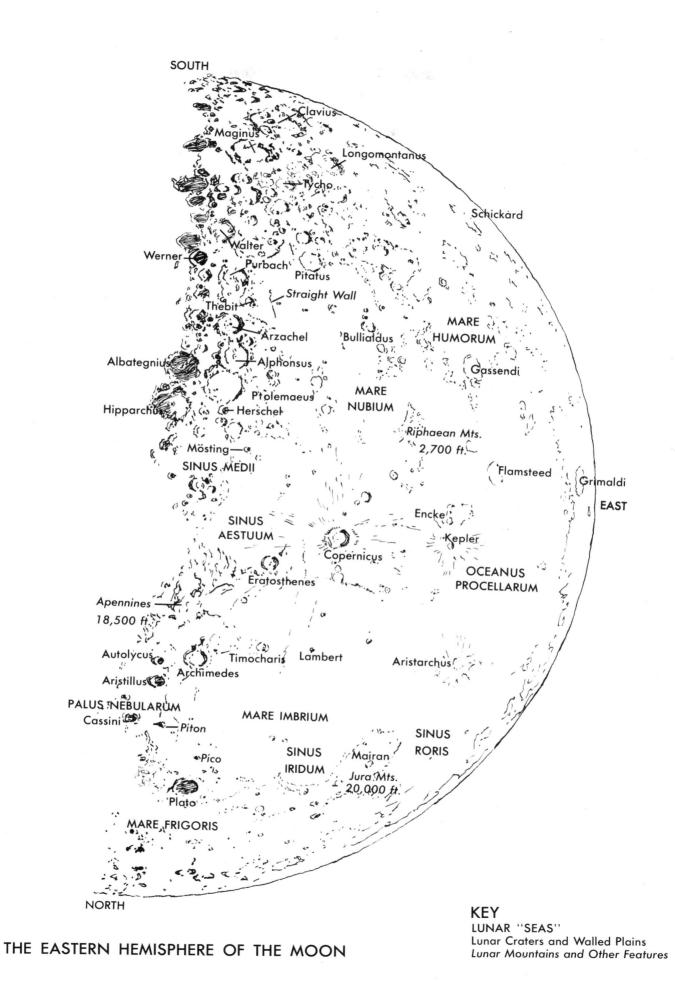

THE EASTERN HEMISPHERE OF THE MOON

Telescopes and How They Work

On the following twelve pages you will find diagrams, photographs, and explanations of several different kinds of telescopes and mountings.

The optical surfaces used in today's telescopes are probably as nearly perfect as anything made by man. Like cameras, telescopes are built in many different forms. Each type, from the simplest binoculars to the most complex observatory telescopes, is designed for a particular use.

Binoculars and hand telescopes are particularly recommended for beginning amateurs for two reasons: these instruments are easy to carry about; and their large field of view makes it easy to study large areas of the sky. Sooner or later each amateur wants a larger telescope so that he can study the Moon's surface in detail, observe the changes of variable stars, study the planets and their moons, and nearby galaxies.

Palomar Observatory in California (shown here) houses the 200-inch Hale Telescope, the largest reflector in the world. Because of its great aperture (see glossary), it has tremendous light-gathering power, which means that it has a great advantage in photographing and analyzing distant galaxies and nebulae. Many of the photographs in this book were taken with the 200-inch telescope.

The largest refracting telescope in the world is the 40-inch at Yerkes Observatory, Wisconsin. Because of its long focal length (see glossary), it can pick up great detail on celestial objects which are relatively "close" to the Earth. Many of the finest photographs of the Sun, Moon, and planets have been taken with this telescope.

Radio telescopes are exciting new tools of astronomy. Unlike optical telescopes, they can be used in the daytime, and even clouds do not interfere with the reception of the radio waves they detect from outer space.

The Sky Through Binoculars

Beginning amateur astronomers usually are pleasantly surprised the first time they sweep the heavens with a pair of binoculars. Advanced amateurs and professionals alike regard binoculars as standard viewing equipment.

For one thing, binoculars are easy to handle, if they are not too heavy. Also they provide surprisingly good magnification for such an inexpensive astronomical tool, and they give you a large field of view. For astronomical work your binoculars should have objective lenses with a diameter of 50mm. The usual power of this type of glass is 7, therefore they are listed as 7 x 50s. These binoculars, by the way, are known as "night glasses." Since the diameter of the objective determines the light-gathering power of your binoculars, 7 x 50 binoculars are better than 7 x 35s.

What can you expect to see with binoculars? If the Moon is your subject, you will be able to see mountain ranges, the "seas," craters, and ray systems. Because of their large field of view, binoculars are excellent for constellation study. If you can hold the binoculars steady enough, you will have a good view of the Pleiades. This star group

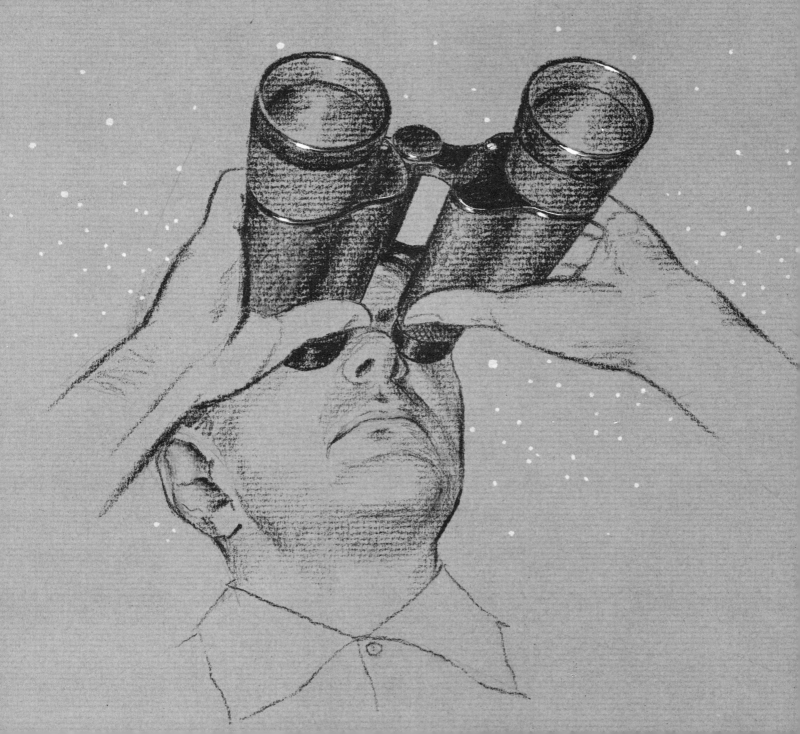

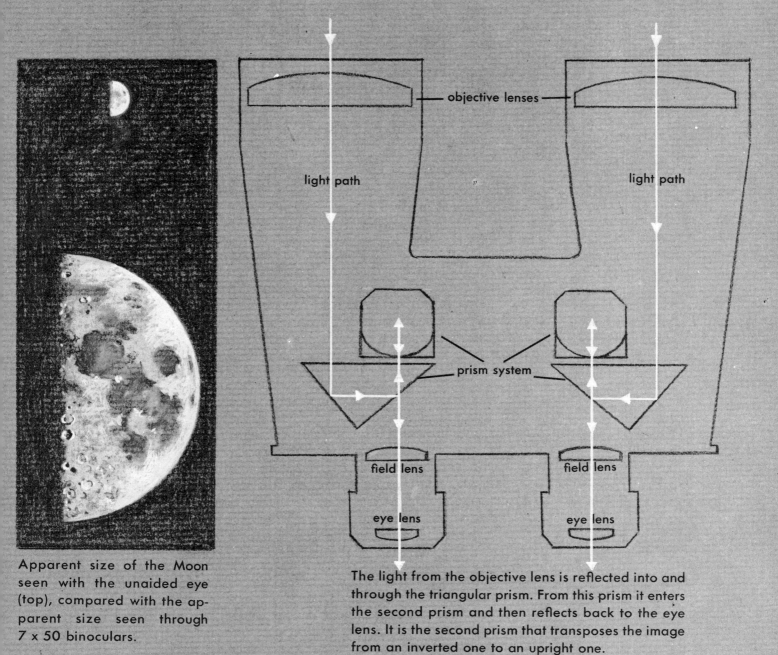

objective lenses

light path

light path

prism system

field lens

field lens

eye lens

eye lens

Apparent size of the Moon seen with the unaided eye (top), compared with the apparent size seen through 7 x 50 binoculars.

The light from the objective lens is reflected into and through the triangular prism. From this prism it enters the second prism and then reflects back to the eye lens. It is the second prism that transposes the image from an inverted one to an upright one.

appears as six or seven stars to the unaided eye but blossoms into a fine cluster when seen through binoculars. And **M 31**, which is a spiral galaxy in the constellation Andromeda, and much like our own galaxy, is revealed as a hazy, glowing spot. In summer, if you study the area of sky near the southern horizon with binoculars, you will find many galaxies, although they will appear tiny and faint. Even so, it is a thrilling experience to see them, when you realize that you are looking at star-worlds very much like our own.

Variable stars and double stars are also good viewing objects for binoculars. With a pair of 7 x 50s you can split several doubles, Epsilon Lyrae being one. (And a telescope will split the

Epsilon Lyrae pair into still another pair. This star is a "double double.") But don't expect to see much if you train your binoculars on the planets. To resolve these objects as proper disks, you need a telescope. You can, however, make out Jupiter's four major moons.

For the beginning amateur, half the fun of using binoculars is discovering new things for himself. If one section of the sky looks particularly interesting to the unaided eye, then look at it in detail with your binoculars. And the next step is to identify the objects you see by referring to the star charts in this and other books. This random observing, incidentally, is a good way to familiarize yourself with the sky.

Two views of an amateur astronomer's telescope. This is an 8-inch Newtonian reflector; "8-inch" refers to the diameter of the main mirror. The tube itself is almost 6 feet long.

Photographs by John Polgreen

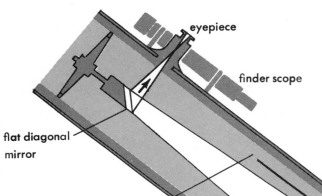

eyepiece

finder scope

flat diagonal
mirror

incoming light

tube

light reflected from
main mirror

main mirror

adjusting screws

The **Newtonian Reflector** gathers light by means of a curved mirror at the bottom end of a tube. The curvature of the mirror directs the light rays onto a second mirror called a "flat." An eyepiece at the side of the tube brings the rays to a focus and magnifies the image they form. This telescope is preferred by most "do-it-yourself" amateurs.

106

The **Cassegrainian Reflector** differs from the Newtonian by having a shorter tube, and by having a greater focal length because of a convex secondary mirror (at right and bottom of page). The big telescopes shown here can be adapted to other optical arrangements by a simple change of lenses or mirrors.

convex secondary mirror

path of light

perforated primary mirror

Cassegrain focus of the 200-inch

The 200-inch Hale Reflector of the Mount Wilson and Palomar Observatories. The furniture seen in these photos gives an idea of the tremendous size of these telescopes.

The 100-inch Hooker Reflector of Mount Wilson and Palomar Observatories.

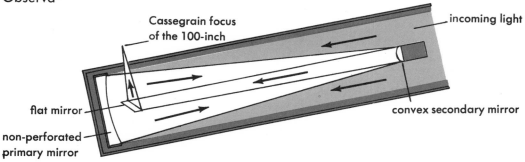

Cassegrain focus of the 100-inch

incoming light

flat mirror

non-perforated primary mirror

convex secondary mirror

107

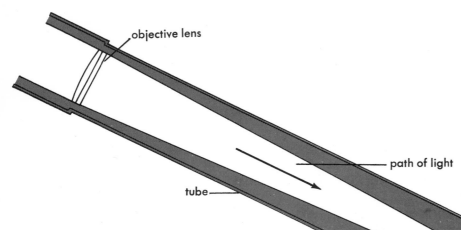

objective lens

path of light

tube

eyepiece

Detail of the mounting of a 4-inch refractor. Note the similarity to the mounting of the giant Yerkes telescope. These are both equatorial mounts and their operation is described on page 113.

Refracting Telescopes gather light by means of an "objective" lens at the front end of the tube. The objective brings the light rays to a focus part way down the tube. At this point the "eyepiece" (made up of a group of lenses) magnifies the image.

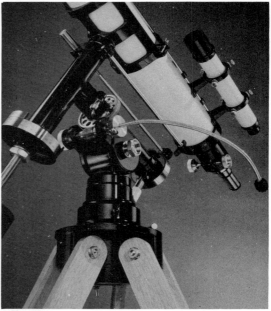

Courtesy of Unitron Instrument Company

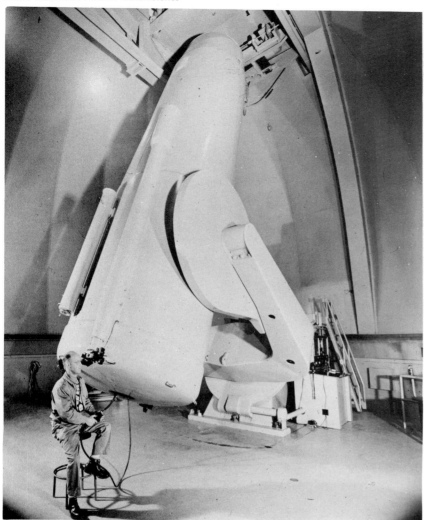

The 48-inch Schmidt Telescope of Mount Wilson and Palomar Observatories.

The 40-inch refracting telescope of Yerkes Observatory. This is the largest refracting telescope in the world.

path of light

correcting lens

tube

spherical primary mirror

curved photgraphic plate

Schmidt Camera Telescope (a reflector) has a "correcting plate" which compensates for defects in the spherical mirror that reflects light rays onto the curved focal surface. The photographic plate, which must be curved also, is placed against the curved focal surface.

109

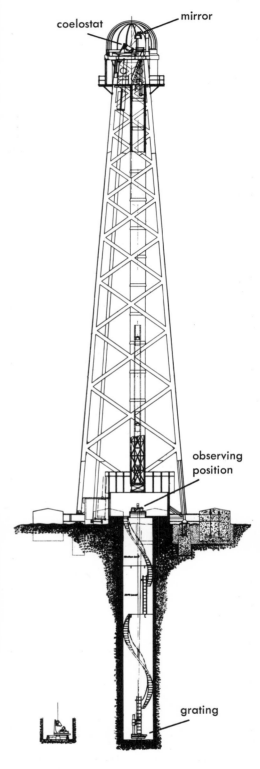

coelostat

mirror

observing position

grating

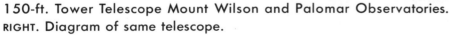

150-ft. Tower Telescope Mount Wilson and Palomar Observatories. RIGHT. Diagram of same telescope.

Solar Tower Telescope at Mount Wilson Observatory, California, is used to study light from the Sun. The light is gathered at the top of the telescope (150 feet high) by a movable mirror called a "coelostat." This mirror reflects the light down the tower through a lens which produces a 17-inch image of the Sun at the ground level. From here the light is passed to a "grating" located 75 feet underground, then reflected back up to ground level where the spectrum is brought to a focus. (See glossary entry Spectroscope—"Diffraction Grating.")

Prism Spectroscope

Spectroscopes separate the individual colors making up white light into their characteristic wave lengths. The prism spectroscope shown here collects light from a source (a star, for instance).

The light is admitted to the instrument through a slit and then passed on to the prism by a collimator which arranges the light in parallel beams. The prism separates the white light into its individual colors and passes them on to the objective lens which focuses the light onto a photographic plate, or forms an image which the observer can see through an eyepiece. (See *Spectroscope* in Dictionary of Terms).

In addition to telling us something about the composition of sky objects, the spectroscope can tell us if a galaxy light source is moving away or approaching the observer. (See *Red Shift* and *Doppler Effect*.)

Telescope Mountings

-Despite the perfection of modern telescope optics they would be useless unless set in a rigid tube (either closed or open) and the tube properly mounted. The mounting must be well balanced and solidly built, to eliminate vibration and to allow the telescope to move easily and smoothly.

The **Altazimuth Mounting,** the most familiar type, incorporates the use of two motions to bring any area of the sky into view. The azimuth axis sweeps a full 360° around the horizon. The altitude axis can be swung from horizon to zenith. An example of this mounting is the surveyor's transit.

The altazimuth mounting is often used for small telescopes. It is useful to amateur astronomers because of the ease with which it can be set up and its comparatively low cost.

Courtesy of Unitron Instrument Company

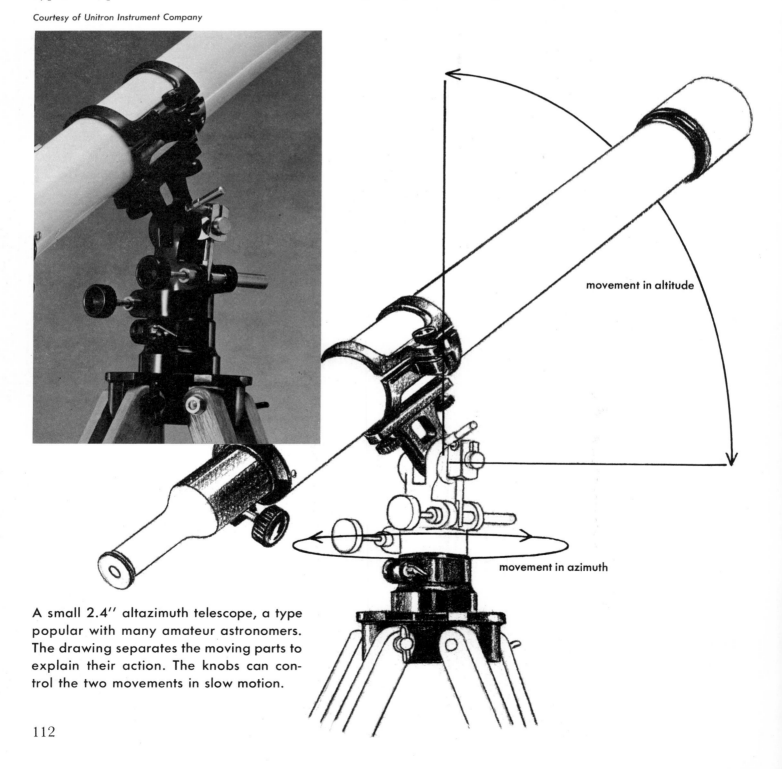

movement in altitude

movement in azimuth

A small 2.4″ altazimuth telescope, a type popular with many amateur astronomers. The drawing separates the moving parts to explain their action. The knobs can control the two movements in slow motion.

The **Equatorial Mounting** is superior to the altazimuth and is used on all big telescopes. There are many types of equatorial mountings, but they all have two things in common. They have one axis, called the polar axis, which is parallel to the earth's axis. They have another axis at right angles to the first, called the declination axis. (See photograph 1 below.)

Because the earth is constantly turning, the stars appear to move across the sky in an east-to-west path. The equatorial mounting is designed and set up to move in such a way that once a star is located, it can be followed across the sky by turning the polar axis alone.

Photographs by John Polgreen

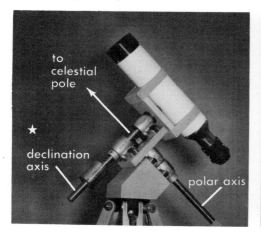

1 A small refractor on a homemade German equatorial mounting. Notice the two rotating shafts, or axes.

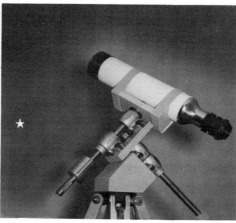

2 The scope is turned on the declination axis. In actual practice, both shafts can be used to aim at any star in the sky.

3 Still turning. Note: on an equatorial mounting, the polar axis *always* points north despite motion of the telescope.

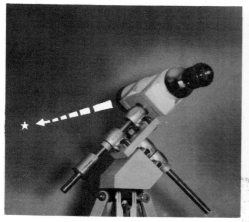

4 Now the scope is pointing directly toward the star. The declination shaft can now be clamped.

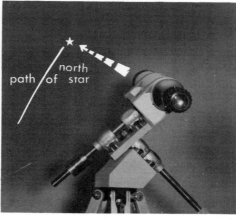

5 The scope is turned on the polar axis to keep the star centered in the field of view.

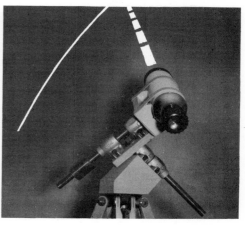

6 The star *seems* to climb in the sky from east to west because of the Earth's movement. The scope is following it.

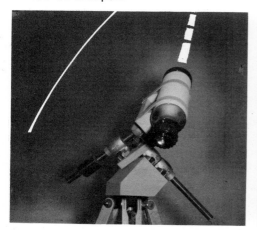

7 The turning of the scope from east to west on its polar axis is compensating for Earth's west to east movement.

8 Hours have passed since we began tracking the star. It continues to climb toward the zenith.

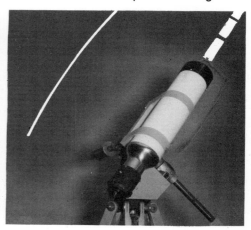

9 The principle of this mounting, combined with a clock drive, made the long exposure photos in this book possible.

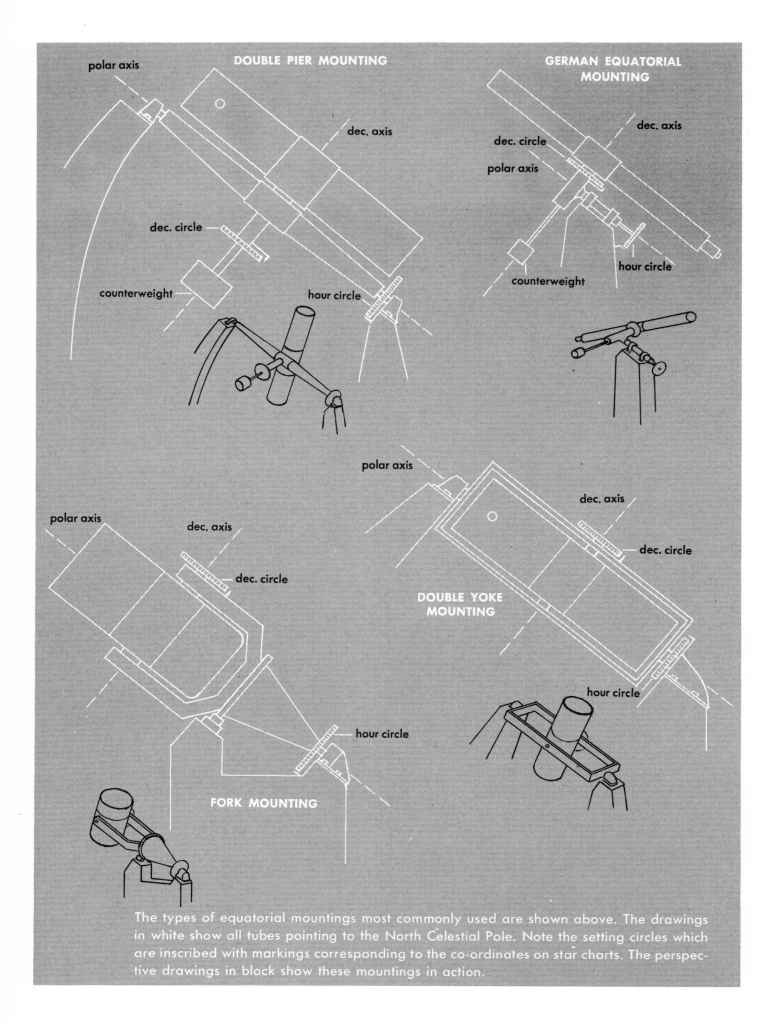

DOUBLE PIER MOUNTING

polar axis

dec. axis

dec. circle

counterweight

hour circle

GERMAN EQUATORIAL MOUNTING

dec. axis

dec. circle

polar axis

hour circle

counterweight

polar axis

dec. axis

dec. circle

DOUBLE YOKE MOUNTING

hour circle

polar axis

dec. axis

dec. circle

hour circle

FORK MOUNTING

The types of equatorial mountings most commonly used are shown above. The drawings in white show all tubes pointing to the North Celestial Pole. Note the setting circles which are inscribed with markings corresponding to the co-ordinates on star charts. The perspective drawings in black show these mountings in action.

250-foot Jodrell Bank Radio Telescope.

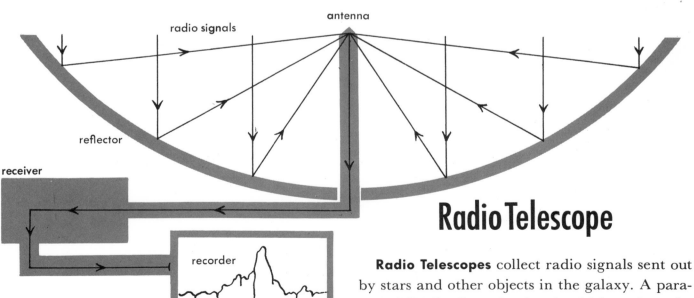

HOW RADIO SIGNALS ARE PICKED UP AND RECORDED ON A MOVING STRIP OF PAPER

Radio Telescope

Radio Telescopes collect radio signals sent out by stars and other objects in the galaxy. A parabolic "dish" collects the signals which are brought to focus on the antenna. After the signal is amplified in a radio receiver, it is sent to a recorder. Here a pen traces highs and lows of the signal's strength.

115

Table of Comets

Each year about five or six comets sweep into view, and most of them have not been recorded previously. Few are visible to the unaided eye, so binoculars or a 3- to 6-inch telescope (low power) are needed. The best search areas for comets are the eastern sky before dawn, and the western sky after nightfall.

While some comets seem to appear only once —possibly they break up and become meteors— others reappear on schedule. Encke's comet returns about every three years, but Halley's comet has a much longer period—76 years. The nucleus of a comet can range from 100 miles to 50,000 in diameter, and the gaseous tails (not all comets have tails) may be millions of miles long.

Name	Number of Appearances	Period in Years
Encke	44	3.30
Grigg-Skjellerup	8	4.90
Honda-Mrkos-Pajduš-áková	2	5.21
Tempel (2)	11	5.30
Tuttle-Giacobini-Kresák	3	5.43
Pons-Winnecke	15	6.12
Kopff	7	6.18
Schwassmann-Wachmann (2)	5	6.53
Giacobini-Zinner	6	6.59
Daniel	4	6.66
Wirtanen	2	6.69
d'Arrest	10	6.70
Finlay	6	6.81
Brooks (2)	9	6.93
Borrelly	6	7.01
Faye	14	7.41
Whipple	4	7.42
Oterma (3)	—	7.89
Schaumasse	5	8.17
Wolf (1)	9	8.42
Comas Solá	4	8.55
Tuttle	8	13.61
Neujmin (1)	3	17.93
Crommelin	4	27.91
Stephan-Oterma	2	38.96
Westphal	2	61.73
Brorsen-Metcalf	2	69.06
Olbers	3	69.57
Pons-Brooks	3	70.88
Halley	29	76.03
Grigg-Mellish	2	164.3

Meteor Showers

You do not need special equipment to observe meteors. During an evening's viewing you should see up to a dozen or so an hour. The best time to observe them is after midnight when the Earth's rotation is carrying you toward the meteors. In early evening the rotation will be carrying you away from them, so fewer are visible.

At certain times of the year (see the table) meteor showers occur in certain constellations. During a shower you may see up to a hundred meteors in an hour. These swarms are sometimes the remains of comets and appear to be raining down from a particular constellation. Those that come out of Leo are called Leonids; those from Orion, Orionids, and so on.

A camera set to a ten-minute or more time exposure will give you a fine photograph of a shower.

A contemporary drawing of the Leonid shower of November 13, 1833. One observer said at the time, "The stars fell like flakes of snow." Another, also believing that meteors were stars, thought that there would be no stars left in the sky the next night. COURTESY OF THE AMERICAN MUSEUM OF NATURAL HISTORY

Name	When They Appear	Rate Per Hour
NIGHT SHOWERS		
Quadrantids	Jan. 3	40
Lyrids	Apr. 20-22	8
δ-Aquarids	May 1-11	12
June Draconids	June 28	12
η-Aquarids	July 24-Aug. 6	20
Perseids	July 27-Aug. 17	50
October Draconids	Oct. 9	—
Orionids	Oct. 15-25	12
Taurids	Oct. 26-Nov. 16	6
Andromedes	Nov. 14	?
Leonids	Nov. 15-20	6
Geminids	Dec. 9-13	60
Ursids	Dec. 21-22	12
DAY SHOWERS		
o-Cetids	May 13-23	15
ζ-Perseids	June 1-16	40
Arietids	May 30- June 18	60
β-Taurids	June 25-July 7	24

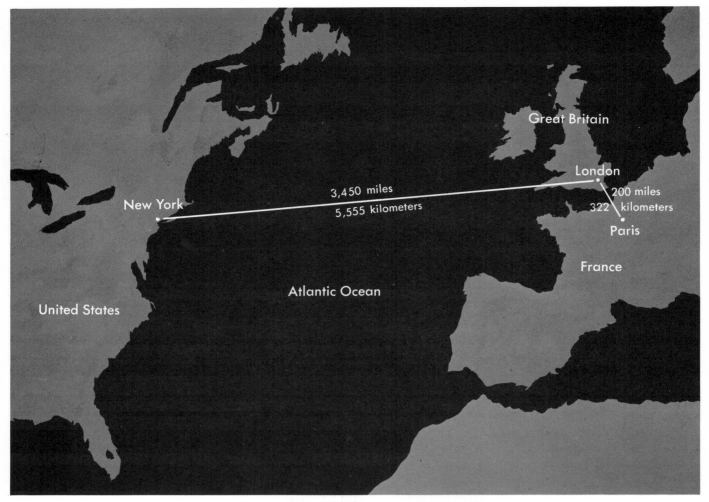

Except for the United States and England, most countries of the world use meters instead of feet, and kilometers instead of miles. This system of measurement is called the "metric" system, and its standard unit is the meter—which is equal to 39.37 inches. One kilometer equals 0.621 miles.

The map above (not drawn to scale) shows the distance in both miles and kilometers between key cities. It will help to remember that one kilometer equals just more than a half a mile.

Kilometers and Miles

km.		mi.	km.		mi.	km.		mi.	km.		mi.
1	=	0.621	15	=	9.321	29	=	18.020	43	=	26.719
2	=	1.243	16	=	9.942	30	=	18.641	44	=	27.340
3	=	1.864	17	=	10.563	31	=	19.263	45	=	27.962
4	=	2.485	18	=	11.185	32	=	19.884	46	=	28.583
5	=	3.107	19	=	11.806	33	=	20.505	47	=	29.204
6	=	3.728	20	=	12.427	34	=	21.127	48	=	29.826
7	=	4.350	21	=	13.049	35	=	21.748	49	=	30.447
8	=	4.971	22	=	13.670	36	=	22.369	50	=	31.069
9	=	5.592	23	=	14.292	37	=	22.991	60	=	37.282
10	=	6.214	24	=	14.913	38	=	23.612	70	=	43.496
11	=	6.835	25	=	15.534	39	=	24.233	80	=	49.710
12	=	7.456	26	=	16.156	40	=	24.855	90	=	55.923
13	=	8.078	27	=	16.777	41	=	25.476	100	=	62.137
14	=	8.699	28	=	17.398	42	=	26.098			

Centigrade and Fahrenheit

The centigrade scale (also called Celsius) is nearly always used in scientific work. On this scale water freezes at 0° and boils at 100°. (On the Fahrenheit scale it freezes at 32° and boils at 212°.) The table below will enable you to convert many readings from C. to F., or from F. to C. If you want to convert a reading not shown in the table, see the entry *Fahrenheit* in the glossary.

Whenever you see a temperature reading with a "K" after it (for example, 6000°K), this stands for *Kelvin*, which is another name for the *absolute* temperature scale which you will find explained in the glossary.

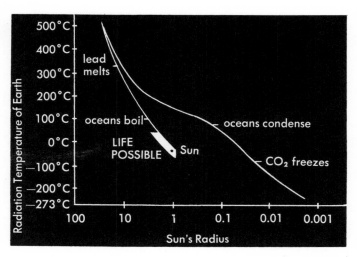

Diagram of the Sun's future shows how the radiation temperature on Earth will change. Sun's radius is shown along the bottom of diagram; Earth's temperature along the side.

C°.	F°.	C°.	F°.	C°.	F°.
−273	−460	180	356	2,500	4,500
−250	−418	190	374	3,000	5,400
−200	−328	200	392	3,500	6,300
−150	−238	210	410	4,000	7,200
−140	−220	220	428	4,500	8,100
−130	−202	230	446	5,000	9,000
−120	−184	240	464	5,500	9,900
−110	−166	250	482	6,000	10,800
−100	−148	260	500	6,500	11,700
−90	−130	270	518	7,000	12,600
−80	−112	280	536	7,500	13,500
−70	−94	290	554	8,000	14,400
−60	−76	300	572	8,500	15,300
−50	−58	310	590	9,000	16,200
−40	−40	320	608	9,500	17,100
−30	−22	330	626	10,000	18,000
−20	−4	340	644	11,000	19,800
−10	+14	350	662	12,000	21,600
0	32	360	680	13,000	23,400
+5	+41	370	698	14,000	25,200
10	50	380	716	15,000	27,000
20	68	390	734	16,000	28,800
30	86	400	752	17,000	30,600
40	104	410	770	18,000	32,400
50	122	420	788	19,000	34,200
60	140	430	806	20,000	36,000
70	158	440	824	21,000	37,800
80	176	450	842	22,000	39,600
90	194	460	860	23,000	41,400
100	212	470	878	24,000	43,200
110	230	480	896	25,000	45,000
120	248	490	914	26,000	46,800
130	266	500	932	28,000	50,400
140	284	750	1,382	30,000	54,000
150	302	1,000	1,832	35,000	63,000
160	320	1,500	2,700	40,000	72,000
170	338	2,000	3,600		

Future of the Sun

If astronomers are correct in their predictions about the Sun, our star has a very bright future, but its effects on the temperature of the Earth are less bright. According to Allan Sandage, the Sun is destined to become bigger, brighter, and hotter. In the process it will burn itself out, ending its visible life as a white dwarf star.

The diagram above, based on one prepared by Sandage, shows the Sun as it is now (at the radius 1 position), at the lower end of the zone of possible life. Over the next six billion years or so the Sun will brighten somewhat, but not so much that the radiation temperature on Earth makes life impossible. But over the following 500 million years the temperature on Earth will rise to about 500°C. During that period the oceans will have boiled and evaporated, and all life will have disappeared. At this stage (the upper point on the graph) the Sun will be a great red globe with a diameter 30 times its present size.

Having used up most of its hydrogen, the Sun will next begin to grow smaller and colder, with the result that the radiation temperature on Earth will fall off rapidly. The oceans will re-form and then freeze. Gradually the Sun will radiate so little energy that the temperature on Earth will fall to more than −225°C.

He
He
H
H
H,Ca$^+$
Mg,Ca$^+$
Fe,Ca$^+$

Spectra of stars can reveal their chemical composition. The vertical lines appearing in these spectra of white dwarf stars represent particular chemical elements as listed below.

The Chemical Elements

At one stage in his study, the amateur astronomer may develop an interest in the composition of the stars, the planets, and their atmospheres. If you do, you will need to know some chemistry. The table below simply lists the elements together with their symbols. You may find it useful if you refer to technical publications which sometimes use only the symbols without naming the elements.

Hydrogen and helium are the two most abundant elements in the universe. Hydrogen makes up about 90 per cent of the material; helium about 8 per cent.

A few compounds that will be useful to know include: CO—carbon monoxide; CO_2—carbon dioxide; O_3—ozone; H_2O—water; CH_4—methane; NH_3—ammonia.

Symbol	Name						
Ac	Actinium	Er	Erbium	Hg	Mercury	Sm	Samarium
Al	Aluminum	Eu	Europium	Mo	Molybdenum	Sc	Scandium
Am	Americium	Fm	Fermium			Se	Selenium
Sb	Antimony	F	Fluorine	Nd	Neodymium	Si	Silicon
A	Argon	Fr	Francium	Ne	Neon	Ag	Silver
As	Arsenic			Np	Neptunium	Na	Sodium
At	Astatine	Gd	Gadolinium	Ni	Nickel	Sr	Strontium
		Ga	Gallium	Nb	Niobium	S	Sulfur
Ba	Barium	Ge	Germanium	N	Nitrogen		
Bk	Berkelium	Au	Gold	No	Nobelium	Ta	Tantalum
Be	Beryllium					Tc	Technetium
Bi	Bismuth	Hf	Hafnium	Os	Osmium	Te	Tellurium
B	Boron	He	Helium	O	Oxygen	Tb	Terbium
Br	Bromine	Ho	Holmium			Tl	Thallium
		H	Hydrogen	Pd	Palladium	Th	Thorium
Cd	Cadmium			P	Phosphorus	Tm	Thulium
Ca	Calcium	In	Indium	Pt	Platinum	Sn	Tin
Cf	Californium	I	Iodine	Pu	Plutonium	Ti	Titanium
C	Carbon	Ir	Iridium	Po	Polonium	W	Tungsten, (see Wolfram)
Ce	Cerium	Fe	Iron	K	Potassium		
Cs	Cesium			Pr	Praseodymium	U	Uranium
Cl	Chlorine	Kr	Krypton	Pm	Promethium		
Cr	Chromium	La	Lanthanum	Pa	Protactinium	V	Vanadium
Co	Cobalt	Pb	Lead			W	Wolfram (Tungsten)
Cu	Copper	Li	Lithium	Ra	Radium		
Cm	Curium	Lu	Lutecium	Rn	Radon	Xe	Xenon
				Re	Rhenium	Yb	Ytterbium
Dy	Dysprosium	Mg	Magnesium	Rh	Rhodium	Y	Yttrium
		Mn	Manganese	Rb	Rubidium	Zn	Zinc
E	Einsteinium	Mv	Mendelevium	Ru	Ruthenium	Zr	Zirconium

Light-years and Parsecs

Because the distances of the planets and stars are so great, astronomers find it more convenient to use light-years and parsecs rather than miles. Both are a measure of distance. They are not a measure of time.

One light-year is equal to about 5.88 million million miles. This is the distance that light (travel-ling at a velocity of 186,300 miles a second) would cross in one year. The star nearest the Earth is the double star Alpha Centauri, at a distance of 4.3 light-years, or 25 million million miles. The Moon is 1.3 light-seconds from the Earth; the Sun 8.3 light-minutes. The parsec is a unit even larger than the light-year; equal to 3.26 light-years.

Parsecs	Light-years	Parsecs	Light-years	Parsecs	Light-years	Parsecs	Light-years	Parsecs	Light-years
1 =	3.259	12 =	39.11	23 =	74.96	34 =	110.81	45 =	146.66
2 =	6.518	13 =	42.37	24 =	78.22	35 =	114.07	46 =	149.91
3 =	9.777	14 =	45.63	25 =	81.48	36 =	117.32	47 =	153.17
4 =	13.036	15 =	48.89	26 =	84.73	37 =	120.58	48 =	156.43
5 =	16.295	16 =	52.14	27 =	87.99	38 =	123.84	49 =	159.69
6 =	19.554	17 =	55.40	28 =	91.25	39 =	127.10	50 =	162.95
7 =	22.813	18 =	58.66	29 =	94.51	40 =	130.36	60 =	195.54
8 =	26.072	19 =	61.92	30 =	97.77	41 =	133.62	70 =	228.13
9 =	29.331	20 =	65.18	31 =	101.03	42 =	136.88	80 =	260.72
10 =	32.590	21 =	68.44	32 =	104.29	43 =	140.14	90 =	293.31
11 =	35.85	22 =	71.70	33 =	107.55	44 =	143.40	100 =	325.90

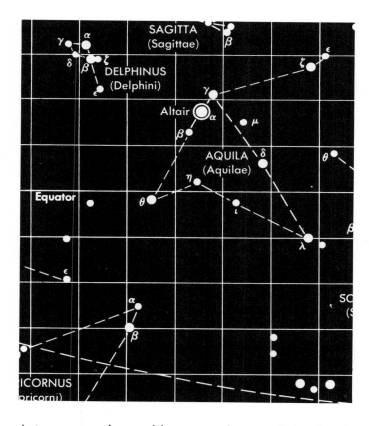

Astronomers the world over use letters of the Greek alphabet to designate the stars making up the constellations. As shown here, Greek letters appear on nearly every star map.

The Greek Alphabet

Capital Letter	Small Letter	Letter's Name
A	α	alpha
B	β	beta
Γ	γ	gamma
Δ	δ	delta
E	ϵ	epsilon
Z	ζ	zeta
H	η	eta
Θ	θ	theta
I	ι	iota
K	κ	kappa
Λ	λ	lambda
M	μ	mu
N	ν	nu
Ξ	ξ	xi
O	o	omicron
Π	π	pi
P	ρ	rho
Σ	σ	sigma
T	τ	tau
Υ	υ	upsilon
Φ	ϕ	phi
X	χ	chi
Ψ	ψ	psi
Ω	ω	omega

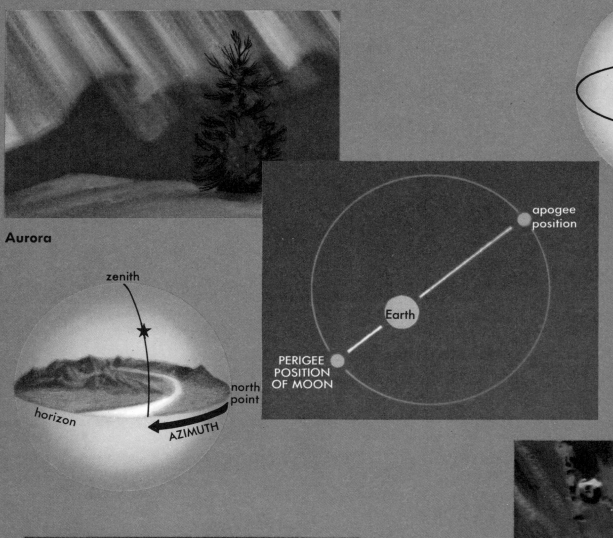

Aurora

Earth's equator

CELESTIAL EQUATOR

apogee position

Earth

PERIGEE POSITION OF MOON

zenith

horizon

north point

AZIMUTH

Lunar Phases

Vanguard I

Artificial Satellite

Rays on Moon

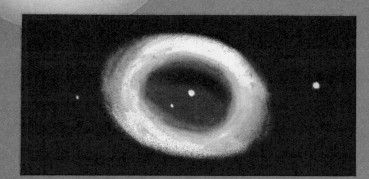

Ring Nebula

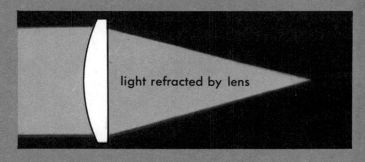

light refracted by lens

Refraction